The Reference Shelf

Substance Abuse

Edited by Joseph Sora

The Reference Shelf
Volume 69 • Number 4

The H. W. Wilson Company
New York • Dublin
1997

Reference Shelf

ints of articles, excerpts from books, addresses on trends in the United States and other countries. bers in each volume, all of which are usually published in the same _____ imbers one through five are each devoted to a single subject, providing background information and discussion from various points of view and concluding with a comprehensive bibliography that lists books, pamphlets and abstracts of additional articles on the subject and an index. The final number of each volume is a collection of recent speeches. This number also contains a subject index to all the articles in an entire Reference Shelf volume. Books in the series may be purchased individually or on subscription.

Visit H.W. Wilson's web site: http://www.hwwilson.com

Library of Congress Cataloging-in-Publication Data

Substance Abuse / edited by Joseph Sora
    p. cm. — (The reference shelf ; v. 69, no. 4)
    Includes bibliographical references and index.
    ISBN 0-8242-0917-6
    1. Drug abuse—United States. 2. Drug abuse—Treatment—United States. 3. Youth—Drug use—United States. 4. Teenagers—Drug use—United States. I. Sora, Joseph W. II. Series: Reference Shelf ; v. 69, no. 4.
HV5825.S8 1997
362.29'0973—dc21   97-24825
                                                   CIP

Cover: Two men lie in an inebriated state in front of a building.
Photo: AP/Wide World Photos

Printed in the United States of America

Contents

IV. Treating Substance Abuse

Bibliography

Preface

Although the statistics vary, it is generally believed that currently: 80 million Americans (nearly 33 percent of the total population) have tried an illegal substance at least once; 12 to 18 million (five to seven percent of the population) drink heavily; more than five million (two percent of the population) smoke marijuana more than once a week; over two million (.08 percent of the population) use cocaine regularly; and an estimated 750,000 (.03 percent of the population) use heroin. While these statistics may not appear shocking, they indicate that the abuse of intoxicating or mind-altering substances is not only present within, but also a relatively prevalent part of, American culture.

However, the statistics do not indicate or portray the characteristics of the substance abuse trend that are specific to today. For example, they do not reveal that substance abuse is shockingly (and ever-increasingly) prevalent among American youth. According to the University of Michigan's Institute for Social Research, currently four times as many eighth-graders use drugs on a daily basis than they did in 1992, twice as many eighth-graders tried crack in 1995 than in 1991, and marijuana use among eighth graders has more than doubled in the past five years. It must be noted that the prevalence of substance abuse by children as young as 13 or 14 years old is a particular manifestation of the current drug problem.

As the characteristics of the users change, so do the drugs themselves. It is estimated that the average purity of heroin has risen 60 percent, and marijuana is more than four times as potent today as it was 20 years ago. In like fashion, attitudes and opinions towards illegal substances have also taken an interesting and unprecedented turn. While there has always been an underground "drug-culture," not until today has there been such a mainstream polarization between those who advocate the continued criminalization of drugs and those who vie for their legalization.

While substance abuse is often understood as a simple and almost general "evil" that affects a certain portion of the population, it is really a changing phenomenon which adopts peculiarities and specifics according to the age in which it occurs. It follows that substance abuse evolves, taking on new forms, affecting different people and arousing different reactions. Substance abuse must therefore be understood not simply as an "evil" that should be eradicated, but as an issue whose characteristics are specific to the particular time period and environment in which we live. This issue of *The Reference Shelf* is meant to portray the fundamental challenge that the present issue of substance abuse poses for: our everyday lives; our children; our government's domestic and foreign policy; our ethical and moral belief systems; and the way we, as Americans, envision ourselves and our country. Aside from simply relaying the negative and harmful aspects of substance abuse, the articles contained herein explain both the overall effect of substance abuse upon the current time and place Americans live as well as its role in our culture.

The first section, Differing Reactions to Substance Abuse, contains articles that discuss the various and often disparate reactions the current increase in substance abuse has evoked. As this section will show, America is not of a single mind when it comes to answering what to do about the present drug problem. While the federal government attempts to both educate as to the negative effects of substance abuse, and stem the flow of drugs into the country, criticism of the value and result of the government's attempts grows. Such criticism often acts as a basis for a belief that drugs should be legalized. The articles in Section I outline both the government's response to the problem of substance abuse and the reactions and questions evoked by that response. Although it is clear that opinions differ over the question of what to do about substance abuse, there is little doubt that substance abuse is currently reaching crisis levels, particularly among our youth.

Section II, Substance Abuse and Youth, contains articles focusing entirely on the current increase of substance abuse among our youth. Today, the use of illegal substances by young children (12 to 14 years old) is increasing exponentially. This is a peculiarity of the present substance abuse problem. One central reason for this, according to the articles in Section II, is that attitudes towards substance abuse have relaxed, and advertising condemning substance abuse (recall the "Just Say No" campaign of the 1980s) has lessened. In addition to asserting the cause for the rise of substance abuse among young children, Section II's articles also provide listings of the types of drugs children are using as well as accounts of the surrounding communities' reaction to the use of illegal substances by their children.

The goal of Section III, The Culture of Substance Abuse, is to provide the reader with the understanding that substance abuse is a pervasive problem that can not be understood as an event or incident that occurs among particular people at certain times. As these articles will demonstrate, substance abuse can be part of an entire stratum of society from the night club filling "E-Heads" to those famous individuals who dominate our newspaper headlines and magazine articles, including professional athletes, models, famous musicians, etc. For these reasons, it should be understood as a culture or a force which embodies a totality of an individual's existence, while providing him or her with a kinship to others engaged in similarly abusive practices.

A work on substance abuse is not complete unless the means by which that problem can be treated are presented. Section IV, Treating Substance Abuse, presents a sampling of the methods by which addiction to illegal substances is treated as well as an overview of the current state of the treatment industry. Containing scholarly articles, personal accounts, and mainstream articles, Section IV provides an account of addiction recovery from the clinical perspective and the personal or internal perspective.

The editor wishes to thank all those who granted their permission to reprint the articles contained in this issue of *The Reference Shelf*. Special thanks are due to Sarah Imbarlina for her patience and assistance in organizing the articles, and Frank McGuckin, also for his patience and time spent bringing this issue to publication.

Joseph Sora
July 1997

I. Differing Reactions to Substance Abuse

Editor's Introduction

Section I of this compilation provides an overview of the differing reactions to the presence of substance abuse in America. In short, these articles demonstrate, as Barry R. McCaffrey notes, "there is no silver bullet, no quick way to reduce drug use or the damage it causes." It follows that government and media responses to drug use are neither unified nor cohesive as they embody a variety of dogma, belief, and theory. While the government has responded by devising and adopting a range of strategies aimed at lessening the presence of drugs in America and thereby protecting "our youth and society from the terrible damage caused by drug abuse," many others believe that such strategies actually add to the violence and bloodshed that accompanies the drug trade. Likewise, many others believe that decriminalizing or legalizing drugs would be tantamount to mass-murder. This section offers both a glimpse into these polar reactions as well as into their governing ideologies and perceptions of what the substance abuse problem truly signifies.

The first article in this section is a statement given by Robert S. Gelbard, Assistant Secretary for International Narcotics and Law Enforcement Affairs, to the House of Representatives' International Relations Committee. Here, Gelbard provides a summary of the government's "drug control efforts in this hemisphere" and, in doing so, outlines the United States government's response to the trafficking of particular substances from nearby countries to inside American borders. Clearly operating from the belief that the presence of certain substances must be eliminated from the national landscape, Gelbard summarizes the government's "Source-Country" strategy, the costs related to it, and the amount of seized drugs resulting from it.

As Gelbard outlines the government's strategy to prevent drugs from entering the country, the next article by Barry R. McCaffrey, Director Designee of the Office of National Drug Control Policy, presents the government's strategy to protect Americans from the drugs that are already within our borders. Such protection, McCaffrey believes, will arise only from a national strategy involving "treatment, prevention, education, enforcement, and interdiction." He is, therefore, concerned with not only enforcing the laws which prohibit the use of certain drugs, but also preventing that use from ever occurring, as well as treating the often devastating effects resulting from that use.

The criminalization of certain substances, and the government's effort to enforce that criminalization as seen in the current "War on Drugs" is not without its critics. The following article in this section presents negative reactions to both the government's present efforts at curbing drug use and the underlying notion that certain substances should necessarily be illegal. Eva C. Bertram and Kenneth E. Sharpe, writing in *The Nation*, assert that "the drug war...merits attack" because its basis in what Gelbard called the "Source-Country" strategy, i.e. the directing of drug-control efforts at those countries which are perceived as producing the largest amount of illegal substances, is futile. This is owed largely to the fact that as one drug producing field or factory is burned, several others rise up in its place. It follows that Bertram and Sharpe believe the government should understand America's substance abuse problem not as a battle with "particular traffickers or producers or dealers" but rather as a battle with "a market in products that are high in demand." In short, these authors assert there is "no enemy" only a desire for illegal substances, and all efforts to combat that desire should be tailored accordingly.

The next article, a study from *Monthly Labor Review,* examines the drug testing being widely implemented in workplaces throughout the United States, particularly in those industries with high-risk or unionized labor forces. Drug testing can be considered one of the most significant reactions by the American corporate sector to the problem of substance abuse. This article presents employers' reaction to both the number and scope of programs, as well as to the movement toward random drug testing. This article further reveals that corporate dedication to systematic identification of, and intervention in, cases of drug, and to a lesser extent alcohol abuse, is constantly being strengthened.

The strategies outlined by Gelbard and McCaffrey, each attacking a different facet of the substance abuse problem, stem from the belief that the use of particular substances must be understood as an illegal activity and therefore a violation of law. In the next article, Paul B. Stares, a non-resident senior fellow in the Brookings Foreign Policy Studies Program, argues against this notion, noting that, at the very least, the legalization of drugs must be considered. Stares asserts that the central problems of "illicit drug markets" are "the crime, corruption, and violence that attend the operation." As the legalization of drugs would effectively remove the need for a black market "operation" much of the violence and bloodshed that surrounds it would be similarly eliminated.

Arguing against Stares' hope for a reconsideration of drug legalization, James A. Inciardi and Christine A. Saum, writing in *The Public Interest,* provide a basis for the criminilization of certain drugs. According to Inciardi and Saum, drug legalization represents what many believe to be "an alternative strategy" to the government's current criminalization of certain drugs. Yet, as these authors argue, the call for such legalization is based on premises which are inherently false. In addition, the effects of such legalization would, according to these authors, escalate violent crime, increase physical illness and "compound any existing psychiatric problems among users and their family members." It follows that the criminalization of drugs is best understood as a belief based, in part, upon the notion that the legalization of drugs would only compound the existing substance abuse problem.

Drug Control in the Western Hemisphere[1]

Good afternoon, Mr. Chairman and distinguished members of the subcommittee. It is a pleasure to be here today to discuss our drug control efforts in this hemisphere. I would particularly like to review the progress we have made on our source country strategy and why it is critical to do more now. As I am sure you all have guessed, this is a topic about which I feel very strongly. It is a sentiment born of the strong conviction that measurable success in the counter-drug effort not only is achievable, but is very much within our reach.

Let me add a cautionary note that I always stress: This effort must be sustained. Success in a single year is not necessarily permanent. You might ask yourselves why we have asked for so little money to combat the drug trade overseas when the magnitude of the threat is so great. The answer, I believe, is that our request for fiscal year 1997, provided it is sustained and incrementally increased over time, provides insurance for drug control programs with measurable results. I know, from my experience in this job and as Ambassador to Bolivia, that uneven funding from year to year produces uneven results.

Before I discuss the source country strategy in depth, however, I would like to put U.S. budget figures into perspective. Our entire international counter-drug budget in fiscal year 1995, including military and Coast Guard support, came to about $850 million—6% of the total $13.3-billion anti-drug budget. At this low price tag, it remains an important demonstration of how U.S. international engagement pays real, cost-effective dividends to our citizens. The U.S. international drug-control budget is the equivalent of 8.5 metric tons of cocaine, given its street value of about $100 million per metric ton. Single cargo flights into Mexico have carried more cocaine than that. The approximately 130 metric tons of cocaine that Latin American and Caribbean nations seized with our help last year have a street value as great as our government's total anti-drug budget. In other words, the 6% of the budget that we invested in international programs last year provided a return of over 1,500%.

When put into that context, the President's 1997 budget request for international drug programs seems not only reasonable, but highly cost-effective. When you consider the costs to the U.S. of drug-related illnesses, crime and violence, and lost productivity—an estimated $69 billion a year—the potential payoff on this investment in drug control and demand reduction pro-

"The U.S. international drug-control budget is the equivalent of 8.5 metric tons of cocaine..."

---

[1] Statement delivered by Robert S. Gelbard, Assistant Secretary for International Narcotics and Law Enforcement Affairs, on June 6, 1996, from *U.S. Department of State Dispatch* 7/24:310-12 Je 10 '96.

grams becomes even more impressive.

Funds appropriated to the Bureau of International Narcotics and Law Enforcement Affairs—INL—the portion of the budget which is invested directly in crop control, alternative development, and support to law enforcement and judicial institutions— represent a very small percentage of the total. In fact, INL's 1997 budget request for international drug and crime control programs totals only $213 million—just over 1% of the total federal drug control budget request. We are most appreciative, Mr. Chairman, for this committee's strong support of our budget in the past and as we look to the future.

Why A Source Country Strategy?

President Clinton's 1993 decision to adopt the source country strategy was, in my view, inevitable. This government had spent some 10 years confronting a growing, increasingly sophisticated and violent group of largely Colombian drug-trafficking organizations. Our efforts were, at first, piecemeal. As we began to understand the threat better, coordination improved.

We helped producing countries build interdiction forces to target production and transportation centers. At the same time, we expanded our own resources in the Caribbean in the hopes of stopping the rising tide of cocaine before it reached U.S. shores. By the early 1990s, we had engaged Mexico in the interdiction effort to bolster our own domestic efforts to strengthen our border defenses—notably with the creation of the Northern Border Response Force. This strategy produced some significant seizures but, more importantly, disrupted trafficking operations and forced constant changes to evade Mexican interdiction activities.

Ultimately, despite successes, it became clear that we would never be able to stem the flow of drugs from South America or Mexico by focusing on interdiction alone—the traffickers would always be able to put another shipment in the air or in the water.

The adoption of the source country strategy was in no sense an abandonment of interdiction or the transit zone. Interdiction in the transit zone remains a critical element of the overall strategy, as can be seen in the vigorous bilateral efforts underway with Mexico. PDD-14 recognized, however, that our resources were finite and were too widely dispersed to have a major impact on trafficking. The President, therefore, directed us to focus on the drug crops, the kingpins, and their organizations, and the production and trafficking networks in the heartland of the trade— the three Andean source countries of Colombia, Peru, and Bolivia. For this reason, during my tenure, we have concentrated 60% to 65% of our annual budget on these countries.

INL: Laying Foundations for Long-Term Success

The ultimate objective of our source country strategy is to stem the flow of drugs to the U.S. Our most effective means of achieving and maintaining positive results are training and assistance programs that help the source countries develop strong legal frameworks and help build credible democratic institutions. Strong institutions will be better prepared to eradicate and control cultivation, to dismantle top crime and drug syndicates through investigation and prosecution, and to interdict drug shipments.

Our other key weapon is eradication of both coca and opium poppy, which provides the means to eliminate the source of this illegal trade completely. In the key source countries, eradication must be combined with sustainable alternative development in order to ensure that producers have viable means of supporting themselves once they abandon the trade. Without this carrot, governments, especially fragile ones, cannot wield effectively the stick of eradication. Even against the backdrop of very limited resources for alternative development in 1995, some substantial strides were made. Colombia continued its U.S.-supported aerial eradication program, eliminating an estimated 9,000 hectares of mature coca and up to 4,000 hectares of opium poppy. Bolivia manually eradicated almost 5,500 hectares of mature coca and destroyed seedbeds and new planting. New planting offset the gains in both countries, but support for eradication has increased, and new plantings are far more fragile than the mature coca that was destroyed. In Bolivia, a successful alternative development program—legal crops in the Chapare now cover double the hectarage of coca—is providing a strong counter-balance to coca. Peru, the world's leading supplier of coca, has yet to adopt a large-scale eradication program, but the government has begun to eradicate all new coca. Mexico made respectable strides against opium poppy cultivation, effectively eradicating over 60% of the 13,500 hectares cultivated in 1995.

"Colombia continued its U.S.-supported aerial eradication program, eliminating an estimated 9,000 hectares of mature coca..."

Strong Institutions Breed Success

In Colombia, with U.S. support and training, the Anti-Narcotics Police—or DANTI—has become one of the region's most skilled units of its kind. The DANTI has spearheaded Colombia's efforts to dismantle the production and trafficking infrastructure of the world's most productive traffickers. The National Police's capability will be upgraded further by the June 2 delivery of six additional UH-1H helicopters for use primarily in support of eradication. The Medellin drug syndicate has been virtually dismantled, and almost all of the top Cali traffickers are dead or in jail. The Prosecutor General's office is building cases against the drug lords and pursuing a wide-ranging investigation of narco-corruption that reaches to the highest levels of Colombian society and government.

Within the next few days, the Colombian Chamber of Deputies will issue a judgment, on the basis of evidence provided by the Prosecutor General, on whether or not President Samper should be tried by the Colombian Senate on charges that narco-traffickers contributed several million dollars to his 1994 presidential campaign. We have expressed our concern about the credibility, impartiality, and thoroughness of the Accusations Commission, which has recommended to the Chamber the President's exoneration. Only a full and transparent review of the charges by the duly elected representatives of the Colombian people could put an end to the current political crisis in the country.

In the meantime, we are reviewing Colombia's cooperation on the counter-drug front and our policy options for securing better cooperation. We will discuss with the Colombian Government this month our expectations for progress this year, in the context of a mid-year review of objectives for certification. President Clinton made it very clear on March 1 that he wanted to see improved Colombian cooperation and would reserve the option for applying additional sanctions if Colombia's counter-drug performance did not improve.

In Peru, the enhanced police and military interdiction operations—made possible in large part because of U.S.-provided helicopter assets and intelligence support—have successfully disrupted air smuggling and raised the cost of trafficking operations. Peru followed through on a threat to shoot down trafficker aircraft that violated its airspace. In so doing, the Government of Peru disrupted the so-called "air bridge" between Peru and Colombia. Consequently, the business in Peru's coca markets has suffered. Coca prices dropped last year because pilots were reluctant to fly, and stocks accumulated. The Government of Peru National Drug Plan calls for a 50% reduction in coca by the year 2000. We are supporting this ambitious goal by making Peru's case for additional resources before the international donor community and pressing the GOP to accelerate its coca reduction plans. Peru has recently created a separate, new court system to deal with drug offenses.

In Bolivia, U.S.-supported rural police, intelligence, riverine, and air units have substantially disrupted the trade—putting behind bars many of the Colombian traffickers that directed the trade there—and now are targeting Bolivian organizations which supply cocaine products to Colombia, Mexico, Brazil, and directly to markets in Europe. At the same time, they carried out an unprecedented campaign to prevent new coca planting in support of the government's reinvigorated eradication efforts. Special investigative units focus on the trade in precursor chemicals used to process cocaine, and a group of special prosecutors now is dedicated solely to dealing with drug-related crimes in Bolivia.

Political Will—The Key Intangible

A less tangible, but no less important factor to the success of the source country strategy is the will and strength of governments in the region to weather the political backlash that effective anti-drug measures inevitably trigger. Political will is the most difficult component of the strategy to generate and the hardest to measure. Despite some setbacks in the last few years, however, I am willing to argue that we have never had a more important opportunity than we do now to advance our counter-drug agenda in the hemisphere.

I do not know a single drug expert who, five years ago, would have been willing to predict the downfall of the Medellin drug syndicate, let alone the progress that has been made throughout the hemisphere in dismantling the Cali organization. Eradication campaigns in Bolivia and Colombia have shown that it is possible to restrict significant expansion of the coca crop, and both governments now acknowledge that the elimination of the drug crop is critical to their national security. In fact, in April of this year, the Bolivian Drug Secretary delivered an unprecedented speech at the UN Commission on Narcotic Drugs emphasizing the necessity of eradication. Meanwhile, despite ill-founded criticism over its force-down policy, Peru stayed the course and produced an interdiction breakthrough which we must now exploit. We must convince the Government of Peru to follow up by containing and reducing the coca grown within its borders.

"Current research shows that roughly 200 hectares of coca eradicated deprives the system of up to a metric ton of cocaine."

Maximizing Our Opportunity

U.S.-supported crop control efforts, training, and assistance under the source country strategy have created policy and operational environments ripe for even greater success. The goal of significantly reducing the supply of illegal drugs is attainable—but not without a sustained commitment. Specifically, we will be unable to fully capitalize on the successes of 1995 without adequate resources to:

- Broaden crop control and interdiction programs;
- Enhance support in Bolivia and Peru for alternative development; and
- Expand training and assistance to the beleaguered judicial and law enforcement institutions charged with implementing and enforcing hosts of new laws.

Drug crop control remains pivotal to the ultimate success of the source country strategy. Eradication, particularly aerial eradication, has the potential to be our most effective tool. The drug crop represents a key vulnerability to the trafficking groups. The crops are detectable and destroyable—tactically easier to target than airplanes or cargo vessels loaded with cocaine—and they are critical to the industry's survival. Current research shows that roughly 200 hectares of coca eradicated deprives the system of up to a metric ton of cocaine. These factors demand that eradication—and related alternative development projects—remain central to our source country strategy.

INL's resources will be devoted to supporting aerial and manual eradication—and to programs designed to develop income-generating alternatives for coca growers to abandon their crops. We will continue to support aviation, police, and riverine units that form the backbone of interdiction forces in the Andes, and will enhance our regional training efforts in order to expand cooperation among the source countries. DoD, by lending consistent support to broad interdiction efforts, has been critical to building cooperation among the Andean nations—some of which have long been adversaries. Continued and expanded support for the interdiction infrastructure—in terms of radars, communications, and training—remains central to the success of our efforts.

In addition to our primary focus on the source countries, we face significant new challenges. Our 1997 budget request reflects our plans for addressing them. Successes in the Andes, particularly against the Cali Cartel in Colombia, have produced shifts in the trade, and have created new opportunities for Mexican, Peruvian, and Bolivian trafficking syndicates, among others.

In this regard, I want to highlight recent Mexican counternarcotics efforts. Under the leadership of ONDCP Director Barry McCaffrey and Mexican Attorney General Lozano, we have launched an effort to develop a comprehensive bilateral strategy to attack the trafficking groups which move the bulk of the cocaine destined for U.S. markets across our shared border. These trafficking groups, which once served Cali and Medellin, now aspire to succeed them. They have not only begun to contract their own multi-ton shipments from Andean suppliers, but are further diversifying their trade with methamphetamines. Mexican-dominated distribution groups now dominate the manufacture and sale of this destructive substance in the U.S. and are expanding their role in the sale of cocaine and other illicit substances.

Combating these transborder organizations, which have strong footholds in both the U.S. and Mexico, will require even greater bilateral cooperation between the U.S. and Mexican Governments. It will require intense legal cooperation, as we achieved with the January arrest and expulsion by Mexico of Juan Garcia Abrego, notorious leader of the Gulf Cartel based in Matamoros, Mexico, but whose empire spread across Mexico and the United States. It will also require increased material and logistics support to interdiction forces, as well as stepped-up training and assistance for law enforcement and judicial institutions in Mexico.

We are implementing a new heroin control strategy and must respond to the President's requirement, expressed in PDD-42, for a comprehensive international crime control strategy which places special attention on the money laundering and financial crimes which enable all of these drug and crime syndicates to continue to operate.

All of these efforts require the commitment of U.S. resources. But as I said at the start, our real investment is small given the long-term payoffs of the source country strategy. Our investment of time and money and the provision of U.S. training reap the added benefit of strengthening these often very new democracies. The institutions we support are less vulnerable to corruption, especially as their leaders see for themselves the benefits of ridding their countries of this corrosive threat. Such changes not only will produce success in eliminating the drug threat in this hemisphere, but will ensure these countries remain viable allies and trading partners.

I know this committee is attuned to the challenges we face. I am confident that, with your help, we can continue to show dramatic results.

The So Called War on Drugs: What We Must Do[2]

It is an enormous honor to appear before this distinguished committee to be considered for the position as Director, Office of National Drug Control Policy. I take very seriously the great responsibility that President Clinton has asked me to accept. The President's instructions to me were to help create a cooperative bipartisan effort among Congress and the Federal, state and local governments. President Clinton and I share the view that the American people can and must both reduce illicit drug use and also protect our youth and society from the terrible damage caused by drug abuse and drug trafficking.

A lot of energy and magnificent leadership has been dedicated to addressing these problems over the years. Many American leaders including President Reagan, President Bush, and now President Clinton have provided a strategic vision and encouragement.

However, I would be remiss to not publicly applaud the positive role that Congress has played in this effort. Senator Hatch and Senator Biden, your leadership and creativity on these issues has been crucial. So too have been the contributions of many other key congressional leaders such as Senator Feinstein, Representative Charles Rangel, and Representative Bill Zeliff.

I would also like to specifically recognize the efforts of attorney Janet Reno, Secretary of Education Dick Riley, Secretary of Health and Human Services Donna Shalala, DEA Administrator Tom Constantine, and FBI Director Louis Freeh.

In the last two weeks I have been encouraged by my preparatory discussions with these superb public servants.

If confirmed by the Senate, I can assure you that we, the senior officials of government, will work together to forge a coherent strategy and in a responsive manner to Congressional viewpoints.

We should have no doubt that illicit drug use is a major menace to public health, the safety of our society, and to the well being of our youth.

In 1962, fewer than 4 million Americans had ever experimented with illegal drugs. Today, more than 80 million have. We are vulnerable. The good news is that most of those 80 million quit using drugs.

In the 1990s alone, illegal drug abuse has cost America more than $300 billion and 100,000 dead.

At least one third of all property crimes, assaults, or murders

---

[2] Speech delivered by Barry R. McCaffrey, Director Designee of the Office of National Drug Control Policy, retired General of the United States Army, at the Senate Judiciary Committee, in Washington, D. C., on February 27, 1996, from *Vital Speeches of the Day* 62:325-6 Mr 15 '96.

have a drug connection.

Today, illicit drug use and tolerance of drug use by teenagers is once again rising dramatically.

The damage caused to America by illegal drug use is intolerable. We must and can reduce this terrible burden on the American people.

And we can't reduce that burden without enforcement. Law enforcement is crucial. Because of it, illegal cocaine costs 15 times as much as the same substance sold in legal form. Without it there would be a catastrophic rise in the availability and usage of illegal drugs.

The metaphor "War on Drugs" is inadequate to describe this terrible menace facing the American people. Dealing with the problem of illegal drug abuse is more akin to dealing with cancer.

Wars are relatively straight forward. You identify the enemy, select a general, assign him a mission and resources, and let him get the job done.

In this struggle against drug abuse, there is no silver bullet, no quick way to reduce drug use or the damage it causes.

Step number one is to mobilize the societal family—the same as when helping a cancer patient. As the President noted in the State of the Union address, "the challenge begins at home with parents talking to their children openly and firmly."

Then we must implement a long-term comprehensive plan that goes to the heart of the problem—reducing the availability of illegal drugs and their use.

It is wrong to sell drugs. This should be punished. It is also wrong to use illegal drugs. However, this is much more than a law enforcement problem. It requires a sustained and coordinated systems approach.

Clearly you can't defeat cancer if you give up hope. Nor can you make progress against illicit drug tracking and use if you give up hope. And the answer to self-destructive proposals such as legalization is an unequivocal no.

Addressing the use and trafficking of heroin, cocaine, methamphetamine, marijuana, or other illicit drugs requires a systems approach. Each facet of the problem will require a focused program that attacks the disease while limiting damaging effects. We must design, test, and implement programs which are affordable and which do not cause unintended consequences while going after the root cause of the problem.

Addressing drug abuse requires a systems-based approach and long-term commitment.

Our current national drug policy is basically sound and features many successful programs. I have been an integral part of this strategy the past two years; we have made progress.

But we need to create an operational construct that links those successes together into a coordinated effort.

We also need to reach a better consensus on our strategy and to establish an active international coalition.

> *"Each facet of the problem will require a focused program that attacks the disease while limiting damaging effects."*

Treatment, prevention, education, enforcement, and interdiction must all be synergistic components of that policy.

In my own view we must be even more successful in our efforts to convince American youth that experimentation with illicit drugs is dangerous. They must understand that casual drug use is like playing Russian roulette. Some of them for sure will be destroyed by addiction.

We must also find ways to reduce drug consumption by both adult casual and hard-core users.

However, we must focus as a priority on reducing consumption among the three million hard core users who consume 75% of the total tonnage of illegal drugs. A focus of treatment programs on hard core addicts can cause a reduction of drug-related property crimes and also drug trafficking and the violence and mayhem it spawns.

"In 1979, more than 22 million Americans used illegal drugs. 5 million used cocaine."

One of my early intentions, if confirmed, will be to examine the evidence on what works and what doesn't in drug treatment programs. We owe our Congress and the American people a full accounting of the costs and payoffs of all components of our drug strategy.

Effective treatment regimes are essential to reducing drug consumption. Specifically, let me underscore my conviction that drug testing and then the treatment of convicted criminals prior to and following release from prison is vital. We simply must provide treatment to these people if we expect to protect the American people from violence and property crimes.

Finally, allow me to offer a judgment that while illicit drug use constitutes a great menace to our society the ways in which we address this challenge must be equitable and respectful of the freedoms and rights outlined by our Constitution. This [is] a free society and we must conduct our public policy with an absolute respect for the law.

A lot of progress has already been made. In many ways we are not losing the so called "War On Drugs."

A decade of hard work and the support of Congress has already substantially reduced illegal drug abuse.

In 1979, more than 22 million Americans used illegal drugs. 5 million used cocaine.

Today, less that 12 million Americans use illegal drugs regularly. Around three million could be classified as hard core users, including those incarcerated. The number of cocaine users has dropped 30 percent in the past three years.

But there are still serious problems to face up to.

While the number of hard core drug users has remained steady at about three million, these addicts are using ever increasing tonnage's of cocaine, heroin, methamphetamines, and other drugs.

Medical costs of drug abuse now exceed $20 billion per year. More than 500,000 emergency room episodes last year were drug related.

Teenage use of marijuana has doubled in the past three years. This statistic tell[s] us that our prevention programs must be more effective. We cannot cut back on these programs.

About 300 metric tons of Latin American cocaine are being smuggled into the U.S. every year along with increasing quantities of Burmese and Colombian heroin and Mexican methamphetamines.

A fundamental principle of American society is that the law must provide equal protection to all. Yet drug abuse and trafficking are having a disproportionate effect on our poor, our minorities and our cities.

We must extend a helping hand to those most in need. Many of our fellow citizens lack secure neighborhoods, safe schools, and healthy work environments. Trust in our public institutions is declining as a result. We must guarantee the safety of the families and working men and women in our urban areas.

We must reduce the harm inflicted on those sectors of our society. There can be no safe havens for drug traffickers and no tolerance for those who would employ children. We cannot tolerate open air drug markets in our cities: markets fueled by suburban money and which exacerbate the drug crisis.

If confirmed, what do I bring to the table? Optimism.

As a member of the President's team, we will demonstrate to the American people that we can actually successfully do something about this problem. We are not helpless. We put astronauts on the moon. We beat polio and the Mafia. We won Desert Storm in 31 days and the Cold War in 45 years.

There is no reason to believe that the American people with our enormous spiritual and moral strength, our respect for law, and our compassion for our children cannot control the menace of drug abuse and the criminality it engenders.

Thirty one years of association with an American military team that demanded results and which overcame a serious drug abuse problem of our own.

Finally, commitment to provide leadership, energy, and organization to our counterdrug efforts.

President Clinton and the legislation that authorized this position have provided me the requisite authority to effectively coordinate the national counterdrug effort.

However this challenge to our youth, to our future, to our safety, and to our health cannot be met by government alone.

It is one we must all collectively face up to: government officials; law enforcement officers; teachers and coaches; religious leaders; parents; family members; health care providers; entertainers; and journalists.

All of us, as Americans, are fed up with the devastation that illicit drug use has brought to American families, neighborhoods, and work places. All of us must share the responsibility to address this problem.

Senators, thank you for the privilege of coming before this

committee.

I will be forthcoming in responding to your questions and will take careful note of your views.

If confirmed I will welcome a continuing partnership with the Congress in creating programs to implement our strategy.

The Drug War's Phony Fix:
Why Certification Doesn't Work[3]

As President Clinton heads for Latin America next month to discuss important issues of trade and democracy in the hemisphere, U.S. relations with the region have been soured by domestic drug war politics—and particularly by recent battles over the "certification" of Mexico as a drug war ally.

The annual certification ritual began in 1986, when Congress passed a law requiring the President to certify that key countries are cooperating in the U.S. war on drugs, and to "decertify" and sanction those that are not. The issues at the center of this year's certification debate were how to evaluate the allegiance of Mexico and Colombia to the drug war and how to pressure them to improve their performance. The outcome was predictable. When the President released his certification list in early March, Mexico made the grade and Colombia did not—despite overwhelming evidence that Mexico is a primary transit route for cocaine and a major producer of heroin, methamphetamines and marijuana, and that its antidrug agencies are steeped in corruption. Just before Clinton's announcement, Mexican drug czar Gen. Jesus Gutierrez Rebollo was arrested for cooperating with one of the country's most powerful drug lords, Amado Carrillo Fuentes.

In defending Mexico's certification, Administration offices paraded a long list of "body counts," showing rising numbers of drug seizures, arrests and tough new laws passed in Mexico. Some argue that decertification—which triggers cuts in U.S. aid, possible trade sanctions and U.S. opposition to loans from international lending institutions—would make Mexico's performance even worse, and could undermine cooperation on issues of immigration, financial stability and NAFTA-based trade.

The move produced a backlash in Congress and launched a heated debate. The House voted to overturn the certification and impose sanctions if Mexico didn't improve its performance in ninety days. But in the end, certification stood: When the debate moved to the Senate, Administration officials intervened and a milder compromise resolution censured Mexico's efforts as inadequate and required President Clinton to report back later this year.

The spectacle of Washington scrambling to circumvent its own drug war laws drew criticism from both sides of the border. Some U.S. critics denounced the certification process as institutional-

---

[3] Article by Eva C. Bertram, a policy analyst in Washington, D.C. and Ph.D. candidate in political science at Yale University and Kenneth E. Sharpe, chair of the political science department at Swarthmore College, from *The Nation* magazine 264:18+ Ap 28 '97. They are coauthors (with Morris Blachman and Peter Andreas) of *Drug War Politics: The Price of Denial*. Reprinted with permission.

ized whitewashing and pointed to the irony of a system that allows the drug-consuming United States to vilify those who supply its habit. Many condemned drug certification as a modern variant of Washington's historic imperialist impulse in Latin America. In Mexico, President Ernesto Zedillo reacted to the foreign intervention implied by the House vote by vowing to "act with all necessary energy to defend the dignity and sovereignty of the Mexicans."

These critics are right to condemn drug certification as arrogant and hypocritical. But it is the drug war that merits attack, not certification itself. The United States invariably sets criteria for determining which countries should receive U.S. assistance and in what amounts. And Congress has used the certification process appropriately—if not always effectively—in the past to hold the President accountable and to elevate certain policy goals. The more important issue is what should be "certified" and when.

"El Salvador's security forces made token gestures to stop the most blatant abuses..."

In the early eighties, for example, Congress required Ronald Reagan to certify El Salvador's commitment to protecting human rights as a condition for continued U.S. aid. Every month, the U.S.-backed military and its death-squad surrogates were murdering, disappearing and torturing hundreds of opposition leaders, peasant and labor organizers and human rights advocates. It was legitimate for Congress to tie continued aid to adherence to internationally recognized human rights standards: The Salvadoran military had the power to stop its brutality, and the interests of Salvadorans and Americans alike in peace and democracy were being undermined.

The process was undeniably compromised. El Salvador's security forces made token gestures to stop the most blatant abuses, and U.S. officials lied about the improvements to justify continued aid. But the certification process put the long-neglected issue of human rights on the agenda. It gave human rights advocates in the United States a chance to challenge government policy publicly every six months, forced the Reagan Administration to demand modest reforms to mollify its domestic opponents and helped create political space for democratic forces in El Salvador.

Certifying El Salvador's progress in meeting international standards of human rights arguably advanced a legitimate foreign policy goal. But certifying Mexico's progress in meeting U.S. drug war goals does not—not because reducing drug abuse isn't a worthy aim but because it is neither an achievable nor an appropriate foreign policy objective.

The test of drug war "commitment" that the United States uses to score Mexico diverts public attention from a disturbing fact: Even if Mexico earned a perfect grade for its drug war efforts, this would do virtually nothing to reduce levels of drug use in the United States, and it could do a great deal to undermine the shared interests of Mexico and the United States in democracy and human rights. The reason is simple: The war on the foreign drug supply is flawed, and no matter how fervently it is fought, it is bound to fail and to bring widespread damage in its wake.

The three fatal flaws in the drug strategy stem from the character of the drug war "enemy." The United States and its allies are not battling particular traffickers or producers or dealers, but a market in products that are in high demand, extremely lucrative and generally cheap and easy to produce and transport. This makes the effort to reduce the supply of drugs to the United States—by eradicating crops, destroying processing labs, blocking trafficking routes and seizing drug supplies—interminable and ultimately futile. Eliminating crops or trafficking routes is like slaying the hydra: Many heads grow back to replace each one that's cut off. Campaigns to suppress drug production and trafficking simply lead producers and traffickers to set up operations elsewhere to meet the demand—shifting or even spreading drug production and trafficking to new routes and regions.

"Between 1988 and 1995, more than 138,000 acres of coca were destroyed."

This explains the recent findings of the Congressional General Accounting Office that net coca and opium poppy cultivation has increased, despite the efforts of the United States and its drug war allies. Between 1988 and 1995, more than 138,000 acres of coca were destroyed. But because "farmers planted new coca faster than existing crops were eradicated," the G.A.O. wrote, production jumped 15 percent. Global production of opium, meanwhile, has doubled in the past decade, according to Barry McCaffrey, director of the Office of National Drug Control Policy.

The hydra effect is not new. Drug-control campaigns against heroin in Turkey in the seventies stimulated heroin production in Southeast Asia, Afghanistan and Mexico. In Peru, success in disrupting the "air bridge" to Colombia led to a switch to river routes; now the Pentagon is studying plans to shift millions in that direction. Closer to home, U.S. officials were proud of the significant drop in cocaine smuggling after intense interdiction efforts in southern Florida in the eighties. But before long, traffickers shifted to air drops over the Caribbean for pickup by boat. When enforcers caught up with this tactic, traffickers switched to routes through northern Mexico, and are now plying new routes in the Pacific. Coast Guard Vice Adm. Roger Rufe Jr. put the problem candidly: "When you press the balloon in one area, it pops up in another.... It's a market economy; with demand as it is in the U.S., they have plenty of incentive to try other routes."

A second flaw compounds the hydra effect. The U.S. drug warriors aim to cut the foreign drug supply—and raise U.S. prices—with tough enforcement strategies that make drug production and trafficking more risky and costly. But their very success in raising production costs and consumer prices also radically inflates black market profits for growers and traffickers. A pure gram of pharmaceutical cocaine that would cost about $15, for example, brings about $150 on the retail black market. Production costs are so low, meanwhile, that "the average drug organization can afford to lose 70 percent to 80 percent of its product and still be profitable," explained one former Drug Enforcement Administration official.

These black-market profits provide a steady incentive for drug suppliers to remain in the trade, and for new suppliers to enter. So the stick (law enforcement) that is intended to discourage black marketeers ironically creates the carrot (enormous profits) that encourages them. This profit paradox insures that producers and traffickers pursuing the trade's high profits will keep the supply of drugs up, and competition among them will keep prices from rising too high—undermining the aim of policy. It is thus not surprising that heroin and cocaine prices have declined, not increased, over the past fifteen years.

The logic of the market defeats the drug war in yet a third way, which could be called the "value-added effect." Most of the price of drugs on U.S. streets is the result of the value added to the drugs after they enter this country—the inflated black-market costs of distributing them here. At the point of export, in fact, the price of cocaine is still only 3 to 5 percent of the price a U.S. consumer will pay. Even the costs of smuggling the drug from Colombia to the United States account for less than 5 percent of the retail price. This means that an extremely successful crop-eradication program that tripled the leaf price of coca would raise cocaine prices in the United States by only 1 percent. It means that if U.S. interdiction programs were to seize an inconceivable 50 percent of all cocaine shipped from Colombia, this would add less than 3 percent to the retail price of cocaine in this country. The effect on drug use in the United States would be barely perceptible.

"The fight against corruption is the clearest example of the drug war's collateral damage."

These three fatal flaws make the drug war efforts of Mexico and other countries irrelevant in stemming abuse and addiction in the United States. At the same time, the inevitable failure of foreign drug war allies to reduce the supply significantly generates continued U.S. pressure to escalate their antidrug efforts—or face sanctions. The consequences of this useless and unending crusade for countries like Mexico are disastrous. Millions of tax dollars are poured down a black hole rather than invested in meeting social needs. The lives of drug enforcement agents are needlessly lost. Delicate relations around bilateral issues of trade, investment and immigration are distorted. And advances in democracy and human rights protections are eroded.

The fight against corruption is the clearest example of the drug war's collateral damage. Democratic forces in Mexico have been struggling to challenge decades of one-party rule, sustained in part by high-level corruption and fraud. But the drug war has complicated these efforts by exacerbating corruption among politicians and security forces. Evidence recently released in U.S. district court in San Diego documented the Tijuana cartel's payoffs to hundreds of Mexican federal and state law-enforcement officials. Pressure from the United States to fight drugs led

President Zedillo, in 1995, to step up the drug war by calling in the military—one of the few armies in Latin America that has historically remained outside politics and respectful of civilian rule.

With the cartels spending an estimated $6 billion a year on bribery in Mexico, however, drug war corruption is likely to overwhelm the Mexican military long before the military overwhelms the drug trade. In February and March alone, two generals were jailed on bribery charges. Soldiers under the command of drug-tainted officers have already been implicated in kidnappings and disappearances. The U.S. government's "success" in pressuring Mexico to increase its commitment to the drug war thus threatens to replace the corrupted police force with a more powerful, unaccountable and corrupt military.

At home, too, the drug certification process takes a toll. The exercise of certifying countries that can never do enough to curb drug problems is politically dishonest, and maintaining the fiction requires gyrations and lies: "What happens is that Congress requires the President to certify that the world is perfect," explains Representative David Obey. "Then when he has to do that to further the interests of American foreign policy," Congress attacks him for not telling the truth.

Worse, drug certification sets the wrong agenda for public debate. Nobody asks whether an overseas war on supply will ever work. No one points out its flaws or tallies the mounting collateral damage. Instead, policy-makers demand more funding and more firepower from foreign drug war allies. And the U.S. public is led to believe that the problems of abuse and addiction at home are the fault of weak-willed foreign governments—denying our own responsibility for the prevention and treatment of what is essentially a domestic problem.

Prevalence of Drug Testing in the Workplace[4]

Substance abuse has compelled many U.S. firms to create strategies that would help keep it out of the workplace. Some firms have sponsored elaborate and extensive programs to control alcohol and drug misuse. However, these programs have tended to rely on a supervisor's, a coworker's, or an employee's judgment about the presence of substance abuse in another individual or themselves. In the 1980s, some firms began to adopt drug and alcohol testing as an objective strategy to detect and control substance abuse. Advocates of this approach assert that an employee's positive test results can be linked to impairments in job performance, safety risks, and absenteeism.

While drug testing programs span many segments of society (including suspected criminal offenders and automobile operators), this article focuses on the prevalence and characteristics of drug testing programs in private-sector workplaces within the United States. First, we describe the proliferation of drug tests as evidenced in earlier studies. We then present our findings from a national telephone survey conducted in 1993, which estimated the prevalence and characteristics of testing programs, and descriptors of worksites most likely to implement them. We discuss the implementation of various types of programs (that is, preemployment, random, regular), the types of worksites that conduct such tests, and the employees who are eligible to be tested in those worksites. Research findings are discussed within the context of social policy and the findings of earlier research studies. Lastly, we offer some comments regarding the future of testing and its integration with other workplace substance abuse control strategies.

Drug Testing Trends

Surveys of worksite respondents indicate a growing trend in the implementation of drug testing programs from the mid-1980s to the present. For example, one study finds that 18 percent of Fortune 500 companies tested their employees in 1985, but by 1991, the proportion had more than doubled to 40 percent. A survey conducted by the American Management Association in 1988 indicated increases in the testing of both applicants and current employees for drugs. Thirty-eight percent of all the organizations in the survey tested job applicants, compared with 28 percent of those in 1987; 36 percent tested current employees,

[4] Article by Tyler D. Hartwell, a senior statistician at the Research Triangle Institute, Triangle Park, NC; Paul D. Steele, a director of research at Vera Institute of Justice, New York, NY; Michael T. French, a research associate professor, University of Miami, Coral Gables, FL; and Nathaniel F. Rodman, a research statistician at Research Triangle Institute, from *Monthly Labor Review* 119:35-42 N '96. Reprinted with permission.

compared with 28 percent in 1986. By 1991, 48 percent of Fortune 1000 firms engaged in some type of drug testing. Another study found that up to 63 percent of surveyed employers performed some type of testing in 1992. And, in a survey of 342 large firms (that is, firms that have more than 200 workers) in the State of Georgia, Terry Blum, and others report that 77 percent of the companies engaged in some type of drug testing between 1991 and 1992. In addition to these relatively small surveys, representative national surveys conducted by the Bureau of Labor Statistics indicate that 31.9 percent of worksites with more than 250 employees had drug testing programs in 1988, and by 1990, that proportion had increased to 45.9 percent. Even with the methodological differences among these studies, it seems reasonable to conclude that the drug testing of job applicants and current employees has become much more common in recent years.

Worksites Linked to Testing

Previous research indicates that drug testing programs are implemented differently, according to company size and industry type. For example, a study conducted by the American Management Association in 1987 reported that while 43 percent of large corporate respondents (sales over $500 million) indicated that they test job applicants, only 16 percent of smaller corporate respondents (less than $50 million in sales) reported any type of drug testing. In the BLS Survey of Employer Anti-Drug Programs, conducted in the summer of 1988, 43 percent of the largest worksites (with 1,000 employees or more) had drug testing programs, compared with 2 percent of the smallest worksites (fewer than 50 employees). Furthermore, the BLS follow-up survey, conducted in 1990, showed an increase in the percentage of larger companies, but no significant increase in the percentage of small firms with drug testing programs.

Firms implementing drug testing programs also can be distinguished by type of industry. The 1989 Conference Board survey showed that three-fourths of the companies with drug testing programs were manufacturers or gas and electric utilities, while nearly half of the companies that reported not having a drug testing program were in banking, insurance, and other financial service industries. The 1988 BLS survey also showed that worksites in mining, communications, public utilities, and transportation were most likely to have testing programs, reaffirming the findings reported by the Conference Board. Worksites least likely to have testing programs were those in the retail trade and services industries. Worksites in the latter industries tended to be small, however, confounding the relationship between the existence of testing programs and specific industry type.

Differences in Programs

Three primary distinctions among drug testing programs relate to
the persons or groups subject to testing, the scheduling of tests,
and the substances for which they are tested. The groups that are
subject to testing are usually job applicants or current employees. Testing of new applicants appears to be a more common policy than any form of testing of current employees. For example,
the Conference Board survey reports that almost half of all organizations screened job applicants by using a drug test. In addition, the study by Blum, and her colleagues found that job applicants were not often subjected to drug testing among the large
firms in Georgia. The firms that did test current employees, but
not applicants were rare, and were probably located in communities with limited labor markets.

*"...the Conference
Board survey
reports that
almost half of all
organizations
screened job
applicants by
using a drug test."*

The scheduling of tests among current employees is usually
classified as random, comprehensive, or for reasonable cause
(including followup testing). Random testing is completed with
all or a specific segment of employees at a particular worksite, on
an unannounced, variable schedule. Random testing seems to be
the approach most commonly implemented by firms affected by
Department of Transportation regulations. The proportion of
larger firms engaged in random testing of employees has
increased rapidly. In fact, one study found an increase from 2
percent in 1987 to 30 percent in 1991. Blum and colleagues found
that 18 percent of the firms in the American Management survey
conducted random tests in 1988.

On a regular basis, companies are likely to conduct testing as
a part of a routinely scheduled annual physical examination.
Alternatively, they may otherwise announce testing dates, or
periods in which tests will be conducted, to employees. This pattern of testing is likely to be conducted with all workers, and
unlike random testing, does not seem to have a detrimental effect
on employee morale (the administrators are tested along with
subordinates). Regular testing is usually more acceptable to
workers and organized labor, and it can enhance the firm's
image in the community. It is less effective than random testing
in detecting substance misuse, however, because employees are
usually notified when the test will be scheduled.

Among companies that test current employees, testing for reasonable cause has been the most common practice, and is based
on suspicion of substance misuse (resulting from unsafe or non-
productive practices, observation of erratic behavior, possession,
or other indications of intoxication or policy violation). If detected, substance abusers are given the opportunity to seek treatment by the firm and retain their jobs. They could be subjected
to return-to-work and followup testing as a condition of employment, for a period of time.

Employers have the option of selecting substances for which
employees are tested, threshold levels of various chemicals in the

body that would constitute a positive drug test, and the option of retesting in the case of a positive result. Of particular interest is the inclusion of alcohol testing in a comprehensive drug testing program. While practically all companies that conduct alcohol tests also test for drugs, only a small proportion of all drug testing programs screen for alcohol misuse.

Other corporate responses. According to the 1989 Conference Board survey, drug testing programs were typically part of an integrated substance abuse strategy, which included a written substance abuse policy, an employee assistance program, and a drug education and awareness program. Coordinated efforts to deal with alcohol and drug misuse in the workplace were far less common in corporations without drug testing programs. Similarly, one study found that 60 percent of companies with a drug testing program also had a comprehensive treatment and education program. Another study reported that more than one-half of companies with drug testing programs also had Employee Assistance Programs. Other research has indicated that organizations with drug testing programs are significantly more likely to also have Employee Assistance Programs than those without drug testing programs.

"The prevalence of worksite drug testing increased approximately 32 percent..."

Results

Table 1 [p.27] presents national estimates of drug and alcohol testing for worksites and employees by worksite size, type of industry, and region. (See appendix for a description of the methodology used in this study. [p.30]) Approximately 48 percent of all private worksites in the United States with 50 or more full-time employees conduct drug tests, and approximately 23 percent test employees for alcohol misuse. The prevalence of worksite drug testing increased approximately 32 percent (that is, from 16 percent to 48 percent) from the 1988 BLS survey to the period of our survey, 1992-93.

Worksite size. Table 1 also shows a positive relationship between worksite size and the prevalence of a drug or an alcohol testing program. Approximately 71 percent of worksites with more than 1,000 employees conduct drug tests and 42 percent test for alcohol misuse. In contrast, 40.2 percent of worksites with 50 to 99 employees conduct drug tests and 16.5 percent test for alcohol misuse.

Because of the relatively greater prevalence of drug and alcohol testing programs in larger worksites, most employees in the United States are in worksites with these programs. As shown in table 1, about 62 percent of all employees in private-sector worksites (with 50 or more workers) are employed by firms which conduct drug tests and approximately 33 percent are employed by firms which test for alcohol misuse. Compared with the BLS survey, this coverage rate is greater in all worksite size categories.

Type of industry. The prevalence of drug and alcohol testing varies across industry groups. As table 1 shows, the manufacturing (60.2 percent); wholesale and retail trade (53.7 percent); communications, utilities, and transportation (72.4 percent); and mining and construction (69.6 percent) industries have the highest prevalence of drug testing, compared with the finance, real estate, and insurance (22.6 percent) and services (27.9 percent) industries, which have the lowest. A similar pattern is demonstrated for alcohol testing programs with the communications, utilities, and transportation (34.9 percent) industries having the highest prevalence rates and the finance, real estate, and insurance industries (7.8 percent) having the lowest rates. Approximately, the same ranking orders apply when percentage of worksite data are compared with percentage of employees (table 1).

Regional areas. The highest prevalence for drug and alcohol testing in worksites, by regional area (as defined by the Bureau of the Census) is in the South (56.3 percent for drugs and 26.3 percent for alcohol), while the lowest is in the Northeast (33.3 percent for drugs and 12.9 percent for alcohol). The Midwestern and Western regions have similar prevalence rates (approximately 48 percent for drugs and 25 percent for alcohol). (The remainder of this article pertains to drug testing programs only.)

Worksites and Employees

Table 2 [p.28] examines the relationship between the prevalence of drug testing and various employee and worksite characteristics. For example, of all employees in worksites with 50 or more full-time employees, 12.7 percent are represented by a union. However, worksites with a larger percentage of union employees are more likely to have a drug testing program than not to have one (16.3 percent, versus 9.2 percent). A similar relationship exists with the percentage of full-time employees. Worksites with a larger percentage of full-time employees are more likely to have drug testing. A reverse relationship exists with the percentage of employees who have a college degree and are under age 30. Worksites with larger percentages of these employees are less likely to have drug testing programs. Neither the percentage of minority employees at a worksite nor those with a high school diploma is related to having a drug testing program.

The worksite characteristics presented in table 2 indicate the following: when a worksite conducts drug testing, it is more likely to have a written alcohol and drug use policy (96.0 percent) and it is more likely to have an Employee Assistance Program (45.9 percent).

Who gets tested? In addition to the overall prevalence of drug testing programs in worksites, we also examined which employees were subject to testing. As table 3 [p.28] shows, 48.4 percent of worksites with more than 50 full-time employees have some type of drug testing program. Of this group, 23.6 percent subject all employees to testing, 14.0 percent test *only* applicants, and 3.6 percent test *only* employees regulated by the Department of Transportation. Not shown in table 3, but interesting to note, is that 0.8 percent of the worksites test only safety or security employees and 6.4 percent test other combinations of groups (for example, job applicants and employees regulated by the Department of Transportation only).

Thus, most programs are designed to test all employees or applicants only. In general, the percentage of worksites that test all employees and applicants only increases by worksite size. The mining and construction industries have the largest percentage of worksites where all employees are subject to testing (49.0 percent), and the manufacturing industry has the largest percentage that test new employees only (21.4 percent). As expected, the communications, utility, and transportation industries have the largest percentage of worksites that test only employees who are regulated by the Department of Transportation (13.4 percent). Of the four regions, the South has the largest percentage of worksites that test all employees (32.7 percent).

Frequency. Table 4 [p.29] presents the percentage of drug testing worksites that test on a regular or random basis. Generally, less than 15 percent of these worksites actually conduct such tests on a regular basis. In contrast, approximately 47 percent of these worksites test on a random basis. The percentage of random testing decreases with worksite size and is the highest in the communication, utilities, and transportation industries (76.1 percent). Regular testing does not appear to be related to worksite size and is highest in the mining and construction industries (20.7 percent). The South has the highest percentage of random testing (53.8 percent), while regular testing is highest in the Midwest (16.2 percent). The West has the lowest percentages for both random (32.7 percent) and regular testing (11.0 percent).

Who conducts the tests? Table 5 [p.29] examines which organization or department is responsible for conducting drug tests at a worksite. Overall, outside contractors are responsible for testing at approximately 79 percent of worksites, while a medical department within a company conducts tests for approximately 11 percent and a personnel or human resources department tests for 6.4 percent. As worksite employment size increases, outside contractors are used less frequently (for example, 86.9 percent for worksites with 50-99 employees, versus 46.3 percent for worksites with 1,000 or more employees), while the use of a medical department increases dramatically (for example, 5.0 percent for worksites with 50-99 employees, versus 40.4 percent for worksites with 1,000 or more employees). Thus, compared with smaller worksites, the larger worksites are more likely to conduct tests internally. The wholesale/retail trade industry reported the largest percentage of tests done by an outside contractor (91.2 percent), while the services industry reported the lowest percentage (69.0 percent). The Northeast had the largest percentage of drug tests done by a medical department (16.8 percent), while there was no noticeable pattern across regions for the percentage of testing by an outside contractor.

"The South has the highest percentage of random testing..."

Conclusion

Drug testing is widely implemented in worksites throughout the United States, and is partially based on the characteristics of the worksite, the characteristics of its employees, and the implementation of other strategies and policies to control substance misuse. Drug testing programs are continually added to worksite policies, as well as the proportion of the labor force subject to testing. Programs that test for illicit drug use are more than twice as prevalent as those that test for alcohol use. This is ironic, in that alcohol misuse is by far the more common personal problem related to impaired job performance. However, testing for alcohol use is a more complex social and legal issue because *alcohol use* per se does not constitute a violation of law or company personnel policies.

"...alcohol misuse is by far the more common personal problem related to impaired job performance."

However, the results of this study confirm that drug testing continues to develop as a preferred strategy to control substance abuse in the workplace. Programs are most prevalent in larger worksites, those industries affected by drug testing legislation, and those employing high risk or unionized labor forces. Random drug testing has emerged as the most common form of testing, and most often, all employees and applicants are now included in testing programs. Drug testing is commonly conducted by external firms, but larger worksites are significantly more likely than their smaller counterparts to conduct testing within their worksites. Proliferation of the number and scope of programs, coupled with the movement towards random testing suggests continued strengthening of the employers' dedication to systematically identify and intervene in cases of drug and, to a lesser degree, alcohol abuse at their worksites. Drug testing has joined with other programs and policies (such as Employee Assistance Programs, health promotion programs, and written drug and alcohol use policies) to form more comprehensive responses to workplace substance abuse. Additional research is recommended to further define the integration of strategies to control worksite substance abuse and to examine the outcomes and effectiveness of these efforts.

Table 1. National estimates of the prevalence of drug and alcohol testing among worksites and employees, by selected characteristics of the worksite, 1992-93

[In percent]

Characteristic	Worksites[1]			Employees		
	Total (in thousands)	Test for drug use	Test for alcohol use	Total (in thousands)	In worksites that test for drug use	In worksites that test for alcohol use
All worksites	162.8 (-)	48.4 (1.2)	23.0 (1.0)	41,127 (1,271)	62.3 (1.6)	32.7 (2.1)
Worksites size						
50-99 employees	61.6 (1.7)	40.2 (2.1)	16.5 (1.6)	4,319 (124)	40.7 (2.2)	16.7 (1.6)
100-249 employees	66.0 (1.8)	48.2 (1.9)	22.9 (1.7)	9,612 (265)	48.9 (1.9)	23.2 (1.7)
250-999 employees	29.0 (.9)	61.4 (2.1)	32.7 (2.1)	12,520 (404)	62.8 (2.1)	33.5 (2.2)
1,000 employees or more	6.2 (.3)	70.9 (3.4)	42.1 (3.5)	14,675 (1,282)	77.1 (3.4)	43.0 (5.0)
Type of industry						
Manufacturing	54.0 (1.0)	60.2 (2.2)	28.3 (2.0)	14,058 (554)	73.5 (2.2)	37.5 (2.8)
Wholesale and retail	32.2 (1.1)	53.7 (3.3)	22.1 (2.7)	4,901 (236)	57.3 (3.0)	27.7 (3.2)
Communications, utilities, and transportation	13.5 (.8)	72.4 (3.3)	34.9 (3.0)	4,202 (435)	85.8 (2.6)	43.9 (5.3)
Finance, insurance, and real estate,	14.2 (0.5)	22.6 (2.1)	7.8 (1.3)	4,369 (563)	50.2 (6.7)	12.2 (3.1)
Mining and construction	5.6 (.4)	69.6 (4.1)	28.6 (3.5)	801 (49)	77.7 (3.2)	32.2 (3.1)
Services	43.3 (1.2)	27.9 (2.0)	17.4 (1.7)	12,796 (998)	47.5 (4.5)	32.7 (5.2)
Region						
Northeast	33.0 (1.5)	33.3 (2.4)	12.9 (1.7)	9,356 (617)	49.1 (3.6)	19.3 (2.6)
Midwest	40.7 (1.8)	50.3 (2.5)	24.0 (2.1)	10,190 (616)	62.4 (3.1)	34.4 (3.2)
South	59.1 (1.9)	56.3 (2.0)	26.3 (1.8)	14,986 (1,168)	71.8 (2.6)	36.9 (4.4)
West	30.0 (1.6)	46.8 (2.9)	26.0 (2.5)	6,594 (460)	59.4 (3.3)	39.7 (3.9)

[1] Worksites of private nonagricultural firms with more than 50 full-time employees at the time of survey.

NOTE: Standard errors appear in parentheses.

Table 2. Employee and worksite characteristics by drug testing status, 1992-93

| | | Worksite has drug testing | | |
Characteristic	All worksites[1]	Yes	No	Statistically significant[2]
Employee				
Full-time	90.2	92.4	88.1	Yes
Under 30 years of age	36.1	34.3	37.7	Yes
High school diploma	85.7	85.1	86.3	No
College degree	27.4	23.4	31.0	Yes
Union representation	12.7	16.3	9.2	Yes
Minority employees[3]	28.4	28.4	28.4	No
Worksite				
Written alcohol and drug use policy	87.1	96.0	78.5	Yes
Population less than 50,000 persons[4]	38.9	41.4	36.6	No (p=.06)
Employee Assistance Program	32.9	45.9	20.6	Yes

[1] Worksites of private nonagricultural firms with more than 50 full-time employees at the time of the survey.

[2] Significant difference in mean percentages for worksites with and without drug testing at the .05 percent level.

[3] Includes black, Hispanic origin, Asian, and Native American.

[4] Worksite is in a community with a population of less than 50,000.

NOTE: Percentages for employee characteristics are means of percentages of employees at worksites with that characteristic; the statistical test was the t-test. Percentages under worksite characteristics are percentages of worksites with that characteristic; the statistical test was the chi-square test.

Table 3. Percentage of worksites where employee groups are subject to testing, by selected characteristics of the worksite, 1992-93

Characteristic	Worksites that conduct drug test	Worksites where all employees are tested[1]	Only applicants are tested	Only transporation-regulated employees are tested[2]
All worksites[3]	48.4 (1.2)	23.6 (1.0)	14.0 (0.8)	3.6 (0.5)
Worksite size				
50-99 employees	40.2 (2.1)	19.9 (1.8)	10.4 (1.3)	5.3 (1.0)
100-249 employees	48.2 (1.9)	24.6 (1.7)	14.5 (1.4)	2.4 (.6)
250-999 employees	61.4 (2.1)	28.3 (2.0)	19.2 (1.8)	2.8 (.7)
1,000 employees or more	70.9 (3.4)	27.2 (3.0)	19.1 (2.5)	3.2 (1.0)
Type of industry				
Manufacturing	60.2 (2.2)	28.3 (2.0)	21.4 (1.8)	2.5 (.7)
Wholesale and retail	53.7 (3.3)	26.6 (3.0)	14.7 (2.2)	5.7 (1.7)
Communications, utilities, and transportation	72.4 (3.3)	27.4 (2.6)	13.0 (2.1)	13.4 (2.2)
Finance, insurance, and real estate	22.6 (2.1)	7.0 (1.2)	12.3 (1.6)	([4])
Mining and construction	69.6 (4.1)	49.0 (4.2)	6.9 (1.7)	4.0 (1.5)
Services	27.9 (2.0)	16.5 (1.7)	6.0 (1.0)	1.2 (.4)
Region				
Northeast	33.3 (2.4)	11.4 (1.7)	12.4 (1.7)	3.5 (1.0)
Midwest	50.3 (2.5)	20.0 (1.9)	16.1 (1.8)	4.8 (1.1)
South	56.3 (2.0)	32.7 (1.9)	13.4 (1.3)	3.6 (.8)
West	46.8 (2.9)	23.8 (2.4)	14.1 (2.0)	2.0 (.8)

[1] Many of these worksites also test applicants.

[2] Employees are regulated U.S. Department of Transportation.

[3] Worksites of private nonagricultural firms with more

than 50 full-time employees at the time of survey.

[4] Insufficient sample size.

NOTE: Standard errors appear in parentheses.

Table 4. Frequency of drug testing for worksites that test current employees, by characteristics of the worksite, 1992-93

Characteristic	Percent that test[1]—	
	On regular basis	On random basis
All worksites with drug testing program[2]	13.7 (1.4)	46.7 (2.0)
Worksite size		
50-99 employees	15.3 (2.6)	54.3 (4.1)
100-249 employees	12.8 (2.3)	46.4 (3.3)
250-999 employees	12.5 (2.3)	38.2 (3.3)
1,000 employees or more	14.6 (3.6)	38.0 (4.6)
Type of industry		
Manufacturing	11.6 (2.2)	35.9 (3.3)
Wholesale and retail	12.8 (3.5)	51.3 (5.4)
Communications, utilities, and transportation	15.9 (2.5)	76.1 (3.5)
Finance, insurance, and real estate	5.8 (4.2)	32.4 (7.2)
Mining and construction	20.7 (4.5)	55.1 (5.2)
Services	16.2 (3.6)	38.8 (4.5)
Region		
Northeast	14.7 (3.5)	45.4 (5.5)
Midwest	16.2 (2.8)	44.4 (4.0)
South	13.0 (2.1)	53.8 (3.1)
West	11.0 (3.1)	32.7 (4.4)

[1] Worksites that test only job applicants are not included in this table.
[2] Worksites of private nonagricultural firms with more than 50 full-time employees at the time of survey.
NOTE: Standard errors appear in parentheses.

Table 5. Department responsible for conducting drug tests, by worksite characteristics, 1992-93

[In percent]

Characteristic	Medical department	Personnel or human resources	Outside contractor	Other[1]
All worksites[2]	10.6 (0.9)	6.4 (0.7)	78.9 (1.2)	3.7 (0.6)
Worksite size				
50-99 employees	5.0 (1.5)	3.0 (1.2)	86.9 (2.3)	4.7 (1.3)
100-249 employees	5.8 (1.2)	6.0 (1.2)	84.3 (1.9)	3.4 (1.0)
250-999 employees	19.7 (2.3)	10.8 (1.7)	66.6 (2.7)	2.6 (0.9)
1,000 employees or more	40.4 (3.8)	9.3 (2.1)	46.3 (4.0)	3.7 (1.8)
Type of industry				
Manufacturing	13.7 (1.6)	7.1 (1.4)	76.8 (2.1)	2.3 (0.8)
Wholesale and retail	3.6 (1.7)	3.0 (1.0)	91.2 (2.4)	2.1 (1.4)
Communications, utilities, and transportation	9.6 (1.7)	8.2 (1.6)	74.2 (2.7)	7.7 (1.6)
Finance, insurance, and real estate	7.5 (2.3)	5.0 (2.1)	85.0 (3.3)	(3)
Mining and construction	3.8 (1.5)	6.1 (1.8)	81.4 (3.1)	6.3 (1.8)
Services	15.9 (2.5)	7.8 (2.3)	69.0 (3.7)	6.2 (2.2)
Region				
Northeast	16.8 (3.2)	3.2 (1.1)	77.9 (3.5)	1.6 (.9)
Midwest	8.4 (1.5)	6.9 (1.5)	80.7 (2.3)	3.8 (1.0)
South	11.1 (1.4)	6.8 (1.1)	77.1 (2.0)	4.2 (1.1)
West	8.1 (1.8)	6.8 (2.1)	81.2 (3.0)	3.7 (1.4)

[1] Includes Employee Assistance Program, Safety Department, and Department Supervisor.
[2] Worksites of private nonagricultural firms with more than 50 full-time employees at the time of survey.
[3] Insufficient sample size.
NOTE: Standard errors appear in parentheses.

Appendix: Methodology

Sample Design

Despite the voluminous literature on drug testing, some of which is cited in this article, the most recent national probability surveys of drug testing prevalence in worksites were conducted by the Bureau of Labor Statistics; one in 1988, and a follow-up of the same worksites in 1990. To ensure that our results would be comparable to these earlier national probability worksite surveys, we designed our study with a similar target population and stratification. The two notable distinctions between the 1988 BLS survey and our survey are that we excluded worksites with fewer than 50 employees (because of data collection costs) and we excluded nonprivate worksites (because of the lack of a comprehensive list).

A worksite represents any business location with a unique, separate, and distinct operation, including headquarter units within an enterprise. Our target population consisted of all worksites with 50 or more employees of private business enterprises in the United States (excluding agricultural enterprises). The sampling frame was constructed using the Dun's Market Identifiers database from Dun's Marketing Services.

The sampling strata were defined on the primary industry at the worksite (manufacturing; wholesale and retail trade; communications, utilities, and transportation; finance, real estate, and insurance; services; and mining and construction) and the number of employees at the worksite (50-99, 100-249, 250-999, and 1,000 or more). The sampling frame included approximately 421,000 worksites. Geographic location (four census regions) was used as a secondary stratification factor within the sample selection procedure. The sample was selected to obtain a proportional allocation within each sampling stratum across four geographic location strata and with equal probability within each stratum. Only worksites that reported 50 or more full-time employees at the time of the survey were eligible for analysis and reporting.

During data collection, the response and eligibility rates were monitored and the sample size in each stratum was supplemented to accommodate differences between projected and actual response and eligibility rates. The final national probability sample ensured adequate sample sizes for estimates defined by the primary industry and the number of employees at the worksite. The final stratified sample contained 6,488 worksites, of which 3,204 were eligible responding worksites. Ineligible worksites included nonprivate worksites, worksites with fewer than 50 full-time employees, and closed worksites. The response rate ranged from 80 percent to 96 percent across the 24 sampling strata, with an overall response rate of 90 percent.

Sampling weights were equal within each sampling stratum, but differed across the strata. The sampling weights were computed from the selection probability of the worksite within the sampling stratum, and, to reduce nonresponse bias caused by the differential response rates, the weights were adjusted to compensate for nonresponse and were poststratified to external counts of worksites.

Response Rates

The excellent response rates for the survey indicated a strong willingness of worksite staff to contribute information related to drug and alcohol testing. The overall refusal rate was only 10 percent. Worksites with fewer than 100 employees and worksites in the services and mining and construction industries refused less frequently than other industries.

Data Collection

Prior to administering the telephone survey, we mailed a lead letter and an outline of the survey instrument to the director of human resources or the personnel department at each selected worksite. The materials a introduced the study, informed personnel of the types of questions we would be asking, and prepared them for the telephone interview. The actual interviewing started approximately 2 weeks after the survey materials were delivered and was conducted using computer assisted telephone interviewing (CATI). The introductory section of the survey instrument confirmed that we contacted the correct worksite, that the worksite was eligible to participate in the survey (that is, a private worksite with 50 or more full-time employees), and that we were speaking with the person most knowledgeable about employee benefits (for example, department heads of human resources, personnel, or an Employee Assistant Program).

After collecting this preliminary information, we then determined whether the worksite had an Employee Assistance Program. If so, we administered 130 additional questions on worksite demographics; characteristics of a worksite's Employee Assistance Program, services provided, and costs; drug and alcohol testing; and employee benefits. For worksites without an Employee Assistance Program, we still collected information on worksite demographics, drug and alcohol testing, and employee benefits. Thus, we collected data on drug and alcohol tests from our entire worksite sample. The average contact time (that is, time to reach and interview a respondent) was 58 minutes for worksites with an Employee Assistance Program and 28 minutes for worksites without one.

Each question on the instrument was displayed for the interviewers in program-controlled sequences on computer terminals, and responses were entered directly into the computer to save time and minimize coding mistakes.

Sampling Weights

The stratification and the differential sampling weights across the strata required that the data analysis take into account the complex survey design and the sampling weights. Thus, we computed unbiased national estimates using sampling weights based on selection probabilities and adjusted to compensate for nonresponse. Weighted totals, means, and frequencies and their standard errors were computed using the Survey Data Analysis computer software package (SUDAAN).

Drug Legalization▶ Time for a Real Debate[5]

Whether Bill Clinton "inhaled" when trying marijuana as a college student was about the closest the last presidential campaign came to addressing the drug issue. The present one, however, could be very different. For the fourth straight year, a federally supported nationwide survey of American secondary school students by the University of Michigan has indicated increased drug use. After a decade or more in which drug use had been falling, the Republicans will assuredly blame the bad news on President Clinton and assail him for failing to carry on the Bush and Reagan administrations' high-profile stand against drugs. How big this issue becomes is less certain, but if the worrisome trend in drug use among teens continues, public debate about how best to respond to the drug problem will clearly not end with the election. Indeed, concern is already mounting that the large wave of teenagers—the group most at risk of taking drugs—that will crest around the turn of the century will be accompanied by a new surge in drug use.

As in the past, some observers will doubtless see the solution in much tougher penalties to deter both suppliers and consumers of illicit psychoactive substances. Others will argue that the answer lies not in more law enforcement and stiffer sanctions, but in less. Specifically, they will maintain that the edifice of domestic laws and international conventions that collectively prohibit the production, sale, and consumption of a large array of drugs for anything other than medical or scientific purposes has proven physically harmful, socially divisive, prohibitively expensive, and ultimately counterproductive in generating the very incentives that perpetuate a violent black market for illicit drugs. They will conclude, moreover, that the only logical step for the United States to take is to "legalize" drugs—in essence repeal and disband the current drug laws and enforcement mechanisms in much the same way America abandoned its brief experiment with alcohol prohibition in the 1920s.

Although the legalization alternative typically surfaces when the public's anxiety about drugs and despair over existing policies are at their highest, it never seems to slip off the media radar screen for long. Periodic incidents—such as the heroin-induced death of a young, affluent New York City couple in 1995 or the 1993 remark by then Surgeon General Jocelyn Elders that legalization might be beneficial and should be studied—ensure this. The prominence of many of those who have at various times made the case for legal-

[5] Article by Paul B. Stares, a non-resident senior fellow in the Brookings Foreign Policy Studies Program, from *The Brookings Review* 14:18-21 Spr '96. Copyright © 1996 The Brookings Institution. Reprinted with permission.

ization—such as William F. Buckley, Jr., Milton Friedman, and George Shultz—also helps. [But each time the issue of legalization arises, the same arguments for and against are dusted off and trotted out, leaving us with no clearer understanding of what it might entail and what the effect might be.]

As will become clear, drug legalization is not a public policy option that lends itself to simplistic or superficial debate. It requires dissection and scrutiny of an order that has been remarkably absent despite the attention it perennially receives. Beyond discussion of some very generally defined proposals, there has been no detailed assessment of the operational meaning of legalization. There is not even a commonly accepted lexicon of terms to allow an intellectually rigorous exchange to take place. Legalization, as a consequence, has come to mean different things to different people. Some, for example, use legalization interchangeably with "decriminalization," which usually refers to removing criminal sanctions for possessing small quantities of drugs for personal use. Others equate legalization, at least implicitly, with complete deregulation, failing in the process to acknowledge the extent to which currently legally available drugs are subject to stringent controls.

Unfortunately, the U.S. government—including the Clinton administration—has done little to improve the debate. Although it has consistently rejected any retreat from prohibition, its stance has evidently not been based on in-depth investigation of the potential costs and benefits. The belief that legalization would lead to an instant and dramatic increase in drug use is considered to be so self-evident as to warrant no further study. But if this is indeed the likely conclusion of any study, what is there to fear aside from criticism that relatively small amounts of taxpayer money had been wasted in demonstrating what everyone had believed at the outset? Wouldn't such an outcome in any case help justify the continuation of existing policies and convincingly silence those—admittedly never more than a small minority—calling for legalization?

A real debate that acknowledges the unavoidable complexities and uncertainties surrounding the notion of drug legalization is long overdue. Not only would it dissuade people from making the kinds of casual if not flippant assertions—both for and against—that have permeated previous debates about legalization, but it could also stimulate a larger and equally critical assessment of current U.S. drug control programs and priorities.

First Ask the Right Questions

Many arguments appear to make legalization a compelling alternative to today's prohibitionist policies. Besides undermining the black-market incentives to produce and sell drugs, legalization could remove or at least significantly reduce the very problems that cause the greatest public concern: the crime, corruption, and violence that attend the operation of illicit drug markets. It would

> "...drug legalization is not a public policy option that lends itself to simplistic or superficial debate."

presumably also diminish the damage caused by the absence of quality controls on illicit drugs and slow the spread of infectious diseases due to needle sharing and other unhygienic practices. Furthermore, governments could abandon the costly and largely futile effort to suppress the supply of illicit drugs and jail drug offenders, spending the money thus saved to educate people not to take drugs and treat those who become addicted.

However, what is typically portrayed as a fairly straightforward process of lifting prohibitionist controls to reap these putative benefits would in reality entail addressing an extremely complex set of regulatory issues. As with most if not all privately and publicly provided goods, the key regulatory questions concern the nature of the legally available drugs, the terms of their supply, and the terms of their consumption.

What becomes immediately apparent from even a casual review of these questions—and the list presented here is by no means exhaustive—is that there is an enormous range of regulatory permutations for each drug. Until all the principal alternatives are clearly laid out in reasonable detail, however, the potential costs and benefits of each cannot begin to be responsibly assessed. This fundamental point can be illustrated with respect to the two central questions most likely to sway public opinion. What would happen to drug consumption under more permissive regulatory regimes? And what would happen to crime?

Relaxing the availability of psychoactive substances not already commercially available, opponents typically argue, would lead to an immediate and substantial rise in consumption. To support their claim, they point to the prevalence of opium, heroin, and cocaine addiction in various countries before international controls took effect, the rise in alcohol consumption after the Volstead Act was repealed in the United States, and studies showing higher rates of abuse among medical professionals with greater access to prescription drugs. Without explaining the basis of their calculations, some have predicted dramatic increases in the number of people taking drugs and becoming addicted. These increases would translate into considerable direct and indirect costs to society, including higher public health spending as a result of drug overdoses, fetal deformities, and other drug-related misadventures such as auto accidents; loss of productivity due to worker absenteeism and on-the-job accidents; and more drug-induced violence, child abuse, and other crimes, to say nothing about educational impairment.

Advocates of legalization concede that consumption would probably rise, but counter that it is not axiomatic that the increase would be very large or last very long, especially if legalization were paired with appropriate public education programs. They too cite historical evidence to bolster their claims, nothing that consumption of opium, heroin, and cocaine had already begun falling before prohibition took effect, that alcohol consumption did not rise suddenly after prohibition was lifted, and that decriminalization of cannabis use in 11 U.S. states in the 1970s did not precipitate a dramatic rise in its consumption. Some also point to the legal sale of cannabis products through regulated outlets in the Netherlands, which also does not seem to have significantly boosted use by Dutch nationals. Public opinion polls showing that most Americans would not rush off to try hitherto forbidden drugs that suddenly became available are likewise used to buttress the pro-legalization case.

Neither side's arguments are particularly reassuring. The historical evidence is ambiguous at best, even assuming that the experience of one era is relevant to another. Extrapolating the results of policy steps in one country to another with different sociocultural values runs into the same problem. Similarly, within the United States the effect of decriminalization at the state level must be viewed within the general context of continued federal prohibition. And opinion polls are known to be unreliable.

"Schemes that risk a continuing black market require more questions..."

More to the point, until the nature of the putative regulatory regime is specified, such discussions are futile. It would be surprising, for example, if consumption of the legalized drugs did not increase if they were to become commercially available the way that alcohol and tobacco products are today, complete with sophisticated packaging, marketing, and advertising. But more restrictive regimes might see quite different outcomes. In any case, the risk of higher drug consumption might be acceptable if legalization could reduce dramatically if not remove entirely the crime associated with the black market for illicit drugs while also making some forms of drug use safer. Here again, there are disputed claims.

Opponents of more permissive regimes doubt that black market activity and its associated problems would disappear or even fall very much. But, as before, addressing this question requires knowing the specifics of the regulatory regime, especially the terms of supply. If drugs are sold openly on a commercial basis and prices are close to production and distribution costs, opportunities for illicit undercutting would appear to be rather small. Under a more restrictive regime, such as government-controlled outlets or medical prescription schemes, illicit sources of supply would be more likely to remain or evolve to satisfy the legally unfulfilled demand. In short, the desire to control access to stem consumption has to be balanced against the black market opportunities that would arise. Schemes that risk a continuing black market require more questions—about the new black market's operation over time, whether it is likely to be more benign than existing ones, and more broadly whether the trade-off with other benefits still makes the effort worthwhile.

The most obvious case is regulating access to drugs by adolescents and young adults. Under any regime, it is hard to imagine that drugs that are now prohibited would become more readily available than alcohol and tobacco are today. Would a black market in drugs for teenagers emerge, or would the regulatory regime be as leaky as the present one for alcohol and tobacco? A "yes" answer to either question would lessen the attractiveness of legalization.

What About the International Repercussions?

Not surprisingly, the wider international ramifications of drug legalization have also gone largely unremarked. Here too a long set of questions remains to be addressed. Given the longstanding U.S. role as the principal sponsor of international drug control measures, how would a decision to move toward legalizing drugs affect other countries? What would become of the extensive regime of multilateral conventions and bilateral agreements? Would every nation have to conform to a new set of rules? If not, what would happen? Would more permissive countries be suddenly swamped by drugs and drug consumers, or would traffickers focus on the countries where tighter restrictions kept profits higher? This is not an abstract question. The Netherlands' liberal drug policy has attracted an influx of "drug tourists" from neighboring countries, as did the city of Zurich's following the now abandoned experiment allowing an open drug market to operate in what became known as "Needle Park." And while it is conceivable that affluent countries could soften the worst consequences of drug legalization through extensive public prevention and drug treatment programs, what about poorer countries?

Finally, what would happen to the principal suppliers of illicit drugs if restrictions on the commercial sale of these drugs were lifted in some or all of the main markets? Would the trafficking organizations adapt and become legal businesses or turn to other illicit enterprises?

What would happen to the source countries? Would they benefit or would new producers and manufacturers suddenly spring up elsewhere? Such questions have not even been posed in a systematic way, let alone seriously studied.

Irreducible Uncertainties

Although greater precision in defining more permissive regulatory regimes is critical to evaluating their potential costs and benefits, it will not resolve the uncertainties that exist. Only implementation will do that. Because small-scale experimentation (assuming a particular locality's consent to be a guinea pig) would inevitably invite complaints that the results were biased or inconclusive, implementation would presumably have to be widespread, even global, in nature.

Yet jettisoning nearly a century of prohibition when the putative benefits remain so uncertain and the potential costs are so high would require a herculean leap of faith. Only an extremely severe and widespread deterioration of the current drug situation, nationally and internationally, is likely to produce the consensus—again, nationally and internationally—that could impel such a leap. Even then the legislative challenge would be stu-

pendous. The debate over how to set the conditions for control-
ling access to each of a dozen popular drugs could consume the
legislatures of the major industrial countries for years.

None of this should deter further analysis of drug legalization.
In particular, a rigorous assessment of a range of hypothetical
regulatory regimes according to a common set of variables would
clarify their potential costs, benefits, and trade-offs. Besides
instilling much-needed rigor into any further discussion of the
legalization alternative, such analysis could encourage the same
level of scrutiny of current drug control programs and policies.
With the situation apparently deteriorating in the United States
as well as abroad, there is no better time for a fundamental
reassessment of whether our existing responses to this problem
are sufficient to meet the likely challenges ahead.

Some Key Regulatory Questions

The nature of the product. Which formerly illicit substances can
be legally acquired and consumed? All, including heroin and
cocaine, or just some, such as cannabis? In what form would the
permitted substances be made publicly available? Would the
purity or potency be controlled? Who would devise such regulations, and how would they be reviewed and revised if necessary?

The terms of supply. Who would produce the permitted substances? Would production be under government or private control? If the latter, what kind of certification, licensing, product
reliability, safety, and security arrangements would take effect?
Would restrictions be applied to the packaging of the product as
well as any self-administration devices? How would consumers
gain access to the drugs—through privately owned businesses,
government-controlled shops, or mail-order services? What regulations would affect the location and operating hours of these
outlets? How would they be monitored? What regulations would
apply to the personnel selling, dispensing, and safeguarding the
drugs? Would public advertising be permitted? If not, would this
contravene constitutional free speech provisions? If advertising
were allowed, what regulations would apply? Could every media
outlet be used? Would the advertising have to conform to certain
standards? Likewise, at the places selling or otherwise dispensing the drugs, would restrictions be placed on their location and
display? Would product liability and safety information be made
available? To whom, how, when, and where? How would the
transactions take place: using money, special credits, ration
cards, medical prescriptions, or some other means? Would transactions be taxed, registered, and otherwise reported? What
would happen to the tax revenues as well as the reported information? What penalties would be set for violating restrictions on
the supply of permitted and unpermitted substances?

The terms of consumption. Would restrictions be placed on who
would have access to the permitted drugs, or on where permitted
substances could be consumed (in special facilities or private

property) as well as where they could not (schools, parks, public transportation)? Would pregnant women be given access; if not, how would this be regulated? Would special identification procedures have to be followed to gain access? Would consent from a parent, guardian, or health professional be required? Would limits be set on the age and occupation of those acquiring drugs? Would restrictions apply to when certain drugs could be consumed? Would restrictions be placed on how the permitted drugs could be consumed? Would information be supplied to help consumers use the drugs safely and tell them what to do in case of accident or adverse reactions? Would limits apply to the amount of drugs that could be consumed at any one time and during a specified period? Would restrictions apply to the amount that could be carried or in one's possession at any time? Would restrictions apply to certain activities—occupational and recreational—that could not be carried out while under the influence of the drugs? Would consumers who suffer adverse reactions have legal recourse? What about people injured and otherwise harmed by others under the influence? In general, what would be the penalties for violating any of the consumer restrictions? Would they be harsher or less severe than existing sanctions?

Legalization Madness[6]

Frustrated by the government's apparent inability to reduce the supply of illegal drugs on the streets of America, and disquieted by media accounts of innocents victimized by drug-related violence, some policy makers are convinced that the "war on drugs" has failed. In an attempt to find a better solution to the "drug crisis" or, at the very least, to try an alternative strategy, they have proposed legalizing drugs.

They argue that, if marijuana, cocaine, heroin, and other drugs were legalized, several positive things would probably occur: (1) drug prices would fall; (2) users would obtain their drugs at low, government-regulated prices, and they would no longer be forced to resort to crime in order to support their habits; (3) levels of drug-related crime, and particularly violent crime, would significantly decline, resulting in less crowded courts, jails, and prisons (this would allow law-enforcement personnel to focus their energies on the "real criminals" in society); and (4) drug production, distribution, and sale would no longer be controlled by organized crime, and thus such criminal syndicates as the Colombian cocaine "cartels," the Jamaican "posses," and the various "mafias" around the country and the world would be decapitalized, and the violence associated with drug distribution rivalries would be eliminated.

By contrast, the anti-legalization camp argues that violent crime would not necessarily decline in a legalized drug market. In fact, there are three reasons why it might actually increase. First, removing the criminal sanctions against the possession and distribution of illegal drugs would make them more available and attractive and, hence, would create large numbers of new users. Second, an increase in use would lead to a greater number of dysfunctional addicts who could not support themselves, their habits, or their lifestyles through legitimate means. Hence crime would be their only alternative. Third, more users would mean more of the violence associated with the ingestion of drugs.

These divergent points of view tend to persist because the relationships between drugs and crime are quite complex and because the possible outcomes of a legalized drug market are based primarily on speculation. However, it is possible, from a careful review of the existing empirical literature on drugs and violence, to make some educated inferences.

Considering "Legalization"

Yet much depends upon what we mean by "legalizing drugs." Would all currently illicit drugs be legalized or would the exper-

> "...violent crime would not necessarily decline in a legalized drug market."

---

6 Article by James A. Inciardi and Christine A. Saum, from *The Public Interest* 123:72-82 Spr '96. Copyright © 1996 National Affairs, Inc. Reprinted with permission.

iment be limited to just certain ones? True legalization would be akin to selling such drugs as heroin and cocaine on the open market, much like alcohol and tobacco, with a few age-related restrictions. In contrast, there are "medicalization" and "decriminalization" alternatives. Medicalization approaches are of many types, but, in essence, they would allow users to obtain prescriptions for some, or all, currently illegal substances. Decriminalization removes the criminal penalties associated with the possession of small amounts of illegal drugs for personal use, while leaving intact the sanctions for trafficking, distribution, and sale.

But what about crack-cocaine? A quick review of the literature reveals that the legalizers, the decriminalizers, and the medicalizers avoid talking about this particular form of cocaine. Perhaps they do not want to legalize crack out of fear of the drug itself, or of public outrage. Arnold S. Trebach, a professor of law at American University and president of the Drug Policy Foundation, is one of the very few who argues for the full legalization of all drugs, including crack. He explains, however, that most are reluctant to discuss the legalization of crack-cocaine because, "it is a very dangerous drug....I know that for many people the very thought of making crack legal destroys any inclination they might have had for even thinking about drug-law reform."

There is a related concern associated with the legalization of cocaine. Because crack is easily manufactured from powder cocaine (just add water and baking soda and cook on a stove or in a microwave), many drug-policy reformers hold that no form of cocaine should be legalized. But this weakens the argument that legalization will reduce drug-related violence; for much of this violence would appear to be in the cocaine and crack-distribution markets.

To better understand the complex relationship between drugs and violence, we will discuss the data in the context of three models developed by Paul J. Goldstein of the University of Illinois at Chicago. They are the "psychopharmacological," "economically compulsive," and "systemic" explanations of violence. The first model holds, correctly in our view, that some individuals may become excitable, irrational, and even violent due to the ingestion of specific drugs. In contrast, taking a more economic approach to the behavior of drug users, the second holds that some drug users engage in violent crime mainly for the sake of supporting their drug use. The third model maintains that drug-related violent crime is simply the result of the drug market under a regime of illegality.

Psychopharmacological Violence

The case for legalization rests in part upon the faulty assumption that drugs themselves do not cause violence; rather, so goes the argument, violence is the result of depriving drug addicts of

> *"Medicalization... would allow users to obtain prescriptions for some, or all, currently illegal substances."*

*they ma/s crim!
not becaus what !
to get grcds.*

drugs or of the "criminal" trafficking in drugs. But, as researcher Barry Spunt points out, "Users of drugs do get violent when they get high."

Research has documented that chronic users of amphetamines, methamphetamine, and cocaine in particular tend to exhibit hostile and aggressive behaviors. Psychopharmacological violence can also be a product of what is known as "cocaine psychosis." As dose and duration of cocaine use increase, the development of cocaine-related psychopathology is not uncommon. Cocaine psychosis is generally preceded by a transitional period characterized by increased suspiciousness, compulsive behavior, fault finding, and eventually paranoia. When the psychotic state is reached, individuals may experience visual, as well as auditory, hallucinations, with persecutory voices commonly heard. Many believe that they are being followed by police or that family, friends, and others are plotting against them.

Moreover, everyday events are sometimes misinterpreted by cocaine users in ways that support delusional beliefs. When coupled with the irritability and hyperactivity that cocaine tends to generate in almost all of its users, the cocaine-induced paranoia may lead to violent behavior as a means of "self-defense" against imagined persecutors. The violence associated with cocaine psychosis is a common feature in many crack houses across the United States. Violence may also result from the irritability associated with drug-withdrawal syndromes. In addition, some users ingest drugs before committing crimes to both loosen inhibitions and bolster their resolve to break the law.

Acts of violence may result from either periodic or chronic use of a drug. For example, in a study of drug use and psychopathy among Baltimore City jail inmates, researchers at the University of Baltimore reported that cocaine use was related to irritability, resentment, hostility, and assault. They concluded that these indicators of aggression may be a function of drug effects rather than of a predisposition to these behaviors. Similarly, Barry Spunt and his colleagues at National Development and Research Institutes (NDRI) in New York City found that of 269 convicted murderers incarcerated in New York State prisons, 45 percent were high at the time of the offense. Three in 10 believed that the homicide was related to their drug use, challenging conventional beliefs that violence only infrequently occurs as a result of drug consumption.

Even marijuana, which pro-legalizers consider harmless, may have a connection with violence and crime. Spunt and his colleagues attempted to determine the role of marijuana in the crimes of the homicide offenders they interviewed in the New York State prisons. One-third of those who had ever used marijuana had smoked the drug in the 24-hour period prior to the homicide. Moreover, 31 percent of those who considered themselves to be "high" at the time of committing murder felt that the homicide and marijuana were related. William Blount of the

"Cocaine psychosis is generally preceded by a transitional period..."

University of South Florida interviewed abused women in prisons and shelters for battered women located throughout Florida. He and his colleagues found that 24 percent of those who killed their abusers were marijuana users while only 8 percent of those who did not kill their abusers smoked marijuana.

And Alcohol Abuse

A point that needs emphasizing is that alcohol, because it is legal, accessible, and inexpensive, is linked to violence to a far greater extent than any illegal drug. For example, in the study just cited, it was found that an impressive 64 percent of those women who eventually killed their abusers were alcohol users (44 percent of those who did not kill their abusers were alcohol users). Indeed, the extent to which alcohol is responsible for violent crimes in comparison with other drugs is apparent from the statistics. For example, Carolyn Block and her colleagues at the Criminal Justice Information Authority in Chicago found that, between 1982 and 1989, the use of alcohol by offenders or victims in local homicides ranged from 18 percent to 32 percent.

Alcohol has, in fact, been consistently linked to homicide. Spunt and his colleagues interviewed 268 homicide offenders incarcerated in New York State correctional facilities to determine the role of alcohol in their crimes: Thirty-one percent of the respondents reported being drunk at the time of the crime and 19 percent believed that the homicide was related to their drinking. More generally, Douglass Murdoch of Quebec's McGill University found that in some 9,000 criminal cases drawn from a multinational sample, 62 percent of violent offenders were drinking shortly before, or at the time of, the offense.

"...in some 9,000 criminal cases drawn from a multinational sample, 62 percent of violent offenders were drinking shortly before, or at the time of, the offense."

It appears that alcohol reduces the inhibitory control of threat, making it more likely that a person will exhibit violent behaviors normally suppressed by fear. In turn, this reduction of inhibition heightens the probability that intoxicated persons will perpetrate, or become victims of, aggressive behavior.

When analyzing the psychopharmacological model of drugs and violence, most of the discussions focus on the offender and the role of drugs in causing or facilitating crime. But what about the victims? Are the victims of drug- and alcohol-related homicides simply casualties of someone else's substance abuse? In addressing these questions, the data demonstrates that victims are likely to be drug users as well. For example, in an analysis of the 4,298 homicides that occurred in New York City during 1990 and 1991, Kenneth Tardiff of Cornell University Medical College found that the victims of these offenses were 10 to 50 times more likely to be cocaine users than were members of the general population. Of the white female victims, 60 percent in the 25- to 34-year age group had cocaine in their systems; for black females, the figure was 72 percent. Tardiff speculated that the classic symptoms of cocaine use—irritability, paranoia, aggressiveness—may have instigated the violence. In another study of cocaine users in New York City, female high-volume users were found to be victims of violence far more frequently than low-volume and nonusers of cocaine. Studies in numerous other cities and countries have yielded the same general findings—that a great many of the victims of homicide and other forms of violence are drinkers and drug users themselves.

Economically Compulsive Violence

Supporters of the economically compulsive model of violence argue that in a legalized market, the prices of "expensive drugs" would decline to more affordable levels, and, hence, predatory crimes would become unnecessary. This argument is based on several specious assumptions. First, it assumes that there is empirical support for what has been referred to as the "enslavement theory of addiction." Second, it assumes that people addicted to drugs commit crimes only for the purpose of supporting their habits. Third, it assumes that, in a legalized market, users could obtain as much of the drugs as they wanted whenever they wanted. Finally, it assumes that, if drugs are inexpensive, they will be affordable, and thus crime would be unnecessary.

"...users are forced to commit crimes in order to support their drug habits."

With respect to the first premise, there has been for the better part of this century a concerted belief among many in the drug-policy field that addicts commit crimes because they are "enslaved" to drugs, and further that, because of the high price of heroin, cocaine, and other illicit chemicals on the black market, users are forced to commit crimes in order to support their drug habits. However, there is no solid empirical evidence to support this contention. From the 1920s through the end of the 1960s, hundreds of studies of the relationship between crime and addiction were conducted. Invariably, when one analysis would support the posture of "enslavement theory," the next would affirm the view that addicts were criminals first and that their drug use was but one more manifestation of their deviant lifestyles. In retrospect, the difficulty lay in the ways that many of the studies had been conducted: Biases and deficiencies in research designs and sampling had rendered their findings of little value.

Studies since the mid 1970s of active drug users on the streets of New York, Miami, Baltimore, and elsewhere have demonstrated that the "enslavement theory" has little basis in reality. All of these studies of the criminal careers of drug users have convincingly documented that, while drug use tends to intensify and perpetuate criminal behavior, it usually does not initiate criminal careers. In fact, the evidence suggests that among the majority of street drug users who are involved in crime, their criminal careers are well established prior to the onset of either narcotics or cocaine use. As such, it would appear that the "inference of causality"—that the high price of drugs on the black market itself causes crime—is simply false.

Looking at the second premise, a variety of studies show that addicts commit crimes for reasons other than supporting their drug habit. They do so also for daily living expenses. For example, researchers at the Center for Drug and Alcohol Studies at the University of Delaware who studied crack users on the streets of Miami found that, of the active addicts interviewed, 85 percent of the male and 70 percent of the female interviewees paid for portions of their living expenses through street crime. In fact, one-half of the men and one-fourth of the women paid for 90 percent or more of their living expenses through crime. And, not surprisingly, 96 percent of the men and 99 percent of the women had not held a legal job in the 90-day period before being interviewed for the study.

With respect to the third premise, that in a legalized market users could obtain as much of the drugs as they wanted whenever they wanted, only speculation is possible. More than likely, however, there would be some sort of regulation, and hence black markets for drugs would persist for those whose addictions were beyond the medicalized or legalized allotments. In a decriminalized market, levels of drug-related violence would likely either remain unchanged or increase (if drug use increased).

As for the last premise, that cheap drugs preclude the need to commit crimes to obtain them, the evidence emphatically suggests that this is not the case. Consider crack-cocaine: Although crack "rocks" are available on the illegal market for as little as two dollars in some locales, users are still involved in crime-driven endeavors to support their addictions. For example, researchers Norman S. Miller and Mark S. Gold surveyed 200 consecutive callers to the 1-800-COCAINE hotline who considered themselves to have a problem with crack. They found that, despite the low cost of crack, 63 percent of daily users and 40 percent of non-daily users spent more than $200 per week on the drug. Similarly, interviews conducted by NDRI researchers in New York City with almost 400 drug users contacted in the streets, jails, and treatment programs revealed that almost one-half of them spent over $1,000 a month on crack. The study also documented that crack users—despite the low cost of their drug of choice—spent more money on drugs than did users of heroin, powder cocaine, marijuana, and alcohol.

"...despite the low cost of crack, 63 percent of daily users and 40 percent of non-daily users spent more than $200 per week on the drug."

Systemic Violence

It is the supposed systemic violence associated with trafficking in cocaine and crack in America's inner cities that has recently received the attention of drug-policy critics interested in legalizing drugs. Certainly it might appear that, if heroin and cocaine were legal substances, systemic drug-related violence would decline. However, there are two very important questions in this regard: First, is drug-related violence more often psychopharmacological or systemic? Second, is the great bulk of systemic violence related to the distribution of crack? If most of the drug-related violence is psychopharmacological in nature, and if systemic violence is typically related to crack—the drug generally excluded from consideration when legalization is recommended—then legalizing drugs would probably not reduce violent crime.

Regarding the first question, several recent studies conducted in New York City tend to contradict, or at least not support, the notion that legalizing drugs would reduce violent, systemic-related crime. For example, Paul J. Goldstein's ethnographic studies of male and female drug users during the late 1980s found that cocaine-related violence was more often psychopharmacological than systemic. Similarly, Kenneth Tardiff's study of 4,298 New York City homicides found that 31 percent of the victims had used cocaine in the 24-hour period prior to their deaths. One of the conclusions of the study was that the homicides were not necessarily related to drug dealing. In all likelihood, as victims of homicide, the cocaine users may have provoked violence through their irritability, paranoid thinking, and verbal or physical aggression—all of which are among the psychopharmacological effects of cocaine.

Regarding the second question, the illegal drug most associated with systemic violence is crack-cocaine. Of all illicit drugs, crack is the one now responsible for the most homicides. In a study done in New York City in 1988 by Goldstein and his colleagues, crack was found to be connected with 32 percent of all homicides and 60 percent of all drug-related homicides. Furthermore, although there is evidence that crack sellers are more violent than other drug sellers, this violence is not confined to the drug-selling context—violence potentials appear to precede involvement in selling.

Thus, though crack has been blamed for increasing violence in the marketplace, this violence actually stems from the psychopharmacological consequences of crack use. Ansley Hamid, a professor of anthropology at the John Jay College of Criminal Justice in New York, reasons that increases in crack-related violence are due to the deterioration of informal and formal social controls throughout communities that have been destabilized by economic processes and political decisions. If this is the case, does anyone really believe that we can improve these complex social problems through the simple act of legalizing drugs?

Don't Just Say No

The issue of whether or not legalization would create a multitude of new users also needs to be addressed. It has been shown that many people do not use drugs simply because drugs are illegal. As Mark A.R. Kleiman, author of *Against Excess: Drug Policy for Results*, recently put it: "Illegality by itself tends to suppress consumption, independent of its effect on price, both because some consumers are reluctant to disobey the law and because illegal products are harder to find and less reliable as to quality and labeling than legal ones."

Although there is no way of accurately estimating how many new users there would be if drugs were legalized, there would probably be many. To begin with, there is the historical example of Prohibition. During Prohibition, there was a decrease of 20 percent to 50 percent in the number of alcoholics. These estimates were calculated based on a decline in cirrhosis and other alcohol-related deaths; after Prohibition ended, both of these indicators increased.

Currently, relatively few people are steady users of drugs. The University of Michigan's *Monitoring the Future* study reported in 1995 that only two-tenths of 1 percent of high-school seniors are daily users of either hallucinogens, cocaine, heroin, sedatives, or inhalants. It is the addicts who overwhelmingly consume the bulk of the drug supply—80 percent of all alcohol and almost 100 percent of all heroin. In other words, there are significantly large numbers of non-users who have yet to even try drugs, let alone use them regularly. Of those who begin to use drugs "recreationally," researchers estimate that approximately 10 percent go on to serious, heavy, chronic, compulsive use. Herbert Kleber, the former deputy director of the Office of National Drug Control Policy, recently estimated that cocaine legalization might multiply the number of addicts from the current 2 million to between 18 and 50 million (which are the estimated numbers of problem drinkers and nicotine addicts).

"With legalization, violent crime would likely escalate..."

This suggests that drug prohibition seems to be having some very positive effects and that legalizing drugs would not necessarily have a depressant effect on violent crime. With legalization, violent crime would likely escalate; or perhaps some types of systemic violence would decline at the expense of greatly increasing the overall rate of violent crime. Moreover, legalizing drugs would likely increase physical illnesses and compound any existing psychiatric problems among users and their family members. And finally, legalizing drugs would not eliminate the effects of unemployment, inadequate housing, deficient job skills, economic worries, and physical abuse that typically contribute to the use of drugs.

II. Substance Abuse and Youth

Editor's Introduction

Ultimately the largest and most painful consequence of America's substance abuse problem lay in the damage it inflicts upon our youth. As Paul B. Stares writes in the previous section "For the fourth straight year, a federally supported nationwide survey of American secondary schools students...has indicated increased drug use." In many ways, the marked and shocking increase in substance abuse among American youth is singular to the age we live in. While young people have traditionally been the largest group of illegal substance consumers, the sheer rate at which illegal substances are infiltrating our youth is staggering. In addition to exploring the particular nature of this phenomenon, the articles contained in Section II also convey a variety of theories as to reasons and origins of the relationship that clearly exists between youth and the abuse of illegal substances.

The first article in this section, from *Reader's Digest*, explores the sudden "upsurge" of marijuana use by young people. The article begins by noting that nearly double the amount of teenagers "had smoked marijuana at least once" in 1995 than had in 1992. This, according to the author, is a result of the "parents, schools, and media" failing to insure that teenagers understand illegal substances, including marijuana, as "dangerous and unacceptable." The author continues, noting that at one time in recent history, most notably seen in the "Just-Say-No" campaign of the 1980s, children were met with a "unified chorus" of anti-drug slogans and warnings, whereas today they are greeted with a "pro-drug message" or a call for legalization that is becoming increasingly strong.

Reiterating concern over the increase in marijuana use by young people, James L. Graff, writing for *Time* magazine, describes marijuana as "an ancillary pleasure of growing up in the '90s." Graff reaches this conclusion after investigating a wealthy suburban high-school in which marijuana use "has become almost boringly conventional." Graff states this is a result of parents who are not adamant enough in their objection to drug abuse coupled with a general belief that marijuana use is simply a part of life and seemingly "without risk." Graff's article also contains a variety of charts and graphs which support the notion that drugs, particularly marijuana, are no longer confined to a single stratum of America's youth but have become notably pervasive.

Graff's conclusions are confirmed by Christopher S. Wren, writing in the *New York Times*. Wren's article notes that marijuana is "the overwhelming drug of choice" of young people. Stringing together a variety of quotes from teenagers in New York and Massachusetts, Wren successfully portrays the darker side of marijuana abuse which includes its negative effects upon memory, grades, and overall achievement in later life. The next article, "Why Just Say No Hasn't Worked," by Roy DeLaMar, presents an alarming series of statistics, all of which confirm that marijuana is no longer viewed by many as being a dangerous substance. Yet, as DeLaMar points out, "marijuana contains 400 health-hazardous chemicals," many of which pose serious health risks.

Yet it is not marijuana alone that has made a resurgent presence in the lives of America's young people. As John Leland points out in "The Fear of Heroin Is Shooting Up," "heroin is now scaring the heck out of people...in cities and suburbs nationwide." Like marijuana, government estimates indicate that heroin use by the young has "doubled since the mid-80s." Leland theorizes that this could be the result of several factors including the new potency levels heroin has achieved despite selling for nearly half the price it did in the 80s. Another theory lay in the notion that "cocaine and opiate waves have suceeded one another" for more than 100 years. Perhaps the current surge in heroin use is merely a consequence of the high rate of cocaine abuse so much a part of the 1980s. Whatever the cause for the increases in heroin use among our youth, the consequences are often lethal. This point is made painfully clear in the next article entitled "The Damage Done" by Richard Jerome and Ron Arias. Here, Jerome and Arias recount the death of Elizabeth Danser, a seemingly normal, well-adjusted teenager who died of a heroin overdose in 1996.

Drugs Are Back Big Time[1]

Eighteen-year-old Mike Woods of suburban Cleveland describes his schedule this way: Every day after school he smokes marijuana. Then he takes a nap or calls a few friends and just "hangs out." Before he started smoking pot three years ago, his grade point average was 3.5, and he was a star sprinter on the track team. Now his GPA is 2.7, and he has dropped track.

"Pot makes you lazy," says Woods. "I don't like to do schoolwork." Even so, he admits he'll continue smoking marijuana. It has also led Woods and his friends to experiment with stronger drugs. "A lot of people move on to acid," he says. When asked how many other students smoke pot, he laughs. "I couldn't count, it's so many. And it's like that at all the other high schools around here."

"Daily use among eighth-graders has quadrupled since 1992..."

• At an Austin, Texas, music festival, the smell of marijuana permeates the air, and a cloud of smoke hangs thick near the stage. Pipes and joints are passed around freely.

Many of the 14,000 fans wander among the concession stands, most of which are selling pot-related products. Displayed at one stand are Phillies Blunt cigars. Some people buy these, hollow them out and fill them with marijuana. Four teen-age girls finger some herbal cigarettes on sale next to the cigars and ask whether they would get high by smoking them. When told "no," one of the teens responds, "Why would you smoke it if it didn't do anything?"

• In Seattle on a sunny Saturday afternoon, two teens walk past the Westlake shopping center. When I approach the pair with questions, they laughingly admit they are on their way to get high. Three blocks later, we stop on the sidewalk. One of them, Jamie Rogers, pulls a joint from a pack of cigarettes, lights it and takes a deep drag. "There isn't a day that I'm not stoned," he says. "Weed is as common as school lunch."

After declining steadily through the 1980s, teen-age drug use, especially of marijuana, has jumped sharply. Daily use among eighth-graders has *quadrupled* since 1992, according to University of Michigan's Institute for Social Research. In 1995, nearly twice as many teen-agers had smoked marijuana at least once during the previous 12 months as in 1992. Half of high-school seniors have used illegal drugs at least once. And drug use is not limited to marginal students or troublemakers. Says Monica Lobo, a 16-year-old junior from West Des Moines, Iowa: "So many people at my high school smoke pot that you can't even label one group 'the stoners' anymore."

---

[1] Article by Daniel R. Levine, Washington Bureau Senior Editor, from *Reader's Digest* 148:71-6 F '96. Copyright © 1996 The Reader's Digest Assn., Inc. Reprinted with permission.

Marijuana is the overwhelming drug of choice among our children, but inhalants—breathable chemical vapors from common household products that produce "psychoactive," mind-altering effects—are also being abused. Twenty percent of eighth-graders admit trying them to get high.

Other drugs being used by teens: LSD and PCP, powerful hallucinogens that can cause prolonged psychotic reactions after being ingested; Rohypnol, also called "roofie," a sedative stronger than Valium; and MDMA, or "Ecstasy," which produces feelings of euphoria. In a recent survey of 12- to 17-year-olds, more than half said heroin and cocaine were readily available.

The reason for this upsurge is increasingly clear, says Dr. Robert DuPont, first director of the National Institute on Drug Abuse. For 13 years, marijuana use dropped because an unrelenting, unified chorus of parents, schools, the media and national leaders made sure teens understood that drugs, starting with marijuana, were dangerous and unacceptable. Then teens began hearing fewer of these messages. Says Susan Acorn, 17, of Omaha: "Nobody talks about it anymore. It's like the subject of drugs is taboo." Meanwhile popular culture, especially music, has portrayed marijuana as a normal, even glamorous, aspect of teen life. As the Washington *Post* commented last May: "Pot is hip." Drug use began to climb.

To better understand why, talk with former teen-agers who did get the message on drugs. One success story is Britt Tunick, 23, a graduate student at American University in Washington, D.C. An outgoing brunette, Tunick graduated from high school in 1990 and never used drugs as a teen-ager. Asked why she refrained, Tunick mentions the dangers. "There were all those ads on TV," she says. " 'Say no the first time and every time.' We all knew the ads by heart. And it was a constant message." There was a clear understanding that drugs were harmful and socially unacceptable. Students who used drugs "were considered losers who were going nowhere.

During the 1980s, the most effective anti-drug message was First Lady Nancy Reagan's advice "Just Say No." Presented to a class of Oakland, Calif., elementary-school children in 1985, the slogan fired the nation's conscience. That year there were just 36 community-based substance-abuse coalitions across the nation. By 1989 there were 650.

The focus on drugs also generated a tidal wave of media coverage. When the Partnership for a Drug-Free America (PDFA) was formed in 1986, communications and advertising experts worked together to create anti-drug ads. The nation's media donated $2 billion in time and space, making it the largest public service advertising drive in history.

In the late 1980s, commercials like this memorable PDFA ad blanketed the airwaves:

A stern-looking man faces the camera and says, "Is there any-

one out there who still isn't clear about what 'doing drugs' does?" Cut to shot of an egg. "This is your brain." Cut to a hot frying pan. "This is drugs." He breaks the egg and drops it into the pan. It sizzles loudly and fries almost immediately. "This is your brain on drugs. Any questions?"

Television advertising has demonstrated that it can play a powerful role in shaping teens' perceptions of drugs. Last year researchers at The Johns Hopkins Children's Center studied the effect of anti-drug TV messages on some 700 middle- and high-school students: 97 percent reported that the ads convinced them using drugs was "more dangerous" than they had thought; 71 percent said the ads would persuade them not to try drugs in the first place.

In the early '90s though, attention moved away from drugs. In 1989, 518 drug stories were aired on the evening news of the three major networks. By 1994, there were just 78. The number of PDFA spots is down 20 percent since 1990. More important, today's PDFA ads are being scheduled by TV stations during off-peak hours—when young people are less likely to be watching. Political leaders also focused their attention elsewhere. Says Herbert D. Kleber, executive vice president of the Center on Addiction and Substance Abuse at Columbia University: "This Administration and Congress have really ignored the drug issue."

At the same time, a pro-drug message is emerging as an increasingly influential lobby promotes radical alternative policies such as legalizing marijuana and heroin. One of these outfits, the Drug Policy Foundation, calls itself a think tank on drug policy reform and is backed by George Sòros, one of the world's wealthiest financiers. Through his Open Society Institute, Sòros has donated over $8 million to the 20,000-member Drug Policy Foundation and other groups.

Sòros, who refused Reader's Digest's request for an interview, says through his spokesman that he "has no position on drug policy." Pressed further, the spokesman added that Sòros believes "law enforcement has been a failure and decriminalization and legalization should be debated."

On the other hand, the president of the Drug Policy Foundation, Arnold Trebach, admits he is a "flat-out legalizer." At the foundation's annual meeting last October, Trebach presented its highest award and a $6000 check to President Clinton's former Surgeon General, Joycelyn Elders. Elders, who resigned her post after making controversial statements about drugs and sexual behavior, was touted by Trebach as "one of our heroes." She responded with a speech in favor of drug decriminalization. Another of the foundation's awardees was enthusiastically applauded when she exhorted the crowd: "Let's hear it for the junkies!"

The media have also contributed to a pro-drug climate. Last April, ABC television aired the prime-time special "America's

War on Drugs: Searching for Solutions." The show put forth "harm reduction," a policy that is supposed to reduce the social and health risks of drug use through such measures as distributing clean needles to addicts.

In August 1994, MTV aired an hour-long news special entitled "Straight Dope" in which marijuana use was put on a par with drinking coffee or smoking cigarettes. As part of its Cable in the Classroom series, MTV distributed tapes of the show to schools around the country.

Drug legalizers often tout "the European model" for relaxing drug enforcement. Throughout the Netherlands, for example, marijuana and hashish are openly sold and consumed in so-called "coffee shops." But the results are increasingly problematic. Dutch adolescent marijuana use, for example, nearly tripled between 1984 and 1992, while the flow of drugs into bordering countries has grown. At the same time the Netherlands is ranked No. 1 in Europe for forcible assaults up 65 percent since 1985.

Legalization of hard drugs has produced similar results. In 1989, the Swiss city of Zurich instituted a harm-reduction program that allowed the use and sale of drugs in a downtown park. It was quickly dubbed "Needle Park" because addicts were given free needles, condoms, medical care, counseling and the opportunity for treatment. The number of regular drug users in the park swelled from a few hundred to thousands. By 1992 the operation had to be shut down because of a sharp rise in drug-related violence and deaths. Today, Switzerland is left with Europe's highest per-capita rate of drug addiction and second highest rate of HIV infection.

"Legalized marijuana in the United States would be a disaster," says Columbia's Kleber. "It would create a pediatric epidemic for which we would pay a dreadful price in terms of more damaged children and more damaged adults when they grow up."

The youthful drug epidemic is further fueled through popular culture, especially by rock music. At the Lollapalooza music festival last July in Great Woods, Mass., the mostly white, suburban teen crowd cheered wildly when rap group Cypress Hill pushed a six-foot-tall "bong," or water pipe, onstage. The group has sold five million copies of its first two albums, one of which included songs titled "Legalize It," "Hits From the Bong" and "I Wanna Get High."

Popular rock star Tom Petty regularly glamorizes marijuana use in concerts and songs. Petty's latest top-selling album includes the lyrics "Let's get to the point. Let's roll another joint." In another he sings, "It's good to get high and never come down."

In a recent study of 12- to 17-year-olds conducted for Columbia's Center on Addiction and Substance Abuse, 76 percent said that the entertainment industry encourages illegal drug use. Phil Cannon, 16, and Steve Logan, 16, both of Broken Arrow, Okla., agree. Cannon started smoking pot when he was

13, and Logan started more than a year ago. They now do it "pretty much every day." Cannon has a persistent cough, and Logan admits, "I forget a lot of stuff, like what happened a couple of days ago." Does popular music promote drug use? Says Logan, "All I know is that almost every song you listen to says something about it. It puts it into your mind constantly." Adds Cannon, "When you see the celebrities doing it, it makes it seem okay."

Children even receive pro-drug messages through their computers. On the Internet, they can find step-by-step instructions on how to roll a joint, bake pot brownies or make LSD.

Some marijuana advocates propagate the notion that hemp—another name for the marijuana plant and for the fiber from it—can "save the world." They promote the plant as our "premier renewable natural resource," which could be used for paper, food, fuel and fiber, and at the same time, according to one pro-marijuana publication, "balance the world's ecosystems and restore the atmosphere's oxygen balance."

"...hemp products, such as wallets, jeans and hats, have proliferated, and their popularity is evident among teens."

Says professor of pharmacology Billy Martin, a leading marijuana researcher at Virginia Commonwealth University, "It's obvious that hemp is a facade to give marijuana a better name." Nevertheless, hemp products, such as wallets, jeans and hats, have proliferated, and their popularity is evident among teens. For example, when German shoe manufacturer Adidas asked young Americans for new athletic-shoe ideas, the result was a shoe made of hemp.

Despite all of these pro-drug messages, the fact remains that marijuana is harmful. Studies show that it disrupts short-term memory and hormonal levels. Young women may find their monthly cycle disrupted. Marijuana alters brain function and harms the lungs-one joint has four times more tar than a tobacco cigarette. During a marijuana high, motor skills such as timing, coordination and alertness are diminished.

Marijuana is also a "gateway" drug: few cocaine, LSD or heroin users did not first smoke pot. One reason is that a teen who uses marijuana is more likely to come into contact with users and sellers of harder drugs. A youngster 12 to 17 years old who smokes marijuana is 85 times more likely to use cocaine than one who does not.

Moreover, teen-age marijuana use is linked to criminal behavior. In 1993, 26 percent of all male teens arrested in 12 major cities tested positive for marijuana. In Washington, D.C., 52 percent of arrested juveniles tested positive for marijuana in 1994—up from six percent in 1990.

Fred Motley of Spring Valley, N.Y., understands just how dangerous marijuana really is. He was a 12-year-old honor student when he first smoked pot. "I wanted to be accepted by the cool crowd," he says. He started smoking pot only on weekends, but

then moved to LSD, cocaine and crack. He grew increasingly bel-
ligerent, routinely skipped school and became depressed. In
January 1993 he entered a drug treatment program, and for two
years he has been trying to put his life back together.

Lloyd D. Johnston, program director of the Institute for Social
Research at the University of Michigan, who has tracked teen
drug trends since 1975, sees the country in the same position
today as it was in the late 1960s when anti-drug attitudes broke
down and use skyrocketed. Says Johnston: "This has all the signs
of another epidemic. In the last one, thousands of lives were lost
and millions adversely affected. We cannot afford another
tragedy like that."

High Times at New Trier High[2]

A Model School Struggles With a Vexing National Issue: Kids on Pot

Even with his leather jacket, wraparound shades and permanent slouch, Matt can't quite pull off the menacing air people attach to drug dealers. Maybe it's the fact that he operates under the stately trees of Chicago's wealthy North Shore, or that he is only 17 and wears braces. He parks his late-model Lincoln in the student lot and saunters through the after-school crowd loitering on "Smokers' Corner," a short block from New Trier Township High School. Matt talks the language of business, not crime. "The way to make a large sum of money is with repeat customers," he explains. "With me, these kids can walk out of school and get good quality at good prices—$35 for an eighth [of an ounce of marijuana]. I'm not a pusher, which is disgusting; I'm a dealer—people who want it can get it from me."

"Getting high has become almost boringly conventional."

Marijuana is Matt's top seller, but today he is hawking some psilocybin mushrooms to two ninth-graders, Russell and Jared. As a bonus, Matt drives his young clients to a Chicago head shop, where they spend $50 on an elaborate porcelain hookah shaped like a mushroom. Afterward they stop at Matt's place, where everyone repairs to the garage for a few bongfuls of "excellent bud" before heading home for dinner.

It is a classic afternoon's adventure for young suburbanites, with a touch—but no more—of peril. In Wilmette, Winnetka, Glencoe and Kenilworth, the posh white suburbs served by New Trier, drug use isn't associated with gang violence, crack houses, addiction or dead-end despair. Getting high has become almost boringly conventional. Drew (names and some other identifying features have been changed), a regular at the Corner, has even kicked around the notion of buying "New Trier Smoking Club" jackets with his friends and awarding mock varsity letters.

Most New Trier kids who smoke pot—by all accounts more than three-fifths of the student body—wouldn't be caught dead in a jacket like that. Only a fraction of New Trier's pot smokers—the denizens of the Corner among them—view getting high as the main part of their identity. For most, marijuana is an ancillary pleasure of growing up comfortably in the '90s, not the least bit incompatible with varsity athletics, the spring musical or advanced-placement chemistry. After all, most of the kids at New Trier will go on to succeed, just as their parents did. The fact that they have tried pot won't cancel out the perks of good breeding

---

[2] Article by James L. Graff, from *Time* 148:33-6 D 9 '96. Copyright © 1996 Time Inc. All rights reserved. Reprinted with permission.

and unbounded opportunity.

Situated in Winnetka, where last year the median sale price for a house was $515,000, New Trier regularly sends 95% of its graduates to four-year colleges, many of them the same elite institutions that produced the lawyers, doctors and corporate executives who live here in large part because of the excellent school system. New Trier offers its students—85% white, 12% Asian, 2% Hispanic and 1% African American—everything from international relations and classical Greek to operatic choir and gourmet food. At New Trier, there's nothing called gym class or phys ed; it's kinetic wellness.

"Everybody here overplays marijuana, like it's some horrible thing," says Melinda, a senior who wants to attend an East Coast college. "It's not just something that 'bad' people do. My dad went to an Ivy League school, and he and my mom both tried it in high school." Her parents' concern, she says, is that she'll buy pot laced with speed or crack. But Melinda, who seems representative of the average user at New Trier, smokes only occasionally and seems able to take it or leave it. "The people with problems are the ones who want being high to be reality," she says. "That's not me."

"The very ordinariness of drug use leads some to conclude that it is without risk."

Once a badge of hipness, marijuana today welcomes everyone at New Trier—jocks and literati, nerds and debutantes. "These days it's everywhere," says Dottie, 17. "Cheerleaders puff. Sixth-graders puff." The very ordinariness of drug use leads some to conclude that it is without risk. But there are plenty of kids on the Corner at New Trier who started out as recreational users and now admit they can't stop. One prematurely wise senior voices disdain for "gumpy sophomores who think it's harmless." Some end up in rehab programs, which far more often than not fail initially with adolescents. The sad fact is that many will have a substance-abuse habit all their lives.

If teenage drug use were the kind of problem a school could solve, New Trier would probably ace it. It was among the first high schools in Illinois to face up to the last teenage drug explosion, in 1981. "We made a decision then to go public and say we have a problem," says Jon White, assistant principal for student services. When school officials decided in 1985 to go outside to hire a full-time person to deal with substance abuse, they opted not for an enforcer or an educator but for Mary Dailey, a social worker from an adolescent treatment center.

Dailey, now in her 12th year as the self-styled "drug czarina" of New Trier, heads the oldest and one of the best-funded student-assistance programs in the state. In 1988 she received an award, signed by William Bennett and presented by Nancy Reagan, honoring New Trier's "excellence in drug-prevention education." "I've devoted a career to this," says Dailey, "but I know that drug use is more prevalent in the freshman class than ever before." Despite all the societal angst generated over drug use during the 1980s, she feels that attitudes since then have

softened. "In the late '70s and early '80s there was plenty of denial but also the idea that drugs aren't good," says Dailey. "Honestly, today a lot of parents don't feel that way. They hark back to the days when they used. And they don't realize what's happened to drug content or what the implications are of using at such young ages."

New Trier has always prided itself on its enlightened policy toward drug infractions. Some schools, such as nearby Glenbrook High, will permanently expel a student for merely having a roach clip. At New Trier, a student found for the first time under the influence of drugs or alcohol is suspended for five days, but four of those days are placed "in abeyance" if the student and his or her parents agree to go through a substance-abuse program together.

If a law is broken—possession of marijuana, for instance—charges are filed by Scott Harty, a Winnetka police officer permanently assigned to the school. For amounts less than 10 grams, that can mean a minor fine under a village ordinance; for more or for dealing, kids land in county court. "I don't give warnings," Harty says. The friend-to-friend commerce is hard to infiltrate, he says, so a bust "really puts blood in the water" as kids try to figure out whether someone was "narked" on. But Harty has been around long enough to know that many kids can't be scared straight by the law. "I've arrested kids who just love to see the squad car pull up," he says. "Some of them see a rap sheet as a badge of honor."

The school does what it can to insulate its students. Two years ago, New Trier, formerly an open campus, started keeping its 3,000 students on school grounds all day, except for about 300 juniors and seniors whose parents give permission for them to leave. But even a wealthy, concerned alma mater like New Trier can't fill the shoes of parents who either don't care that their kids are smoking or fail at the task of stopping them. "How could a school eradicate it?" asks New Trier's superintendent, Henry S. Bangser. "Schools have a responsibility to address the problem, but students didn't learn to do drugs here, and mostly they don't do it here."

There are many cooler places for them to do it. Most evenings a party evolves at Dottie's apartment. She moved there after her parents forbade her to smoke marijuana at home. The scene is right out of the '70s: a black light, a beanbag chair and an African drum in the corner. Pink Floyd is cranked up loud. There seems to be a curious lack of sexual tension among the 15 or so adolescent boys and girls, most of them from New Trier, sitting in a rough circle on the floor in the eerie light. No one necks in the corner; attention is focused on the bong slowly circling the assemblage. Everyone who has pot shares it. "The ethics here is if you're 'holding,' you contribute," explains a kid as he fills the bong one more time.

Among kids who admit they can't control their pot smoking,

trouble at home often lurks in the background. Even in Chicago's relatively tranquil North Shore, dysfunction blooms in a thousand ways. Drew, for instance, a thoughtful 16-year-old junior who began getting high in the eighth grade, has had trouble handling marijuana from the start. He claims that his absent father once had a substance-abuse problem. By the ninth grade, he says, "my priorities were totally screwed up. I didn't even buy the books I needed. I was selling pot in the boys' room."

Drew ended up in outpatient rehab. "They tell you you're a drug addict, and if you say you're not, you're in denial," he says. "If you say you only use it occasionally, they say you're rationalizing." Still, things improved. Some therapy sessions included Drew's mother. "There was complete honesty," he recalls. "It was the best our relationship has ever been."

Last school year Drew not only stayed clean, he even talked to younger kids about the perils of drug use. But doubts were gnawing at him. "I didn't think my use justified a whole life in a 12-step program," he remembers. He started to think, as he still does, that recovery was "a blue-collar thing." He says, "It's fine for people who are going to take their dads' places on road crews, but as a creative person, it holds you back. Just look at groups like Aerosmith or the Red Hot Chili Peppers—they got sober, and they started to suck."

When school was out, Drew gave his demons free rein: he rented a cheap cottage in Wisconsin with some friends and laid into a quarter-pound of pot and lots of booze. "We got sick all over everything—it was definitely my failure self. I was like a dog that had been tied up in front of a steak and then finally let loose." Late last summer, a grandparent interceded to put him in a residential treatment center out of state. A week after his return, he says, he was using again.

Drew knows he has an addictive personality. "Even as a kid, I was the one who had to have every baseball card, every comic book," he says. And while he thinks about quitting every day, he doesn't believe he can just stop. So he converts his vice into a twisted virtue. Bolstered by a smattering of existentialism, Beat poetry and rock 'n' roll, Drew and plenty of teenagers like him justify what they do as a glorification of immediate pleasure over conventional restraint, a familiar theme from the '60s. For Drew, smoking copious quantities of pot confers membership in the select club of "the failures," people who were dealt a good hand of money, talent and support but who opt for a path of all-but-deliberate self-destruction.

While some New Trier parents are disengaged, as Drew claims his were, others are more hands-on—and angry. But the results of greater parental discipline are not necessarily much better. Michael, a preternaturally bright 16-year-old sophomore, is a case in point. Last year he was smoking up to five times a day, and his grades were suffering. But it wasn't until his scoutmaster caught him getting high on a Boy Scout outing that his par-

ents found out. Their reaction was to ground him for the summer. The punishment gave him a chance to read Dante's *Divine Comedy* and some Shakespeare but did nothing to change his attitude; his friends came over to his place to get high.

At the end of the summer, Michael says, "I realized this wasn't good for me," and he stopped smoking. In what he now describes as a cry for help, he came clean with his parents and told them about the pot, the acid, the mushrooms, everything. "I thought they'd help me, but they were furious," he says. Michael has shelved further attempts to bridge the gap. "It's one thing to punish me and another to alienate me," he says. "Now there's no way I'm going to talk straight with them again. I do, and I'm heading right for a military academy." Michael seems neither disposed nor able to quit entirely. "I've been cutting down a lot, and really only do it on the weekends," he says. "But I can't go cold turkey."

Many parents seem similarly unable to turn their outrage about drug use into a clear and compelling message. When Marta, a willowy junior who sports a nose ring, was caught smoking pot on the street last spring, her mother arrived at the police station in a fury. "She just kept slapping me in the face, left and right," the 17-year-old remembers. But the anger only went so far. "My mom and I didn't tell my dad," Marta says. "He would have gone ballistic, and I would never get my car." Marta figures her mother thinks getting busted has scared her straight, but it has not. And she still expects her promised new car.

The cops on Chicago's North Shore see that kind of enabling behavior all the time. "Parents tell me they never go into their kids' rooms—then they wonder why they have a problem," says Officer Harty. No student has been convicted of a drug felony at New Trier in recent memory. When a kid does get caught in the prosperous communities of the North Shore, police and prosecutors frequently come up against formidable legal talent. "The first reaction of any parent is protection," says John Fay, juvenile officer for the Glencoe police department. "They hire the best because they can afford it. And let's face it, we've got judges who live in this area. They'll explore every avenue before sending a suburban kid to [Cook County Jail at] 26th and California."

The school and the police can't do much about pot use without the support and concern of parents, many of whom can't seem to decide whether to be the good cop or the bad cop with their kids. Emily, 48, turned into an enforcer when she found a pipe as she was redecorating her 16-year-old son's room. "I told him I didn't approve, that I didn't think it was necessary," she says. Emily's reaction wasn't as cool when another parent called to tell her that her 14-year-old daughter was smoking pot too. "That really shocked me," says Emily. "I didn't try it until I was 20, and she's all of 14—that's a big difference. What I worry about is the acceleration of gratification: if she's doing marijuana now, what'll she do as a senior?"

Before she caught her kids, Emily attended several meetings of Parent Alliance for Drug and Alcohol Awareness, which is linked to the New Trier school district. "I remember thinking these parents seemed so radical about marijuana," she says. Now she wonders whether random searches of lockers and mandatory drug testing ought to be introduced at school, two options Superintendent Bangser regards as unnecessary. But while she still considers the tone of PADAA too apocalyptic, she finds other parents too lackadaisical. "There's a definite head-in-the-sand attitude here," she says. "People figure our kids' SAT scores are so high they can't be doing it." PADAA sponsors public forums and blankets the community with literature to combat precisely those attitudes, but it's an uphill battle. "It used to be that the parents who got involved were the ones who had problems," sighs PADAA activist Sandra Plowden. "Now it seems like it's the ones without them."

The dilemma for Emily and many other parents of her generation is that she wants to enjoy her children, to be liked by them, so she feels constrained not to crack down too hard. "When we were growing up, there was a big black line between us and our parents," she says. Now she wears sandals, socks and jeans, just like her kids. In the car with her husband and two children, they can all agree on music by Santana, the Beatles and the Doors. "In a way, that makes things easier," says Emily, "but on the other hand, when we tell them something, they just say, 'Whatever.'" Emily even bought a T shirt emblazoned with that word for her son, who refuses to wear it.

So Emily and her husband, a doctor, are left in a parental limbo familiar to her peers: she is on to her kids about smoking marijuana, but she knows that won't be enough to stop them. Next time she catches them, she swears, "I'll lock them in every afternoon"—but she looks doubtful even as she says it. Ultimately, she hopes, the striving for success they've grown up with will check the urge to rebel. "I want to be like Holden Caulfield in *The Catcher in the Rye* and stop these kids from going off the cliff," she says. "But then I look at the breadth of the problem and think I can't do it."

*I agree strongly with the statements:

Taking drugs scares me	1993	1995
	47%	36%

I don't want to hang around drug users	1993	1995
	55%	39%

* From studies of more than 6,000 teens in 1993 and 1995 by the Partnership for a Drug-Free America.

HAVING NO FEAR

A study of 12th-graders shows that availability of marijuana is fairly constant, but usage increases as students' fear of harming themselves declines.

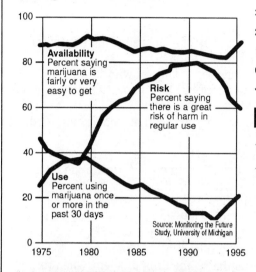

Availability
Percent saying marijuana is fairly or very easy to get

Risk
Percent saying there is a great risk of harm in regular use

Use
Percent using marijuana once or more in the past 30 days

Source: Monitoring the Future Study, University of Michigan

POTENCY

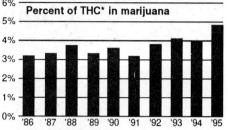

Percent of THC* in marijuana

'86 '87 '88 '89 '90 '91 '92 '93 '94 '95

*The chief intoxicant in marijuana

SEIZURES

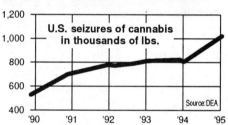

U.S. seizures of cannabis in thousands of lbs.

'90   '91   '92   '93   '94   '95

Source: DEA

PROBLEMS

What is the most important problem facing teens?

Drugs	31%
Social pressures	14%
Crime	14%
Sexual issues	7%

Source:
CASA survey
of Teens and Adults

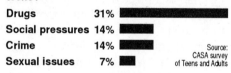

JUVENILE ARRESTS

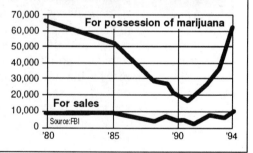

For possession of marijuana

For sales

Source: FBI

'80   '85   '90   '94

Teenagers Find Drugs
Easy to Obtain and
Warnings Easy to Ignore[3]

Nicole, a high school junior with short brown hair, soft eyes and a delicate chin, has smoked marijuana since she was 13 years old. Many of her friends at her Massachusetts high school use it too, and sometimes her father joins her.

"I smoke weed with my dad," Nicole, who is now 16, said. "Obviously he feels fine about it. Since I started smoking weed, we've gotten closer."

Marijuana has become so routine that Nicole admitted, "I smoke every single day."

The rising use of illegal drugs by teenagers like Nicole was confirmed in August by the Department of Health and Human Services, which reported that marijuana use by young people had more than doubled since 1992.

That report set off a running debate between President Clinton and Bob Dole, his Republican challenger, over the reasons for the increase. Mr. Dole has accused Mr. Clinton of causing the increase by being inattentive to the drug problem. The President has said the Republican-controlled Congress cut financing for his programs to reduce drug use.

Interviews with teenagers show that, indeed, many use marijuana, perhaps even more than is reflected in the Government report and in others. Last month the National Center on Addiction and Substance Abuse at Columbia University reported that by the time young people turn 17, 62 percent know someone who uses marijuana. Fewer than one in three said their schools were free of drugs.

The interviews also show that the political debate is not lost on teenagers.

"Look at Bill Clinton," Nicole said. "He smoked marijuana and became President. He said that if he tried it again, he'd inhale," she said, referring to an interview that Mr. Clinton gave in June 1992 to MTV, which Mr. Dole has resurrected in a campaign television commercial.

During the interviews, conducted over the last week and a half in Massachusetts and New York, 30 teenagers from inner-city, working-class and suburban neighborhoods said marijuana can be as easy to buy as beer or cigarettes, often from schoolmates. The usual price is $5 a joint. "It takes one phone call," said Matt, a 16-year-old in Gloucester, Mass. A 16-year-old boy in

"...by the time young people turn 17, 62 percent know someone who uses marijuana."

---

[3] Article by Christopher Sale Wren, from the *New York Times* A20 O 10 '96. Copyright © 1996 The New York Times Company. Reprinted with permission.

Bronxville, N.Y., said he could find marijuana by walking a mile in any direction from his high school. Angel, 17, said it is sold under the counter in groceries and flower shops around his South Bronx neighborhood in New York City.

Most of the young people spoke on condition that they not be identified beyond first names and ages. Because drug use is illegal and because of fears about parental anger, a few asked for complete anonymity.

Their comments confirmed that marijuana remained the overwhelming drug of choice, with cocaine and heroin use far less common.

Those who smoke marijuana said they started not because of peer pressure, but because it seemed fun and offered them temporary escape from the angst of growing up. They disparaged anti-drug advertisements and drug-prevention classes as ineffective and expressed skepticism that parents, teachers or other adults could make much difference.

"...most teenage drug users confine themselves to marijuana, some confess to wider experimentation."

Some teenagers argued that marijuana could not be that bad if so many adults used it, and mentioned Mr. Clinton. "He must have tried it more than once," said Isa, a 17-year-old high school senior. "I bet maybe 50 percent of the Congress has tried it. I mean, some adults still use."

"If you're smoking marijuana, you're not using drugs. I don't think that marijuana is the same thing as using cocaine or heroin."

The growing acceptance of marijuana is not lost on even younger students. "Some people tell you how it feels so good and stuff," said Ryan, a blond 13-year-old who reported that marijuana had piqued interest in his eighth-grade class.

The teenagers who grew up with drugs in New York City were less sanguine. "In my neighborhood, all you see is just drugs," said Angel, who has childhood memories of crack cocaine buyers lining up around his block. He tried marijuana when he was 13, and soon graduated to "blunts," cigars hollowed out and stuffed with marijuana. One day, he recalled, he smoked 11 blunts.

"I was really messing up," Angel said. "I wasn't going to school. I was disrespecting everybody." After running afoul of the law, he was accepted by Phoenix Academy, a residential high school in Yorktown Heights, N.Y., run by the drug treatment and prevention agency Phoenix House.

While most teenage drug users confine themselves to marijuana, some confess to wider experimentation. "My mother did drugs and I said I never would, but when I was 12, I started doing drugs," said Misty, a dark-eyed high school senior in Massachusetts. "At the time I had a boyfriend who was much older than I."

By the time Misty turned 14, she found herself in a drug treatment program. "I was straight, like for two years," she said. "I didn't smoke weed or nothing. Then I went out with another guy, and I started doing it again."

Now 17, Misty said she has chopped up pills "real small" and sniffed them to get high. "My nose started bleeding, but I didn't care," she said. She laughed about how her latest boyfriend slipped LSD, a hallucinogen, into a beer she was drinking. And she has snorted cocaine.

"If it's given to you, obviously you're going to do it," Misty said. "A couple of weeks ago, I was really depressed and I did a line. I just hate it so much, but I keep doing it when I'm feeling all down and out." She feels high for a couple of seconds and then feels terrible, she said.

While surveys indicate that the majority of teenagers do not use drugs, some abstainers admitted to feeling awkward around friends who do. "Sometimes they might think you're too good for them, like you have a prissy attitude," said Jennifer, a blond 16-year-old in Gloucester.

""I just hate it so much, but I keep doing it when I'm feeling all down and out.""

"There are a lot of kids who don't like drugs and who think it is actually stupid," Jennifer continued. "But who are we to say, 'Get that needle out of your arm'? When it comes down to stopping them from doing drugs, they've got to stop their own addictive behavior."

Ben, a lanky 17-year-old from Cambridge, attributed the experimentation at a younger age to lack of self-confidence. "In the eighth grade, smoking marijuana would be an easy ticket to being cooler," he said. "I know there would be a good social result if I'd started smoking."

But marijuana users who were interviewed said that they started out of curiosity. "One day I was playing basketball and someone said, 'Let's get high,' so we did, and I loved it," said Matt, a sophomore who wore a baseball cap, brim backward, over his blond hair.

"I don't need to impress anybody," Matt said. "If I want to get high, I just get high. People say weed makes you stupid. I smoke weed, and I'm smart."

Errika, a 16-year-old sophomore in Gloucester, said some of her friends considered marijuana safer than tobacco. "People say, 'Why smoke cigarettes and get cancer when you can smoke weed and just lose a few brain cells?'" she said. As for marijuana's effect on academic performance, she said, "People will come to school high and say, 'Oh, I did awesome on my test.'"

But grades do suffer, said Raquel, a 16-year-old sophomore who flaunts an enamel marijuana pendant. "I started to be a straight-A student and then I started smoking pot and my grades went straight down," she said. "I'll go home now and not be able to do my homework."

Kay, a 15-year-old classmate who wore a studded leather collar and nose ring, said, "If you want to find out what it's like, you're going to do it."

Kay sloughed off criticism. "I've adjusted to friends who call us the freaks of the school," she said. "Someone told me we were worthless forms of life, and we just laughed in his face."

Robert, a 20-year-old New Yorker who smoked his first joint at 13, attributed much of the teenage drug use to rebellion. "When someone tells you not to do it, that makes you want to do it even more," he said. Marijuana was so abundant in his Queens neighborhood, Robert said, that "it's like going to the store and buying some gum or candy."

After being caught selling cocaine to support his appetite for blunts, he quit drugs and, like Angel, enrolled in Phoenix Academy. "Marijuana has really messed my mind up, because it makes it hard for me to remember something," said Robert, who is trying to finish high school. "If you want to become something in life, don't use it. If you don't want to become anything, go right ahead."

The advertising campaigns against illegal drugs pitch the same message, but few of the teenagers seemed to take them seriously. Isa dismissed them as "a good laugh." And Mr. Clinton's warnings against drug use drew snickers. "For him to say don't do drugs, then to say he did it but he didn't inhale, that's a kind of far-fetched story," Jennifer said.

While professing indifference, many of the teenagers acknowledged, however tacitly, that parents do matter. "If I had an addiction problem," Errika said, "I would trust my friends not to get my parents involved, because it would hurt them more than anything,"

In rejecting drugs, 15-year-old Daren credited his mother, a single parent struggling to bootstrap them both out of a tough Boston neighborhood. "I've been asked to try drugs and I say no, I don't want to start that," he said.

"If I was ever using drugs and my mom found out, it would be all over for me, because she's strict," Daren said with a hint of pride. "When my mom talks to me about drugs, she really puts a lot of emotion into it. She was choking up when she told me not to use drugs. I think it would really hurt my family."

Graph (on pg. 68): "AT ISSUE: Teenagers and Marijuana Use" tracks percentage of teens who reported using marijuana in the past month, from 1985 through 1996. Graph also compares percentages who say they have been solicited to buy or share marijuana and those who can buy marijuana within a few hours. The latter figures are broken down according to age, from 12 to 17. Graph also shows breakdown of the reasons that 17-year-olds say their peers use drugs. (Sources: National Center on Addiction and Substance Abuse, Columbia University; Substance Abuse and Mental Health Services Administration, Dept. of Health and Human Services)

Teenagers and Marijuana Use

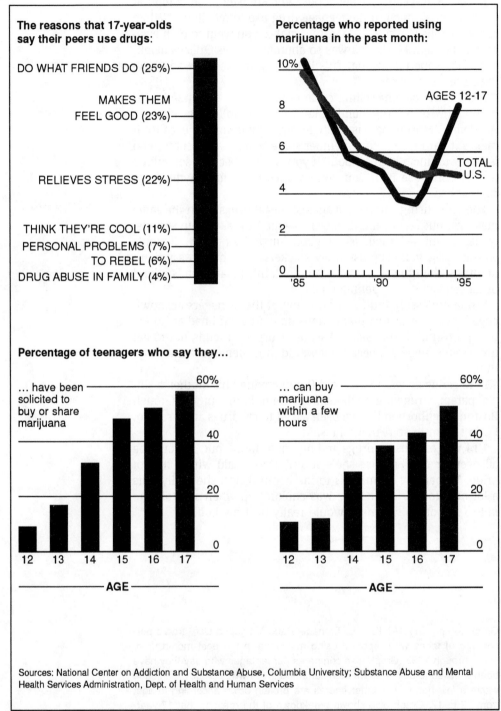

The reasons that 17-year-olds say their peers use drugs:

DO WHAT FRIENDS DO (25%)

MAKES THEM FEEL GOOD (23%)

RELIEVES STRESS (22%)

THINK THEY'RE COOL (11%)
PERSONAL PROBLEMS (7%)
TO REBEL (6%)
DRUG ABUSE IN FAMILY (4%)

Percentage who reported using marijuana in the past month:

AGES 12-17

TOTAL U.S.

'85   '90   '95

Percentage of teenagers who say they...

... have been solicited to buy or share marijuana

12 13 14 15 16 17
AGE

... can buy marijuana within a few hours

12 13 14 15 16 17
AGE

Sources: National Center on Addiction and Substance Abuse, Columbia University; Substance Abuse and Mental Health Services Administration, Dept. of Health and Human Services

The New York Times

Why "Just Say No" Hasn't Worked[4]

Sixteen-year-old Cheryl Petyo is like most teenagers. She hangs out with her friends, deals with boy problems, and sometimes she keeps secrets from her parents. "I used to smoke pot," Cheryl admits. "But I only did it a couple of times. I just wanted to know what it was like."

Cheryl and her friends would get high after school, but she was careful to let the buzz wear off before heading home. "I was afraid of getting in trouble," says Cheryl, who lives in Jackson, New Jersey, with her parents and younger brother.

For a year Cheryl kept her secret well hidden. But a few months ago she gathered her courage and confessed to her mom that she had tried marijuana. "I felt deceived," admits Cheryl's mother, Glory. "It was a very rebellious period for Cheryl," she recalls. "But I never saw any sign of substance abuse."

"Twenty-nine percent of high school sophomores and 35 percent of seniors smoke pot."

After years of declining popularity, pot use among teens is on a serious upswing. According to 1995. Monitoring the Future Study, an annual survey of 50,000 students conducted by the University of Michigan Institute for Social Research, marijuana use has more than doubled among eighth graders (up to 16 percent) over the last few years. Twenty-nine percent of high school sophomores and 35 percent of seniors smoke pot. Teens are also drinking alcohol and smoking cigarettes in alarming numbers. "It's not right that marijuana is often glorified as cool," says Donna E. Shalala, U.S. Secretary of Health and Human Services. "Whether it's from TV, movies or music, young people are receiving too many mixed messages about marijuana."

The Peer Pressure Myth

Teens who get high and those who don't agree that peer pressure has little to do with it. "My saying no now is fine with my friends," says Cheryl. "Nobody tries to force me." Experts concur that although peer pressure may be a factor, it is possible that adults have relied too heavily on it as the *main* reason why kids try drugs. "It's almost a cop-out," says Doug Hall, vice president of the Parents' Resource Institute for Drug Education in Atlanta. "The fact is, the largest teen peer group doesn't use drugs. Kids probably think their friends are using more than they actually are."

Fifteen-year-old Allison* agrees. "I'd always wanted to try it," she says. "So I just went up to someone who dealt." Her friends played no part in it. "I like to do what I like to do," says Allison,

* Name has been changed.

---

[4] Article by Roy DeLaMar, freelance writer, from *Family Circle* 112-117 Mr 12 '96. Copyright © 1996 Gruner + Jahr USA Publishing. Reprinted with permission.

...who lives in Pennsylvania. "Peer pressure is something in text-...

...first time I smoked pot, though, it wasn't the best expe-... friend told me it was laced with PCP," adds Allison. ...to deter her, however. In fact she doesn't consider ...marijuana a health risk at all.

..."'This stuff can't hurt me,'" explains Kelly ...son, M.D., a psychiatrist at North Shore Hospital in Chicago. But it can. The pot kids smoke today is much more potent than the pot of a generation ago. In the 1960's, when mar-ijuana first became popular, its THC (delta-9-tetrahydrocannabi-nol—the key mood-altering substance in pot) level was around 0.2 percent. Today's pot contains THC levels as high as 5 percent, making it 25 times stronger.

So why do teens smoke marijuana? Experts say curiosity is often the first reason. "Once they try it, they realize it can make them feel good," says Jeri Goodman, M.S.W., director of youth drug/alcohol prevention programs with the Single Parent Resource Center in New York. "If a teen's life isn't going the way he wants, he may keep using pot to get that 'good' feeling."

"Some kids turn to drugs to avoid pressure, numb pain or han-dle depression," adds M. Duncan Stanton, Ph.D., a professor of psychiatry and psychology at the University of Rochester Medical Center in New York.

Jason,* a bright 18-year-old from Glencoe, Illinois, who attends a high school that is renowned for academic excellence, claims smoking pot helps him relieve stress. "There's a real high-pres-sure, competitive atmosphere at my school," says Jason. "Pot helps me get 'unlearned.' It's like a little vacation from reality."

Marijuana Health Hazards

The marijuana of the 90's often gives teenagers more than they bargained for. "Pot is not pure anymore; these days it's often laced with other substances or filler," says Dr. Johnson.

In fact, marijuana contains 400 other chemicals that can pose major health hazards, affecting the brain, heart, lungs, and immune and respiratory systems, says Cincinnati pediatrician Richard Heyman, M.D., chairman of the American Academy of Pediatrics' Committee on Substance Abuse. "Puff for puff, there are more pollutants and toxic chemicals in marijuana than in cig-arettes." Since pot users tend to hold smoke in their lungs longer than cigarette smokers, research suggests a greater potential for damage. Marijuana use has also been linked to irregular heart rhythms, disruption of the endocrine and reproductive systems, impaired judgment and motor skills, short-term memory loss and depression.

Misconceptions about Pot

During the 1980's, at the height of the "Just Say No" campaign, when there were increased concerns about marijuana's health risks, experts saw a sharp decline in the drug's use. In recent years, however, there has been a steady and rapid drop in the perception of pot as dangerous. The Michigan study shows that only 61 percent of 12th graders now believe that smoking pot regularly is harmful—down from 79 percent in 1991. "There's a clear trend here," says Secretary Shalala. "As the perception of harm goes down, more young people begin using marijuana." Teens have been scared off harder drugs, adds Dr. Johnson. "To them marijuana is the lesser of the evils," he says. Many adolescents also dismiss the idea that pot is a gateway drug that may lead to more lethal substances. "That's some thing the Government made up to fool people," says Allison. Yet she admits that she has tried acid, PCP and crack since she started smoking pot.

While most marijuana users do not move on to harder drugs, smoking pot does increase a teen's chances of being exposed, according to the National Institute on Drug Abuse in Washington, D.C. The use of harder drugs—LSD, inhalants, stimulants, barbiturates, cocaine, crack—is, in fact, on a gradual rise among teens, according to the Michigan study. "I know one dealer who sells pot, crack and PCP," says Allison. "And he makes you a deal—buy an eighth of pot and try a rock of crack for free."

"...students who drink alcohol are less likely to graduate from high school than their peers who don't."

Binge Drinking on the Rise

Seventeen-year-old Jennifer Dandrow doesn't drink. The Chepachet, Rhode Island, teenager's reason for staying sober is as simple as it is startling. "My grandmother was killed by a 17-year-old driver who decided to get drunk on a Tuesday afternoon," she says. Unfortunately many teens don't follow Jennifer's example. Seventy-one percent of high school sophomores and 80 percent of seniors drink, according to the Michigan study. What's more, 30 percent of the seniors, an increase from last year, admit to binge drinking—downing more than five alcoholic beverages in a row.

With every drink, these teens put their futures—and their lives—at risk. According to the National Bureau of Economic Research in Massachusetts, students who drink alcohol are less likely to graduate from high school than their peers who don't. And about 22 percent of fatally injured 15- to 20-year-old drivers in 1994 were intoxicated.

As with marijuana use, many teens drink as an escape, but the majority simply think it's cool. "Alcohol is around my school more than weed," says Cheryl Petyo. "People still think of pot as a drug, but not alcohol." She admits that she occasionally drinks at parties or with friends. "There's usually beer, because it's easy to get," explains Cheryl.

Teen Tobacco Use Declining

Smoking among teenage girls has decreased. The most recent research from the American Lung Association (ALA) found that the rate of first-time smoking among girls ages 12 to 17 dropped from 24 percent in 1974 to 10 percent in 1991. Yet the ALA study still shows that every day 3,000 kids in the United States try cigarettes, and the highest rate occurs between the ages of 11 and 15. (The good news: If kids aren't smoking by 19, they probably won't start.)

Jennifer says cigarettes are a big problem at her school. "Teachers know about it; they notice the girls coming out of the bathroom smelling like smoke," she says. "But the administration doesn't punish anyone."

Steps need to be taken to induce teens to quit, since studies indicate a direct link between smoking cigarettes and the eventual use of alcohol, marijuana and other drugs. *Preventing Tobacco Use Among Young People: A Report of the Surgeon General* indicates that 12- to 17-year-olds who had smoked cigarettes in the past 30 days were 3 times more likely to have had alcohol, 8 times more likely to have smoked marijuana, and 22 times more likely to have used cocaine in the same time period.

"There is definitely a relationship," Hall notes. "Once adolescents are comfortable with the process of smoking, it's a short step from a regular cigarette to marijuana."

How Parents Can Help

"Parents need to realize that sometimes teenagers are going to experiment in ways adults don't want them to," says Dr. Johnson pragmatically. "But if you come down too hard on a kid, it might actually further his desire to rebel." Instead of pouncing on your teenager or trying to monitor and control his every move, experts advise talking to your child about the long-term health, legal and emotional consequences of substance use.

"It is important to confront your child if you suspect he is using, but you also need to look at why he is getting involved with drugs," advises Goodman. "Ask yourself, 'Is there something going on in my child's life that has caused drugs to become an outlet?' In our programs we teach coping skills. We want to help kids avoid using drugs to feel good or to escape. But we also need to give them other ways to handle their problems."

She suggests that you help your teen build her own extensive support systems. That way, when there is a problem, it isn't just the child and the parents. Encourage your children to establish solid relationships with other adults—relatives, teachers, athletic coaches, counselors, clergy. "Sometimes kids need alternative sources for help, other adults they trust and respect, especially in situations where they might feel uneasy coming to their parents," she says. Try not to feel threatened if your child does go outside the family for support, cautions Goodman.

If you work hard to develop openness and trust with your teenager, however, chances are she'll turn to you. Glory Petyo always hoped her children would feel able to confide in her, but Cheryl says sometimes it's not that easy. "Most kids probably aren't comfortable going to their parents because they're afraid of getting in trouble. I know I was scared when I finally told my mom that I'd smoked pot." But she did. Now Cheryl and Glory are building a stronger, more trusting relationship.

Is Your Daughter Getting High?

Seventy-six percent of teenage girls who responded to our survey, done with *YM* magazine, say they've tried marijuana, beer or other drugs.

- When asked if they have ever smoked pot, nearly one-third of daughters say yes, yet only 12% of mothers believe they have. (Eleven percent of girls have tried other substances as well.)

- Seventy-five percent of girls confess to drinking beer or wine, and 53% have moved on to hard liquor. Here, too, moms are out of the loop. Less than half of them (48%) feel their daughter drank beer and wine, and even fewer (19%) are aware of any use of hard liquor. What's more, well over half of the daughters (64%) say they attend parties where alcohol is readily available and almost a third (31%) have ridden in a car with a drunk driver.

- Six in 10 girls (60%) admit that they have smoked cigarettes, but far fewer moms (29%) think they had.

What Are the Warning Signs?

Telling the difference between the normal noncommunicative phases teenagers go through and the red flags indicating substance abuse is not always easy. "It can be hard for parents to decipher because many 'symptoms' of drug use may just be normal adolescent changes," says social worker Jeri Goodman. How to be sure? If you notice several of the following signals and behaviors, it could indicate that your teen has a drug problem.

- Signs of drug paraphernalia-posters with marijuana leaves, rolling papers, pipes, incense-around teen's room.

- Unexplained changes involving school, grades or extracurricular activities.

- Failure to adhere to curfews or other family rules.

- Defensiveness about the topic of drugs and drug use.

- Sudden disappearance of money, or appearance of large sums of cash.

- Personal possessions (stereo, TV, jewelry, sports equipment, computer, etc.) missing from home.

- Trouble with school authorities or the police.

- A change in teenager's circle of friends.

- Noticeable changes in weight, appetite, sleeping habits or other health-related fluctuations.

- Isolation from family; increased secrecy.

- A change in attitude toward siblings.

- Cigarette smoke or alcohol on the breath.

If you suspect your child may be involved with drugs, alcohol or tobacco, Catherine Seward, executive director of the Hazelden Center for Youth and Families in Plymouth, Minnesota, suggests you speak directly to your teen. "Find the right time to talk, and do it in a caring environment," she says. "Try to avoid being accusatory. Look for an opening for conversation."

Calmness is the key. "You need to process and understand your own feelings before you talk to your teenager," explains Seward.

If you are unable to get your child to open up, seek help from a school counselor, athletic coach, clergy member, family doctor or other adult whom the teen trusts.

One of the reasons it took Cheryl Petyo a year to tell her mother she'd tried marijuana was that she was "afraid of what my mom would think of me." Kids really do want your trust, respect and guidance. Fostering the kind of relationship that encourages teens to share their secrets takes open and honest communication. And talking to your child often about difficult issues like drugs helps her make positive decisions on her own.

For More Information

• **The Hazelden Foundation** offers *A Guide for Teens*, a free booklet designed to help teens assist a friend who has a drug or alcohol problem. Call 1-800-I-D0-CARE, to request a copy.

• **The National Clearinghouse for Alcohol and Drug Information (NCADI)** offers material for both parents and teens. Call 1-800-729-6686 to learn more.

• **Mothers Against Drunk Driving (MADD)** is a national organization with chapters across the country. Check your phone book or write national headquarters: 511 E. John Carpenter Freeway, #700, Irving, TX 75062.

• **The American Lung Association** offers information on helping young people quit smoking and stay smoke free. Call 1-800-LUNG-USA to locate your local chapter.

• **Parents' Resource Institute for Drug Prevention (PRIDE)** teaches 8-hour courses to parents on drug and alcohol use in over 800 communities nationwide. Call 770-565-5257 for more information.

The Fear of Heroin
Is Shooting Up[5]

Jane Howland likes to try an experiment when she talks to kids about drugs. Howland is a middle-school guidance counselor in Greenwich, Conn., one of the wealthiest suburbs in America. The kids are maybe 10 or 11. "I ask them who knows what it means to be a high-risk-taker," she says. Every hand goes up. Then she asks those who consider themselves high-risk-takers to go to one part of the room, low- and middle-riskers to another. Invariably, every boy goes to the high-risk group. "They push each other out of the way to get there first. It's cool." These are just preteens; to them risk means shoplifting, vandalism, marijuana, maybe inhalants. But many of her fifth graders are in the thrall of Kurt Cobain; they think he was "really cool," she says. Howland worries that, by the eighth and ninth grades, the biggest risk-takers might want to fol-low Cobain's path into heroin.

"...U.S. heroin consumption has doubled since the mid-'80s..."

After a decade in low relief, heroin is now scaring the heck out of people like Howland, in cities and suburbs nationwide. "The bad news," says Gen. Barry McCaffrey, the new drug czar "is heroin is back." Schools that used to discuss heroin in the late high-school years now teach it in the eighth grade. The Partnership for a Drug-Free America, best known for its "This is your brain on drugs" campaign of the '80s, now worries that heroin will be *the* drug of the '90s. (James E. Burke, chairman of the partnership, sits on the board of The Washington Post Company, *Newsweek's* corporate parent.) Earlier this summer the organization rolled out the most expensive publicity campaign ever to target heroin. Spurred by images of junkie celebs, and anecdotes about middle-class heroin use, the press has touted a new epidemic since 1989. Now, says Yale medical historian David Musto, "this is the nearest we've come."

How near are we? The answers are not so clear. There are an estimated 500,000 to 750,000 heroin addicts in this country, a fig-ure that has held steady for decades. But for the past five years, heroin use has been, on the rise. Since heroin is illegal, no one knows just how many people use it. But by rough government estimates, U.S. heroin consumption has doubled since the mid-'80s, to about 10 to 15 metric tons per year. Last year 2.3 percent of *eighth graders* said they had tried heroin, nearly double the rate of 1991. (Note: eighth graders always show higher rates than high-schoolers, because heroin users tend to drop out of school.) "Obviously this is not a runaway epidemic among teens," says Lloyd Johnston of the University of Michigan, who monitors ado-

---

[5] Article by John Leland, with Peter Katel in Miami and Mary Hager in Washington, from *Newsweek* 128:55-6 Ag 26 '96. Copyright © 1996 Newsweek, Inc. All rights reserved. Reprinted with permission.

lescent drug use. "But it should give rise to some caution."

Most heroin users today are still old-timers, battered by decades of addiction, arrest and rehab. As crack use has stabilized, many crack smokers have also turned to heroin to ease their cocaine jitters. Dealers, increasingly, are "double breasting," or selling both—bringing crack's widespread availability to heroin. But in many cities, a new class of user is emerging. Drug ethnographers Ansley Hamid and Ric Curtis of John Jay College of Criminal Justice note that as residents of black and Latino communities turned away from heroin in the early '90s, white people started to show up, "infatuated with it," says Curtis. The numbers of new, more affluent users are especially elusive. Because they have resources, they tend not to show up in jail or public treatment centers. "Heroin may be flying *above* the radar," says Mark A.R. Kleiman, a drug-policy analyst at UCLA.

"Heroin booms, by contrast, move slowly."

Why Heroin and Why Now?

If the U. S. auto industry cut the price of its sedans by half and redesigned them to go 180 mph, no one would wonder why sales hit the roof. In the past five years the heroin industry—a $7 billion-plus retail market in the United States—has wrought a similar revolution, offering a more powerful, cheaper and safer product. In the '80s average $10 bags ran about 2 to 8 percent—pure; by 1994 average purity in New York hit 63 percent—pure enough to snort or smoke, without the risk of getting AIDS from dirty needles. This made the drug seem less deadly, more approachable. At the same time, the price has fallen to a historic low. The street price of a milligram in New York fell from $1.81 in 1988 to just 37 cents in 1994. Globally, heroin production has doubled in the past decade, flooding the United States from Burma, Afghanistan, Laos, Pakistan, Colombia and Mexico—and ensuring a competitive market with low prices and high purity. As a recent White House report conceded, "We have yet to substantially influence either the availability or the purity of cocaine and heroin within the United States."

Heroin's rise is also historically predictable. Since 1885 cocaine and opiate waves have succeeded one another, each relieving the chronic maladies of the last. Cocaine epidemics tend to be fast and short, accelerated by binge use. "You can't take cocaine for long periods of time," says Herbert Kleber of the Center on Addiction and Substance Abuse at Columbia University. "It burns you out. People need a sedative to mellow out: sometimes alcohol, sometimes heroin." Heroin booms, by contrast, move slowly. Users take an average of three to 10 years to progress from regular use to treatment or arrest. The heroin-horror stories circulating now suggest a rise in use four or five years ago, and may signal the start of a decline. As Kleber notes, "All drug cycles carry the seed of their own destruction."

New users typically begin by snorting. But many progress to the more efficient method of injecting. According to General

McCaffrey, about 50 percent of users seeking treatment last year used needles; this year, the figure has grown to 75 percent. This is doubly dangerous. Injection-drug users now have the highest rates of new HIV infection, nearly twice that of gay men. And wild fluctuations in street purity raise the risk of overdose. Between 3,000 and 4,000 users die of heroin overdoses annually—many using the heroin in lethal combination with alcohol or other drugs. The expanding drug market and the criminal justice system unwittingly conspire to push this figure higher. As police arrest drug consumers by the thousands, as part of the war on drugs, users are likely to come out of jail with reduced tolerance and a lower threshold for overdose. Also, says John Jay College's Curtis, some new dealers don't have experience with the substance. He mentions one experienced Brooklyn dealer known as Half, for the way he cuts the dope. "The new guys turn to him to show them how it's done." Others, though, "use too much adulterant, or too little," giving people unpredictably strong doses. "I attribute deaths to that instability."

It is too soon to say how high the current heroin wave will rise, or how long it will last. Musto of Yale contends that it "won't be as alarming as the last [in the '70s], because we're much better informed about drugs now. The number of people the 'chic' aspect applies to is very small." But many professionals believe we can't wait around to find out. Already there are too few treatment slots for the addicts on the streets, a woeful shortage of treatment beds in prisons-and no money for more. Wayne Wiebel, an epidemiologist at the University of Illinois at Chicago, offers a chilling scenario. We are unprepared, he says, especially to help the young users just getting hooked. "There are only two pots of money," says Wiebel. "One is for prevention, mostly through schools; and the other is treatment for casualties that have already been fully impacted by the problem. There's virtually nothing in the middle for early intervention." Wiebel has been studying drug trends for more than 15 years. From where he stands, the new wave of heroin use, and our reaction to it, looks horrifyingly familiar. It's going to "unfold like the crack epidemic," he says, "and we're not going to do a hell of a lot about it."

Drug Usage

Eighth graders who have used drugs in their lifetime (in percent)

	1991	1995	Percent Change
Crack	1.3	2.7	+ 108
Heroin	1.2	2.3	+ 92
Marijuana	10.2	19.9	+ 95
Cocaine	2.3	4.2	+ 83
Hallucinogens	3.2	5.2	+ 63
Stimulants	10.5	13.1	+ 25
Tranquilizers	3.8	4.5	+ 18
Cigarettes	44.0	46.4	+ 5
Been drunk	26.7	25.3	-5

Opiate Overdoses and Detox

Emergency room heroin/morphine cases (in thousands)

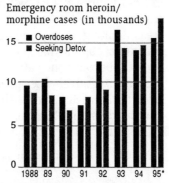

■ Overdoses
■ Seeking Detox

1988 89 90 91 92 93 94 95*

*Estimate based on Jan.–June figures. Sources: University of Michigan, Monitoring the Future Study; SAMHSA, Drug Abuse Warning Network

The Damage Done[6]

A Jersey teen falls victim as cheap, potent heroin moves to the suburbs

At a glance, 17-year-old Elizabeth Danser seemed no more troubled, no more in the grips of teenage angst than any of the other kids in her affluent hometown of Princeton Junction, N.J. She wrote dark poetry, had a taste for grunge fashion, and, being a pretty girl, was seldom without a boyfriend. A senior at West Windsor-Plainsboro High School, Elizabeth also liked to party. In fact, that's exactly what she did on Friday night, April 26, at the home of Cesar Casal, a boy she knew from school. It was about 1 a.m. when she returned to the four-bedroom colonial she shared with her parents—Bill, a former corporate headhunter turned limousine driver, and Linda, an office manager—and Kate, her 15-year-old sister. Climbing the stairs to her bedroom, Elizabeth shed her jewelry, put on her pajamas and set the alarm for 8 a.m.

"Elizabeth had died from an accidental overdose of heroin."

The clock buzzed on cue—and kept buzzing until Linda Danser came in to shut it off and found her daughter lying motionless, facedown in the pillow.

"When I touched her, she was cold, stiff," recalls Linda. "And I went into denial right away. I said, 'Oh, the problem is, she can't breathe. I'll turn her head.' Then I knew, and I screamed at Bill, 'I think she's dead! Call 911.'"

Her parents' sadness became more crushing four weeks later with the release of the toxicologist's report: Elizabeth had died from an accidental overdose of heroin.

Around Princeton Junction, Elizabeth Danser's death was viewed as an aberration. Heroin was supposed to be a vice of the inner cities, not the recreational drug of choice for middle-class schoolkids. But in fact heroin use has exploded. In 1994, according to the federal Substance Abuse and Mental Health Services Administration, 27,300 people were admitted to hospital emergency rooms after ingesting heroin—up from 1,250 in 1988. Moreover, smack has infiltrated suburbia. Cheap, powerful heroin from Latin America, which can be snorted rather than injected, has changed the user profile in the past few years. In certain areas, among the young and upwardly mobile, smack has become a popular party drug. "Purity is up, the price is down, and it's become the latest sexy, chic thing," says Dr. Herbert Kleber, executive vice president of the National Center on Addiction and Substance Abuse at Columbia University. "People don't understand this drug. They think if you don't use needles,

[6] Article by Richard Jerome and Ron Arias, from *People Weekly* 46:131-4+ N 4 '96. Copyright © 1996 Time Inc. All rights reserved. Reprinted with permission.

you don't get addicted, you won't die. Wrong."

"Hey, the stuff is here," adds Greg Eldridge, the West Windsor Township police captain. "And the frustrating part is, a lot of parents would rather talk to their lawyers to get their kids off than get help for them."

That was not the case with Elizabeth Danser. She had been receiving treatment for clinical depression and marijuana and cocaine use. "Intellectually, we know we did everything we could do," says Linda. "But emotionally I feel we should have seen what was coming." Perhaps misleadingly, Elizabeth had appeared to be on the upswing in her final weeks. "I truly felt she was all right, that she was clean," says Korean-born Kate, whom the Dansers adopted in 1985. Adds her father: "We'd all felt we had turned a corner. Elizabeth was becoming this new person."

In early childhood the Dansers' older daughter hadn't seemed marked for a short, anguished life. "She was an easy, placid kid from the start—as an infant, all dark hair and blue eyes," Linda says. Through eighth grade she was a straight-A student and an enthusiastic field hockey player. But in 1992 Elizabeth entered the highly competitive West Windsor-Plainsboro High School and began to lose her way. She started failing tests and cutting classes and seemed "distracted," according to a ninth-grade evaluation. "She got into that high school and hated it," recalls Linda. "She didn't like the people. They were snotty."

Steadily, Elizabeth sank into a serious depression. "At first we didn't realize what was happening," says Linda. Midway through Elizabeth's freshman year, her parents finally took her to a therapist, then to a psychiatrist, who treated her with antidepressants. But sometimes, says her father, she would "self-medicate" with marijuana. Over the next several years, Elizabeth experimented with cocaine as well. "She couldn't stand the school and preppy pretensions, and she used drugs to escape," recalls Liz Keenan, a close friend who is not a drug user. Elizabeth may also have been embarrassed when, in 1992, her father had to find a new job because the market for corporate headhunters had collapsed. "We both had a hard time getting over his driving a limo," Kate admits. "I mean, like, he was driving the fathers of my friends."

In the spring of 1993, the Dansers checked Elizabeth into the Carrier Foundation in Belle Meade, N.J., for one month of treatment for depression. Two years later she spent two weeks at the White Deer Run rehab clinic in Allenwood, Pa., to help wean her off marijuana. After that she briefly attended sessions of Narcotics Anonymous. But she also kept up an active social life, dating a succession of boyfriends, partying or hanging out at a local Denny's. Although she was often attired in obligatory grunge, Elizabeth made more radical fashion statements— notably by way of a tattoo of a small, blue sun above her navel and another one of Chinese lettering on her right upper arm. She began wearing pierced rings in her eyebrow and tongue. (She would carefully remove the ring in her tongue before going home.)

"We found out about the tongue and the tattoos and some other stuff after she died," says Linda. "We really felt kind of angry. What was hurtful was the secret side to her." But there were admirable qualities as well. "She was very kind to this retarded boy who worked at a local supermarket—he had a crush on her," says Bill. "She wouldn't let others pick on him. She didn't tolerate bigotry, gay-bashing, racism. I was proud of that."

By the middle of her senior year, however, Elizabeth, to all outward appearances, seemed finished with drugs. "I didn't see any of the usual signs," says Linda, "like being sleepy, eyes and nose running. She actually looked healthier than she had in years." Sharon Kulick, an administrative assistant at Princeton University, where Elizabeth clerked as part of her high school's work-study program, agrees: "Her appearance sharpened up— she was happy, spunky. She was flourishing." Accepted into two-year Mercer County College, Elizabeth had planned to study photojournalism. Just a week before she died, she accompanied her senior class to Disney World—and returned elated to have enjoyed the company of so many preppies—the very kids she had so long resented. Still, she never made a clean break from her friends who were trouble. "They were the druggies," says Liz Keenan. "And when she told me, I got really upset. So she stopped telling me."

On the night she died, Elizabeth took an overdose of heroin that she had purchased sometime earlier with friends. (The police, who may prosecute the person or persons who provided the heroin, refuse to comment on the case.) Why would Elizabeth, whose life suddenly seemed to be in order, return to drugs with such a vengeance? "I think it was a boy," says her mother. "She was trying to impress him."

On Monday morning, Elizabeth's death was announced over the high school PA system. "I saw teachers crying," her sister Kate says. "The bathrooms were full of smoke—people who didn't even smoke were smoking to relieve the stress." Says Nancy Himsel, a school counselor who thought Elizabeth had turned a corner: "One night of poor choices took away her hopes, her dreams, her future."

A shrine of flowers was laid on Elizabeth's school parking space—No. 37—and on April 30, 500 people, including most of the senior class, filled Prince of Peace Lutheran Church for her funeral service. She was buried in Brainerd Cemetery in Cranbury, N.J., next to her grandfather, with Kangy the Kangaroo, her favorite stuffed animal, nestled in the casket. Scores of friends and relatives paid their respects at the Danser home, but not all their comments were comforting.

"We just got back from the funeral, and people were already

saying there was no drug problem around here," says an angry Bill Danser. "Goddammit! My daughter just died! The hell there isn't a problem! Unless somebody does something, Elizabeth won't be the last."

III. The Culture of Substance Abuse

Editor's Introduction

As noted in Section I, the creation of an altered state of mind and the abuse of illegal substances is not a simple or isolated act. It, in fact, is the basis of a culture with a deep and intriguing history about which a variety of films, novels and music have been made. Movies with a clear basis in substance abuse include *Less Than Zero*, *Bright Lights Big City*, *Drugstore Cowboy* and the immensely popular *Trainspotting*. In addition, countless rock and roll songs from Lou Reed's "Heroin" to Eric Clapton's "Cocaine" all discuss, and sometime extoll, substance abuse. Regardless of the stance towards drugs these works may take, their presence indicates that substance abuse is the basis for more than the simple act of consumption.

Yet despite the allure and sometime glamour given off by the so-called drug culture, there is a lethally dark side, which, more often than not, leaves a wake of wasted lives and ruined dreams. Articles in Section III explore both the complex culture which has arisen around the practice of substance abuse as well as the horrible price that is often paid by those who become too much a part of it.

In the first article of this section, Karen Schoemer, writing in *Newsweek*, discusses the dangerous allure of heroin that has succeeded in damaging or ending the lives of so many in the music spotlight. From Charlie Parker and Billie Holiday to Keith Richards and Kurt Cobain, heroin has been a consistent part of the music industry. While such addictions have been romanticised and glorified by countless fans and hangers-on, the truth of the matter is, "it's gloom and doom."

In the next article, "Our Hero, Heroin," Rich Lowry notes that the current romance with heroin, as pointed out in Schoemer's exposé, is probably owed to the fact that "heroin is in our cultural bloodstream," in our movies and in our music. The question remains: Why is heroin so popular today? Lowry theorizes that much of our current fascination with heroin is owed to the pain of divorce that dominated the lives of so many who grew up in the 1980s. Heroin has the power of turning the "isolation and inadequacy," so much a part of a child who has witnessed divorce, into glamorous and "hip" virtues.

Heroin is not the only drug from which a definable culture emanates. The next article, by Toby Manning, discusses a drug known as Ecstacy around which an ideology and lifestyle have sprung. Manning calls the culture that surrounds Ecstasy the "E-Culture" and defines it as being primarily about "escape, the moment, self: style without content." One of the hallmarks of this culture, according to Manning, is the creation of a type of music which, while unavailable commercially, dominates the clubs and "raves" most commonly frequented by those who regularly take Ecstasy.

Gordon Marino, writing for *The Christian Century*, considers whether the millions of Americans who take legally prescribed uppers and downers are also part of the U.S. drug problem. The more understandable a behavior becomes the more difficult it is to condemn, but the American appetite for drugs, and the quickness and persistence with which they resort to pharmaceutical solutions suggests that such people must be considered part of a drug culture.

Interestingly, a culture of substance abuse is not only manifest in the habits of young people, musicians, and particular movies. The last article of this section, "Bitter Pill" by Peter King for *Sport Illustrated*, discusses Brett Favre's battle with pain-killers. King points out that Favre, "Like many pro football players...would...take a numbing injection or pain-killing pill to get through a game." The fact is, taking painkillers such as Vicodin are simply an often overlooked part of the culture of professional athletics. At some point, however, the practice could no longer be ignored as Favre had a life-threatening seizure thought to be brought on by his habitual consumption of those very same painkillers.

Rockers, Models and the New Allure of Heroin[1]

I never tried heroin, but I used to think I wanted to. White and middle class, just out of college in 1987, I read Jim Carroll's *"The Basketball Diaries,"* a cornerstone of modern heroin mythology: he made it seem like the ultimate rite of passage, a drug that made you funnier, wiser, cooler and full of hilarious stories about running wild on New York's Lower East Side. I listened obsessively to the Rolling Stones' "Exile on Main St." and read accompanying literature like Stanley Booth's "The *True* Adventures of the Rolling Stones" that told how strung out Keith Richards was during this peak of genius. I even knew someone, a musician, who did heroin. For a long time he didn't do it around me. I nagged him to let me try it, and he laughed. "You're not starting." he said.

When he finally did use it around me, my romantic image of heroin collapsed. He nodded out on my couch midway through a sentence; he threw up in my bathroom; he went face down on a restaurant table in front of my friends. From then on, I hated heroin. When at last he offered it to me, holding a knife point piled with ivory powder under my nose, I backed away. "I thought you wanted to try it," he said. "Not anymore," I said. Now I'm old enough to know better. I have a husband and a house and a nice life. When I hear that a musician I admire uses it, I'm concerned but no longer curious. When I hear of a tragic rock overdose, like Jonathan Melvoin of Smashing Pumpkins, I feel sad and shake my head, just like anybody would. I can enjoy a heroin movie like "Trainspotting," and all the while I'm secretly thinking: Whew! Glad it's not me!

Yet no matter how smart we think we are heroin's allure persists. In the past two or three years, its presence in pop culture has risen dramatically. Maybe it's Kurt Cobain's fault. His was the most high-profile drug-related rock-star death since the '70s, and he was battling heroin when he committed suicide in April 1994. Maybe it's his wife Courtney Love's fault: her torn dresses, matted hair and bruisey demeanor put a fashionable spin on junkie chic. Maybe it's the rock world's fault. In the past few months, Smashing Pumpkins drummer Jimmy Chamberlin, Stone Temple Pilots singer Scott Weiland and Depeche Mode frontman David Gahan have all been busted for heroin and/or cocaine. (All three pleaded not guilty; Weiland and Gahan entered rehab.) Aerosmith could be the latest drug-troubled band: they just fired longtime manager Tim Collins, an anti-drug

[1] Article by Karen Schoemer with Gregory Beals in New York, Allison Samuels in Los Angeles, CA, Mark Miller in Seattle, WA, and Steve Rhodes in Chicago, IL from *Newsweek* 128:50-4 Ag 26 '96. Copyright © 1996 Newsweek, Inc. All rights reserved. Reprinted with permission.

crusader credited with helping singer Steven Tyler and guitarist Joe Perry get off heroin in the mid-'80s. Sources say Tyler may have relapsed this year. *Newsweek* has obtained a copy of a pained letter the band wrote to Tyler in June, citing his childishness, negativity and denial. The band members threatened to break up Aerosmith, telling Tyler to "get the help that you need" and "reach out" for counseling. The band is said to have spent weeks with Tyler at Steps, a treatment center in California. Tyler denies all this. "I'm still sober and have remained sober for the last nine years, going on 10," he says. "Sometimes the creative zone and *joie de vivre* I get into throws people. If that's what they see in me, so be it, but I'm as sober as I'll ever be." Collins hopes Tyler is clean. "Steven's an icon of recovery," he says. "If he dies of an overdose, the people around him are going to be in big f—ing trouble."

The resurgence is Hollywood's fault, too. Quentin Tarantino revived John Travolta's career when he cast him as a dope fiend in "Pulp Fiction." (And we got to watch Uma Thurman's lips turn overdose blue.) "Trainspotting," a techno-color trip through Scotland's junkie underbelly, is the most hyped film import of the summer. Actor Robert Downey Jr., so effective on screen as a druggie in 1987's "Less Than Zero," got busted in June for coke and heroin possession, arrested in July when he wandered into the wrong house and now resides in a lock-down detox center. (He's pleaded not guilty to the June charges.) CAA, a top agency, has dropped three clients because of alleged drug use, including Downey.

Meanwhile, there have been growing complaints about "heroin chic" in fashion. Designer Jil Sander drew flak when her catalog showed a druggy-looking woman with one sleeve pushed up. Waif extraordinaire Kate Moss has made a career out of looking wasted. Model Zoe Fleischauer, 21, developed a heroin habit almost immediately when she moved to New York three years ago, and she says she wasn't alone: "There are a lot of junkies in the industry. It's very hush-hush." Now clean, she blames the fashion world for glamorizing the problem. "They wanted models that looked like junkies," she says. "The more skinny and f—ed up you look, the more everybody thinks you're fabulous."

What all this cultural noise means is that heroin is back up from the underground. Back in the '80s, higher prices, lower purity and the AIDS-crisis fear of needles kept it out of the mainstream. Part of the resurgence is simple economics: heroin is now cheaper and purer, and the volume being imported into the country has doubled to around 10 to 15 metric tons since the mid-'80s. Abundant supplies of high-grade blends attract everyone from hipster rock stars to Wall Street executives to inner-city addicts. A new government report scheduled for release this week will show that overall drug use among those 12 to 17 years old has risen almost 80 percent since 1992…. Baby-boomer parents may be shocked by the new casual attitude toward heroin, which even in the drug days of the '60s carried a stigma that seemed to set it apart from pot, acid and the Summer of Love.

But alternative rock has its roots in the punk movement, not the hippie era. When Nirvana's 1991 album "Nevermind" hit No. 1, a range of attitudes and behaviors from the fringe of pop culture suddenly hit the mass market: dressing rebelliously, flouting conventions, screaming real loud, taking drugs if you want to. The most revered bands carry out the message in their lives as well as their songs. Since kids emulate rock stars, they're liable to emulate their drug use. The number of top alternative bands that have been linked to heroin through a member's overdose, arrest, admitted use or recovery is staggering: Nirvana, Hole, Smashing Pumpkins, Everclear, Blind Melon, Skinny Puppy, 7 Year Bitch, Red Hot Chili Peppers, Stone Temple Pilots, the Breeders, Alice in Chains, Sublime, Sex Pistols, Porno for Pyros, Depeche Mode. Together these bands have sold more than 60 million albums—that's a heck of a lot of white, middle-class kids in the heartland. Bob Dole is making drugs a campaign issue. How long is it going to take him to turn on MTV?

"The idea is for executives, managers and agents to stop looking away when an artist clearly has a drug problem."

The music business, it seems, is already anticipating an attack. Ten years ago cocaine was so widespread that one former label executive reports getting hired after doing a line in the president's office. Today attitudes have changed. Ask executives if there's a heroin problem in the music business, and more than one will answer, "Absolutely." "It's worse than it's ever been," says one record-company vice president. Art Alexakis, singer for Everclear, has been drug-free for 12 years, but he still has to deal with other bands' problems. "I've walked into my dressing room and had people sitting on my amp, shooting dope," he says. "That was two years ago, when we were still at the opening stage. They wouldn't shoot up in their own dressing room, being the headliner. They'd come over to our place."

Mike Greene, the head of the National Academy of Recording Arts & Sciences, which puts together the Grammy Awards, is leading the charge by pushing an outreach program called MusiCares. Last December and again in June, he called together 400 members of the industry for closed-door symposiums to discuss the issue. The idea is for executives, managers and agents to stop looking away when an artist clearly has a drug problem. "It's a moral question," says the label vice president, "and we don't like to talk about morality and rock and roll. But the f—ing right wing does, and if we don't clean our own house, then we become vulnerable to them."

This moral question has deeply shaken the music business. Judging from some of the responses to Greene's initiatives, the industry is far from a consensus on how the problem should be handled. Many musicians are suspicious of the executives' motives. "They don't want their artists taking dope because they won't be able to milk more platinum out of them next season,"

says singer Henry Rollins. Even among executives, bitter factions
are emerging. Conspicuously absent from Greene's symposiums
were key members of Kurt Cobain's management team, John
Silva and Danny Goldberg of Gold Mountain. (Goldberg is now
the president of Mercury.) In the wake of Cobain's suicide, former Aerosmith manager Collins, who is closely allied with
MusiCares, wrote a save-our artists editorial in Billboard magazine that implicitly accused Cobain's people of allowing him to
die. Neither Silva nor Goldberg will discuss the situation publicly. But Ron Stone, another manager at Gold Mountain,
responds angrily. "I find it the height of hypocrisy that people
run around grabbing headlines about how they're going to do all
these things," he says. "The reality is, none of the record companies are going to let go of a platinum artist because they're on
drugs. And if they would take a position saying 'We don't want
to do business with you,' then there's 20 other record companies
that would do it in a second."

At the heart of this conflict is anguish and guilt over Cobain.
Two and a half years later, emotions remain raw over his loss.
Cobain was like the star pupil at a high school full of promising
young talent. He was a brilliant musician and a nice person. No
matter how many Pearl Jams, Stone Temple Pilots and Bushes
reach the top 10, he can't be replaced, and his decision to commit suicide has left a terrible pall over the industry. "We constantly tried to get him help," says Stone. "The truth is, when he
sobered up, when he made a serious attempt to get his life in
order, he took a real good look at his life and he killed himself."

Despite all this, heroin's rep soars. People mistakenly think
that it's not addictive if they snort it or smoke it. "In L.A., people are doing it on a real casual basis," says Rollins. "Like, 'Oh,
me and my girlfriend did heroin this weekend.' Like it's a trip.
Like it's a vacation. And I'm looking at them, going, 'Are you out
of your f—ing mind?'"

The fear is that the drug is becoming just another trend. "You
got a million needles tattooing kids," says singer Exene
Cervenka. "You got a million needles piercing their ears, piercing
their noses, piercing their lips. You got a million needles shooting drugs into their veins. And to them it's all the same thing. I
don't think kids can differentiate between behaviors." The
streets of Seattle are cluttered with kids who've moved there to
do heroin, just because Cobain did—and this at a time when
people in the Seattle music scene claim drug use among musicians is tapering off. Singer-songwriter Paul K, who's been clean
for six years, finds the "I have to do it because Keith
Richards/Lou Reed/Kurt Cobain did it" excuse pretty lame. "It's
like buying Paul Newman's salad dressing," he says. "Have you
tasted it? I mean, it's not very good." But even he admits the
power of a junkie idol. When did he start using? "Probably the
day I put down 'The Basketball Diaries'."

Unfortunately, cool images in books, movies and magazines

don't jibe with the reality of addiction. While Sid Vicious was being mythologized as junk's favorite casualty in the '80s, Sex Pistols guitarist Steve Jones was strung out on the streets of L.A. "I lost everything, financially and emotionally," he says. "Lost *everything*. I was literally walking up and down Hollywood Boulevard with one pair of jeans and one pair of tennis shoes, looking to steal a handbag off some old lady to get another fix." With the help of a 12-step program, Jones cleaned up 12 years ago. And even when the images are negative—"Trainspotting" conscientiously focuses on the drug's unglamorous side—the degradation can be part of the appeal. "It has to do with being young and self-destructive," says Tim Foljahn of Two Dollar Guitar, who quit using three years ago. "It's got the reputation as the meanest, dirtiest drug—which I would not necessarily agree with, because I've seen them all destroy people. But it's got that death tag on it. It's as bad as you want to get."

"Heroin ruined my dreams..."

And once someone is addicted, it doesn't matter who he is. "An addict is an addict," says Dave Navarro, guitarist for Red Hot Chili Peppers. Clean for four and a half years, Navarro used heroin while in Jane's Addiction, an influential first-wave alternative band. But he started long before that. "When my mother died when I was 15, I discovered I didn't feel it as badly when I was loaded." People speculate that the pressures of success and touring contributed to the deaths of Cobain and Shannon Hoon of Blind Melon, but Navarro says it works the other way around. "In Jane's Addiction I felt very unsure, very uncomfortable," he says. "By the time we were successful I was so down in the depths of despair that I didn't experience any of it. Perhaps the level of success we did reach enabled me to get through the destructive side of my use quicker, because I was able to spend more money and go down faster. Whereas who knows how many years it would have gone on had my habit been $50 a day?"

Recovery has allowed Navarro to see his addiction in clear terms. "Heroin ruined my dreams," he says. "It made my work life an unhappy experience. Basically turned the one thing that I had worked my whole life for into the thing I wanted to get away from most." He tried to detox several times before entering a long-term rehab program after Jane's Addiction broke up in 1991. "Being in the Chili Peppers, I'm able to experience what I'm doing," he says. "I'm able to be present for it. And happy with what I'm doing for the most part. I would never trade that feeling for anything in the world. It's a long road, but it's well worth it. At least it was for me."

Some L.A. musicians in need of recovery turn to Gloria Scott. A 67-year-old former beatnik, biker chick, hippie chick and junkie with fluffy blondish hair, thick round glasses and dentures that click when she chews gum, Scott is the kind of person a cool, tough, rebellious rocker could connect with, because she's cool, tough and rebellious herself. Her war stories could make any self-obsessed 27 year-old look like a wimp. In the '60s she lived across the canal from Jim Morrison in Venice Beach, and Morrison used to put his head on her pregnant belly and listen to her son, Solo, moving around. In the '70s she and jazz drummer Buddy Arnold, now a bigwig at Musician Assistance Program, ran a scam trading phony prescriptions for pharmaceutical heroin. She got clean 17 years ago, and works as a counselor at Socorro, a treatment center in East L.A. She can't name the young musicians who've come to her, due to the tenets of the 12-step program, but she understands their plight. "I don't think it makes any difference if it's Keith Richards or Kurt," she says. "They're all idols. It sounds romantic, it's gloom and doom, it's like a secret organization. Then it gets ugly. You've got a band you love, a career you love, but *this comes first.*"

Scott helps take some of the scariness away from getting well. She doesn't preach the 12-step program; in fact, she doesn't mind pointing out some of its flaws. "I hated being clean," she says. "Hated those goddam meetings," she says. "We'd go to Beverly Hills, and these women all had sport coats and long f—ing nails. I said, 'Give me a break! I wouldn't use with people like this. Why would I get clean with them?'" She had an additional problem with recovery: she doesn't believe in God. When she was told to focus on a higher power, she tried to think of something that was bigger and stronger than she. First she decided on Neil Young, who sang the anti-junkie anthem "The Needle and the Damage Done."

Later, she chose the ocean. Sometimes Scott walks along the Venice boardwalk, past apartments and alleys where she used to shoot up and deal drugs, and the memories don't bother her. The water nearby takes her out of herself. She doesn't swim in the ocean. She hasn't since she got sober. She's learned a lesson that many young musicians are still struggling with. When something's more powerful than you, it's best to stand back and leave it alone.

> *"It sounds romantic, it's gloom and doom, it's like a secret organization. Then it gets ugly."*

Our Hero, Heroin[2]

Kurt Cobain, the late lead singer of the breakthrough grunge band Nirvana, used to steal drugs from pharmacies when, at age twenty, he worked as a (listless and unreliable) janitor in Olympia, Washington. He became something of a connoisseur. Cocaine and speed, he later explained, weren't his favorites: "I felt too confident and too sure of myself. Just too sociable." Not his style. Cobain's drug of choice, found in his bloodstream after he blew his head off with a shotgun in 1994, became heroin.

The supposedly impending heroin epidemic has been the subject of countless news stories in the last four years. By all accounts already under way among the tragically hip, the epidemic certainly makes great copy. *Newsweek* reports: "The 31-year-old screenwriter looks like she's en route to a dinner party in her $300 dress." (Actually, that's heroin in her compact). One *New York Times* article begins: "Even with her striking beauty, hardly anyone seemed to notice the young model as she glided through the swarm of heroin dealers and glassy-eyed addicts on a patch of steamy pavement in East Harlem."

"What's clear is that heroin is in our cultural bloodstream."

The numbers—heroin-related emergency-room visits are up more than 150 per cent since 1990—do seem alarming, although it's always difficult to gauge where hype ends and reality begins when drug-starved models are involved. What's clear is that heroin is in our cultural bloodstream. The hit British novel and now film *Trainspotting* follows a group of Edinburgh smack addicts, one of a series of recent movies (including *Pulp Fiction* and *Basquiat*) to feature the drug. Yet another grunge rocker died of an overdose this July. And the bitter-almond smell of heroin is reportedly inescapable at hot Hollywood parties.

Drugs always reflect the era in which they achieve their vogue. In the late 1960s and early 1970s LSD was the emblematic drug. Its alleged power to raise one's consciousness appealed to the spiritual pretensions of the hippies and New Left. It was the drug of tuning in and dropping out, of passive revolt and keen self-awareness. The cocaine of the 1980s, in contrast, was a social stimulant, promoting aggressiveness and self-confidence. The protagonist of Jay McInerney's *Bright Lights, Big City* snorts cocaine whenever his energy flags at a downtown nightclub, refueling to continue the endless pursuit of good times.

The culture of heroin is different. When Mark Renton, the main addict in *Trainspotting*, and his mates take the drug, they fall back on the floor to enjoy their hit staring at the ceiling. It is a drug of isolation and oblivion (hence its appeal to the aggressively shy Cobain)—and even pain. First-time users typically

---

[2] Article by Rich Lowry, *National Review*'s national political reporter, from *National Review* 48:75-6 O 28 '96. Copyright © 1996 National Review, Inc. Reprinted with permission.

throw up. Heroin's needlework parallels the self-mutilating body-piercing now all the rage. And addicts experience excruciating pain, described in terms of muscles being ripped from bones, etc., if they don't feed their habit. The pointlessness of heroin, its invitation to oblivious solitude, and its danger make it the drug of grunge "authenticity," tapping into a powerful current in today's popular culture.

Grunge, as articulated in 1990s "alternative" music (the mix of punk and heavy metal that is now the rock mainstream), is about feeling good about feeling bad. The lyrics celebrate failure and inadequacy. Cobain, the urgrunge rocker, sang songs with lines like "I think I'm dumb," repeated in a numb, flat voice. Sarah Ferguson of the *Village Voice* argues: "The empowered feeling you [read: teenage white kid] get from listening to these songs lies in unearthing [an] essential nugget of shame." The songs let the listener sample and even enjoy his own perceived worthlessness, like pressing your tongue against a sore tooth.

Grunge shares some qualities with the old 1960s counter-culture. It is hostile to the bourgeois and consumer culture. It is at the same time, like 1960s activism, an outgrowth of wealth and leisure (it's not easy to be a tortured victim of ennui working on a factory floor). But there are important differences. Grunge is for the most part shorn of ideals and the impulse for political action. Whereas 1960s student rebels were mostly the product of middle-class two-parent families, the defining family for grunge kids is the broken home, a consistent theme in their music.

When Kurt Cobain was eight his mother divorced his dad; she then lived with an abusive and unbalanced boyfriend, and then married a drinker and womanizer. "I'm a product of a spoiled America," Cobain once said. "Think how much worse my family life could be if I grew up in a depression or something. There are so many worse things than a divorce. I've just been brooding and bellyaching about something I couldn't have, which is a family, a solid family unit, for too long." The complaints about divorce do slip into whining, a victimology for white kids. And if the pain of divorce is real, the grunge solution is to revel in it, creating an upside-down world where isolation and inadequacy are virtues, and where a drug like heroin acquires a romantic cachet.

Trainspotting's Mark Renton, a character who suffers from vague, uncharted psychic wounds and who, like Cobain, despises the middle class, explains (in Scottish dialect) the appeal of heroin: "Life's boring and futile... We fill up oor lives wi s—, things like careers and relationships tae delude oorsels that it isnae aw toally pointless. Smack's a honest drug, because it strips away these delusions. Wi smack, whin ye feel good, ye feel immortal. Whin ye feel bad, it intensfies the s— that's alredy thair. It's the only real honest drug. It doesnae alter yir consciousness. It just gies ye a hit and a sense ae well-being. Eftir that, ye see the misery ae the world as it is, and ye canae anaesthetise yirself against it."

Heroin saves Renton and his pals from worrying about the daily routine—"bills, food, bailiffs, these Jambo Nazi scum beat-in us, aw the things that ye couldnae gie a f— aboot whin yuv goat a real junk habit." But it's the nature of pop culture that such an antibourgeois protest immediately gets caught up in the everyday consumerism it reviles. Tortured grunge bands become instant commercials on MTV—and get very rich. On the TV show *The Simpsons*, a member of the band Smashing Pumpkins tells the suburban dad Homer Simpson that he envies his simple domesticity—because all the band has is hordes of adoring fans, millions of dollars, and its youth. Even Cobain's suicide, sup-posedly motivated in part by disgust with success, has become a sort of posthumous stage stunt and marketing gimmick.

Authenticity, when it is equated with a stance against the world—and especially once it becomes hip—invites posing and self-deception. A friend of Renton's tells him: "You just want tae f— up on drugs so that everyone'll think how deep and f— com-plex you are. It's pathetic, and f— boring." Renton allows as how this explanation is as good as any. It certainly applies to the denizens of those Hollywood parties, not otherwise noted for their lives of deep feeling and despair. "Their selfdoubts tell them they're getting rich because of their cheekbones," a screen-writer told the *New York Times*. "You become consumed with doubts about your authenticity and look for authenticity in areas that are, unfortunately, cliches, such as the heroin-using artist."

This, then, becomes heroin's ultimate appeal: it's the *fashion-able* way to be authentic, the latest ticket to being alienated and with-it at the same time. Irvine Welsh, the author of *Trainspotting*, denies nasty rumors that he himself was never a problem user. In *Pulp Fiction* John Travolta, a self-assured char-acter miles away from angst-ridden twenty-year-olds, uses hero-in. And so did that 21-year-old model on the August cover of *Newsweek*, beckoning to us with her fine and innocent features. Being driven into the arms of a dangerous drug by the conviction that life is a pointless bore never looked quite so good. If Kurt Cobain had it to do over again, no doubt he'd be careful to become addicted to something else.

Meet the E-culturati[3]

There's more to Ecstasy than style and scandal, says Toby Manning—there's social bonding, protest and ideology

In the popular imagination Ecstasy is, at best, just a drug a lot of young people take at weekends; at worst an illegal and dangerous substance responsible for more than 50 deaths. Both views miss the point. Ecstasy isn't simply a substance that can be consumed, that can be banned: it's a culture.

The most obvious parallel is with psychedelia, but it's arguable that drugs lie behind most subcultures, be it skinheads (glue), rastafarians (marijuana), or mods (speed). Just as psychedelia had a particular cultural profile, so does Ecstasy. From club fashions to the E-influenced style (ravey editing; dance soundtracks) of film makers Danny Boyle (*Shallow Grave, Trainspotting*) and Paul Anderson (the disappointing *Shopping*); and from drug/dance culture-saturated authors Irvine Welsh (*The Acid House*) and Jeff Noon (*Vurt*), to the cyber-delic imagery of increasing numbers of book covers and magazine layouts, E-culture is everywhere to be observed.

"Claims that drugs raise consciousness or offer useful insights are total twaddle."

Sixties nostalgists will point out what the counterculture's style and drug-use derived from a specific ideology, all about breaking down barriers, freedom of expression and, er, peace and love, while Ecstasy is a classic product of the nihilistic, feel-good 1980s, all about escape, the moment, self: style without content. But most subcultures operate primarily at a stylistic level, their "resistance" symbolic rather than material (though none the less frightening to the establishment for that). Although nostalgists crow that the counterculture aimed higher, the overwhelming number of 1960s icons turned right-wing demagogues suggests that revolutionary rhetoric was, for many, simply stylistic statement. And it's as true of acid as of Ecstasy that the main incentive for indulging was and is getting blitzed out of your brain. Claims that drugs raise consciousness or offer useful insights are total twaddle. And we could do without a lot of the new age mysticism popular within E-culture. But if you look beyond E's grinning surface and beyond the tabloid (and broadsheet) coverage, there *is* an ideology at the culture's core, evolving from the music that the drug itself both compliments and inspires.

The mainstream position that E-consumption and dance music have attained may make such claims hard to credit. High-street nightclubs host "raves"; pop tracks are routinely remixed into "dance" tracks by record companies; and adverts, even super-

---

[3] Article by Toby Manning, from *New Statesman & Society* F 23 '96. Copyright © 1996 *New Statesman & Society*. Reprinted with permission.

market Muzak, have gone techno. Psychedelia was similarly absorbed and nullified by the mainstream, "underground" rock being put to rest long before Jerry Garcia croaked his last croak—after all, how could America's biggest-grossing concert attraction ever be regarded as "underground"? And surely few musicians/club promoters/DJs will be content to remain underground (read "marginal") for long?

All true, except that there's a fundamental subversiveness at the very heart of dance music. While acid opened up pop music's instrumental, rhythmic and lyrical parameters, E-culture (following on from the pioneering work of dub reggae and hip hop) has reconceived the very notion of "music". No longer is pop music something produced and—crucially—*owned* by musicians recording "original" tracks based on melodic and harmonic principles. Ambient and techno can be made on computers in bedrooms, and are more concerned with *texture* than melody. House music can be created purely by mixing together other people's records, using sampling technology. Many records central to E-culture aren't even available commercially—they're DJ-only "white labels". Much of what's played at dubs is created on the spot by DJs. There is no "original". Dance music can be imitated even co-opted, but it remains by nature, subversive.

The DIY ethos of dance music quickly translated into a DIY club ethos: ravers linking up with travellers and their sound systems and organising free raves culminating in Spiral Tribe's Castelmorton event in 1992. The reaction of the establishment was predictably draconian: raids, arrests, then the Criminal Justice Act (CJA). Intricate systems were devised to avoid the police's scrutiny, involving telephone trees, computer linkups, mobile phones and neutral, secondary meeting points. Ravers' opposition to the Criminal Justice Bill may have begun as a subjective libertarian "freedom to party" schtik, but the campaigns politicised, many some of whom then went on to organise anti-roads protests and Reclaim the Streets demonstrations, employing a tactical ingenuity that had been developed on the rave scene (a fact little recognised by the media). The DIY ethos has also translated into projects like Justice? and Exodus' community centres.

Those E-culturati who constitute the underground are, of course, a minority but it's from the underground, not the major labels or the high street that the best music best clubs and best ideas emerge regularly reinvigorating the scene. While there's no denying that the DIY, opt-out, self-help philosophy can offer only micro solutions the cynicism of the denizens of E-culture about formal politics is not surprising given mass unemployment, the CJA (tacitly supported by Labour) and parliamentary attitudes to the drugs so central to this subsulture.

For most young people it's less "Should I or shouldn't I?" than "Which one tonight?" Risk is just part of the culture: "You could walk under a bus." And given the "democratisation" of dealing in E (lots of people score for their friends, taking a small cut here and there), the notion of a killer in the shape of whoever gave poor Leah Betts the pill her body couldn't cope with is perceived as nonsense.

Taking Ecstasy isn't itself a radical act. It doesn't subvert much more than your sleep patterns, and the experience—*and* a lot of E-heads—can be incredibly boring. But pills, dancing and safety are only part of the story, and in many ways the least interesting. It is time the parameters of discussion were opened up.

In the Drug Culture[4]

The notes my kids have been bringing home from school lately declare this to be the era of "values." The television stations I've been cruising all suggest that Americans feel they are in the midst of a moral crisis. The strange thing is that all the people I know see themselves as part of the solution to the crisis. No one considers themselves part of the problem. A venerable tradition holds that moral renewal must be preceded by an act of repentance. If we have indeed become morally unstrung, perhaps what we need is not a new book of virtues but more honesty.

A few months ago I watched a television interview with the firebrand Republican congressman Robert Dornan of California (who just lost his re-election bid). An accomplished orator, Dornan generally is unflappable in interviews. Dornan was batting all the questions out of the park as usual until a reporter threw the congressman a knuckle ball. He asked Dornan about his wife's problems with drugs. Dornan lurched in his chair and sputtered that on five separate occasions, his wife had come very close to being killed by drugs. Though he typically appeals to the theme of responsibility, this time he explained that his wife was not to blame for her close encounters with the reaper. It was her male physicians who were at fault. "Excuses, excuses," Dornan might have muttered if someone else had used a similar rationale for his family's plight.

"...a conservative estimate places American users of Prozac at 5 million..."

A moralist if ever there was one, Dornan has loudly decried the U.S. drug problem. However, he does not seem to regard the millions of Americans taking legally prescribed uppers and downers to be part of that problem. When someone covered by health insurance is in despair, he goes to the clinic and gets a prescription for Xanex or Prozac. About this the moralists, many of whom themselves rely on some pharmaceutical assistance, are less judgmental then Pilate.

Yet when someone who is not covered by health insurance buys a bag of forgetfulness, the indignant virtuecrats are ready to put the scoundrel away for life. Some of us who have more ways and means ought to acknowledge that we, no less than the indigent crack addict, turn to drugs to make life more bearable or, sometimes, just to make ourselves more successful. Judging by the figures on the use of psychoactive medications (a conservative estimate places American users of Prozac at 5 million), even those of us who take two-week vacations pop pills to take the harsh edge off of our lives.

I am no exception. For five years I have been filling and refilling a prescription for Dalmane, a potent sleeping pill. I suspect

---

[4] Article by Gordon D. Marino, teacher in the department of philosophy at St. Olaf College in Northfield, MN, from *The Christian Century* 114:5-6 Ja 1-8 '97. Copyright (c) 1997 Christian Century Foundation. Reprinted with permission.

that I will be filling this prescription for the rest of my days, though I might have been better off if I had learned to cope with my sleeping problems without resorting to a bottle of dark blues. I also have a prescription for dealing with the red-faced terror I feel when I give a public speech. I dip into this bottle whenever I feel as though I am about to blow my top, which is about once a week.

Does this make me part of the drug problem? Most of the people I eat lunch with would insist that it does not. I am, after all, not about to rob anybody to get my Xanies. And yet our appetite for drugs and the quickness and persistence with which we resort to pharmaceutical solutions suggest that I and tens of millions of others must be considered part of the drug culture.

The more understandable a behavior becomes the more difficult it is to condemn. Those of us who resort to crutches from the Lilly Company to help us through our enviable lives ought to understand why people in harder circumstances try to medicate themselves. Is it any wonder that subscribers to health plans are much less likely to use illicit drugs than are folks who have to rush to the emergency room when they get the flu?

While I am not suggesting that snorting cocaine is an acceptable cure for the blues, I do submit that many of us are in no position to say anything more than "there but for the grace of God go I."

The philosopher Richard Rorty has argued that improving communal moral life has little to do with spinning moral arguments and everything to do with expanding our sense of solidarity. Those of us who have allies in the medicine cabinet to help us deal with our problems ought to recognize that we share something important with people who go to the local dealer to cop a few moments of feeling that everything is going to be all right.

When I go to the pharmacy to buy a balm for my despair or diffidence, I act on the same impulse that drives a father to sell his kid's bike for money to buy something to calm himself down. Neither of us can cope with our troubles and pain.

Bitter Pill⁵

Packer Brett Favre tells SI how the pain of playing in the NFL led to his addiction to painkillers and, nearly, his death

Green Bay Packers quarterback Brett Favre can pinpoint when, where and why he got scared straight. It happened on Feb. 27 in room 208 of Bellin Hospital in Green Bay, where he had just undergone surgery to remove one bone spur and several bone chips from his left ankle. One minute Favre, the NFL's MVP last season, was talking to his girlfriend, Deanna Tynes, their 7-year-old daughter, Brittany, and a nurse. The next thing he knew, there were tubes and IVs coming out of him everywhere.

He doesn't remember the 20 minutes in between, during which his limbs thrashed, his head banged backward uncontrollably, and he gnashed his teeth. During those minutes his body told him in a loud wake-up call to stop popping painkillers as if they were Lifesavers. He never heard Tynes scream to the nurse, "Get his tongue! Don't let him swallow his tongue!" He never heard a terrified Brittany ask, as she was being whisked from the room, "Is he going to die, Mom?"

"...once he took 13 tablets in a night."

After the seizure had ended and he had come to his senses, Favre looked into a sea of concerned medical faces and saw Packers associate team physician John Gray. "You've just suffered a seizure, Brett," Gray told him. "People can die from those."

Favre's heart sank. Upon hearing from doctors in the room that his dependence on painkillers might have contributed to the seizure, he thought, I've got to stop the pills, I've just got to.

Last season Favre went on such a wild ride with the prescription drug Vicodin, a narcotic-analgesic painkiller, that Tynes feared for his life. He scavenged pills from teammates. At least once he took 13 tablets in a night. But on Tuesday of last week, during his final telephone call before entering the Menninger Clinic, a rehabilitation center in Topeka, Kans., to treat his dependency (and also to evaluate his occasional heavy drinking), Favre told SI that he hadn't taken Vicodin since the seizure. "I quit cold turkey," he said, "and I entered the NFL substance-abuse program voluntarily. I don't want a pill now, but I want to go into a rehab center because I want to make sure I'm totally clean. The counselors I've seen think it's best for me. The one thing they've taught me is that there will always be a spot in your brain that wants it."

A source close to Favre told SI that Favre initially balked at

---

⁵ Article by Peter King, from *Sports Illustrated* 84:24-30. Reprinted courtesy of *Sports Illustrated*, May 27, 1996. Copyright © 1996 Time Inc. "Bitter Pill" by Peter King. All rights reserved.

"...painkillers aren't detected in annual NFL drug screenings."

entering a rehab facility. The source said Favre also did not want to comply with a demand from his NFL-appointed addiction counselors to sign a 10-part treatment plan that called for him, among other things, to stop drinking for two years. Favre claims he doesn't have an alcohol problem. However, the league's substance-abuse policy mandates that a player who turns himself in for treatment comply with his counselors' recommendations. Had he refused to sign the treatment plan and enter a rehab center, Favre could have been considered in noncompliance with the policy. That could have triggered the penalty clause, under which he could have been subject to a four-game suspension in 1996 without pay (which would cost him $900,000). So he signed the document, revealed the depth of his problem in a press conference in Green Bay on May 14 and traveled by private jet to Kansas at 5 a.m. the next day.

The news hit the quarterback-starved NFL hard. Favre is the newest star in the NFL galaxy, a fresh-faced 26-year-old savior with Bradshawesque leadership skills, charisma and Deep South backwoods likability. Outside of the Dallas Cowboys' Troy Aikman and Emmitt Smith, he's probably the most significant player in football, both for what he has done on the field at a young age and for what he means to the league long-term. Many of the NFL's star quarterbacks, including John Elway, Jim Kelly, Dan Marino and Warren Moon, are in the twilight of their careers, and most of the Generation Xers—Drew Bledsoe, Trent Dilfer, Rick Mirer, Heath Shuler et al.—are struggling to make an impact. Not Favre. In the last two seasons he has thrown 71 touchdown passes, including a team-record 38 in 1995. His two-TD machine-gunning of the San Francisco 49ers in a 27-17 playoff victory last January put the Packers in the NFC Championship Game, their first title contest in 28 years, which they lost to Dallas 38-27.

But in building the longest starting streak among active quarterbacks, 68 games, Favre has paid a painful price. He has had five operations in the last six years, dating back to a July 1990 car accident before his senior season at Southern Mississippi. "Brett's not coming out of the game unless a bone's sticking out," said Ty Detmer, his Packer backup of four years, who signed with the Philadelphia Eagles in the off-season.

Like many pro football players Favre would—almost without thinking—take a numbing injection or a painkilling pill to get through a game. It's tough to determine just how widespread this practice is, because painkillers aren't detected in annual NFL drug screenings. But in the wake of Favre's revelation, Robert Huizenga, a former team doctor for the Oakland Raiders and a past president of the NFL Physicians Society, said, "This is not an isolated incident. We want people to play hurt, and when someone doesn't play hurt, he's no longer our hero. We need a system where a physician, without fear of losing his job, can say to an athlete, 'The injury is not healed. You cannot play.'"

As he walked out of the Chicago Bears' training complex last Thursday carrying a small box of club-prescribed anti-inflammatory pills for a bulging disk in his back, linebacker Bryan Cox said that he thought half of the players in the NFL needed painkillers or anti-inflammatories to make it through a season. Phil Simms, who quarterbacked the New York Giants for 14 seasons before retiring in 1993, estimated that each NFL team would need a roster of 250 players to make it through a season if games were played with only healthy, nonmedicated players.

"I'm sure there are a ton of NFL players out there—I mean it, a ton—who'll watch me come out and say to themselves, 'Man, that's me,'" Favre said last week. "That's one reason I'm talking. I hope I can help some players get help. I realize now how dangerous it is to keep using these things."

It didn't seem so dangerous to Favre when he first experienced the wonder of painkilling medication, in his seventh NFL start, on Nov. 15, 1992, against Philadelphia. A second-year player at the time, he had separated his nonthrowing shoulder in the first quarter, and the pain was so intense that he didn't think he could go on. "I saw [backup] Don Majkowski rarin' to go, and if he'd gotten back in there, I may never have gotten my spot back," Favre said. "At halftime the doctors said, 'It's your choice, but we can shoot it up [with Novocain] without further injury.' I said, 'Let's do it.' They had to pull my shoulder out, and they stuck the needle way down in my shoulder. In a little while I didn't feel any pain. I played well, and we won the game. I thought, damn, that was easy."

"Doctors estimated it would take 12 months for the muscle to heal normally..."

He was thinking much the same thing in the wake of surgery in January 1995 to repair a herniated muscle in his right side. Doctors estimated it would take 12 months for the muscle to heal normally; Favre played a preseason game less than eight months after the surgery.

As the injuries mounted during the 1995 season, Favre began using Vicodin heavily. By Week 7 he had a throbbing turf toe, a bruised right shoulder, an arthritic right hip, a bruised left knee and a sore lower back. "I knew there was something wrong," Tynes said last Saturday. "He'd ask me to ask friends for Vicodin, but I wasn't going to do that."

Favre said he believed he was hiding his addiction well, but Tynes, then-Packers quarterbacks coach Steve Mariucci, and best friends and teammates Mark Chmura and Frank Winters sensed late in the season that he had a serious problem. Mariucci even told the Green Bay training staff to monitor Favre's Vicodin use. However, according to Tynes and Favre's agent, Bus Cook, in addition to the prescribed doses he received from the team, Favre also scored Vicodin from teammates who didn't finish their prescriptions and from doctors outside the organization, including one who had treated him for a past ailment. "I started finding pills everywhere," Tynes said. "I'd catch him throwing up so badly, I'd be looking for blood. And he didn't come to bed at a normal time all season long. He'd just sit there in front of the TV for hours. Sometimes I'd wake up at four o'clock and find him in front of the TV or playing solitaire on the computer. I'd say, 'What's wrong with you? You've got meetings at eight, and you haven't been to bed.'"

Despite the heavy use of painkillers, Favre was playing the best football of his life, and that complicated Tynes's efforts to get him to quit taking the pills. He was also working out like a madman with strength coach Kent Johnston. "I'm in the best shape of my life," he said in October. When Tynes would beg him to stop—she flushed down the toilet countless pills she found in his hiding places—he would reply, "Why should I stop what's helping me get through this?"

Said Chmura, Green Bay's Pro Bowl tight end, "We'd tell him time and again: 'You've got to cut this out.' But players think they're invincible, and Brett was no different. He'd be fine for the games because I think he didn't do much of it on the weekend. But some weekday nights he'd be zapped."

Tynes, whose relationship with Favre dates back to 1985, said she considered leaving Favre but worried that he might increase his Vicodin consumption if she did. Finally, at the Pro Bowl in early February, she demanded that he quit taking the pills. Favre promised he would. He didn't. At the ESPY Awards in New York on Feb. 12, she noticed that despite the fact he had not been drinking, he was slurring his words more and more as the night went on. When they returned to their hotel room Tynes confronted Favre. "Why are you acting like this? What have you been taking?" she said.

"I took a couple of Vicodins," he said.

"A couple? No way!" she said angrily.

"Well, five or six," he said.

"How many? Tell me the truth!"

"Thirteen."

Later, Tynes said Favre told a doctor he was in pain and that the Packers usually prescribed Vicodin for it. According to Tynes, the doctor wrote him a prescription for 30 pills and four refills.

"I was worried he was going to die," Tynes said.

She called Gray to tell him of Favre's dependency. Yet only after the seizure did Favre realize that getting professional help was the only way out.

For the next $2^1/_2$ months Favre was on a roller coaster, confronting the addiction in sessions with his NFL-assigned counselors in Chicago and New Orleans. Tynes said Favre has beaten himself up emotionally. In one down moment he told her, "I may be a successful football player, but I feel like such a failure. How could I let this happen?"

"He told me he could feel we were disappointed in him," said Chmura on Friday. "He told me if it took not drinking for two years to help beat this, he'd do it. I told him, 'No problem. We'll just drink Coke with our pizza instead of Miller Lite.'"

"Maybe I'll find out in two years I can drink," said Favre, who after he leaves rehab will be subjected to as many as 10 unannounced urine tests a month for drugs and alcohol. "I don't know. But I'll find out. That's what this treatment is for." Tynes, who was prompted to quit drinking as a result of Favre's problems, said that all alcohol will be removed from their Green Bay house. Among other things, that means emptying the rec room refrigerator, which was stocked with only one thing: light beer.

Oddly enough Favre may get help in fighting his addiction from the negotiation of a new contract with Green Bay. His current deal expires after the 1998 season, but the Packers are talking about extending it into the 21st century. The Pack may try to tie a significant bonus clause to a stipulation that Favre, who splits his time between Green Bay and his hometown of Kiln, Miss., make his off-season home in Wisconsin.

NFL player after NFL player last week expressed sympathy for Favre, who was worried he would be cast as a druggie if he stepped forward and admitted his addiction. "I'm not blaming anyone," he said. "It's my fault. The only reason I ever did this was because I had to. *Had to*. I had to play. Injuries have cost a lot of guys their jobs in this league, and there was no way an injury was ever going to cost me my job. Then it just got out of hand."

Said Arizona Cardinals quarterback Boomer Esiason, "The worst thing in this league is getting an injury tag. I hope this opens the eyes of some players, but I doubt anyone will show the guts Brett showed in standing up there and admitting his problem."

After his news conference Favre spent much of the night on the phone calling stunned friends. Only once in his conversation with SI did his voice dip a few octaves and show how deeply his tough outer shell has been dented. "I'm 26 years old, I just threw 38 touchdown passes in one year, and I'm the NFL MVP," he said. "People look at me and say, 'I'd love to be that guy.' But if they knew what it took to be that guy, they wouldn't love to be him, I can guarantee you that. I'm entering a treatment center tomorrow. Would they love that?"

Counselors denied Favre's request to delay reporting to rehab so he could host the first Brett Favre Celebrity Golf Tournament in Gulfport, Miss. The event went on without him last Friday and Saturday at the Windance Country Club. Tynes was there. As she sat in a golf cart under a shade tree near the 18th green, she talked about why she had hope for Favre. "A couple of years ago Brett told me he wanted to be the best quarterback in the NFL," she said. "He committed himself to it, and he did it. He'll commit himself to this. He knows his career and his life are at stake."

Tynes wiped her eyes. She took a deep breath. She sniffled a few times. "You know," she said, "he's changed already. He talks to me again. He takes Brittany and me out. He pays attention to us. A few days ago he hugged me and he thanked me for everything I've done, and he said some really nice things to me."

She wiped her eyes again. "I said, 'I can't believe it. The old Brett's back!'"

Time will tell. The true test will start in September. [Brett Favre and the Green Bay Packers won Superbowl XXXI vs. the New England Patriots in January 1997.]

IV. Treating Substance Abuse

Editor's Introduction

The last section of this compilation is devoted to an exploration of the means and methods by which addiction to particular substances is overcome. The grim reality of any addiction is that it comes to encompass the totality of one's life as no facet of that life is left untouched by that addiction, be it family, home, work, or play. By removing oneself from that addiction one comes to a new understanding of what it means to be alive.

The first article, "Kicking Crack," is a series of statements told to Teresa Wiltz from *Essence* magazine. In this article Wiltz points out that while "the headlines have died down, we're still reeling from the impact" of crack cocaine. Those hit hardest by the epidemic include African-American women. What follows are the stories of those women who, after months or years of being controlled by the drug, managed to get themselves clean and lead healthy, fulfilling lives. It must be noted though that such redemption was achieved only after all of these women hit the painful and life threatening place known as "rock-bottom."

Marianne Apostolides, writing for *Psychology Today*, describes a means of overcoming addiction known as holistic therapy. Fast "gaining greater mainstream acceptance" holistic therapy attempts to correct the internal "imbalance" which led the user to addiction in the first place. Rather than simply treat the addiction as a singularity to be overcome, holistic therapy attempts to find and then correct the desire which leads one to compulsive, addictive behavior. A similar approach is explored by Carolyn Morell in the next article, entitled "Radicalizing Recovery: Addiction, Spirituality, and Politics." Here, Morell discusses a "sociospiritual approach" which strives to initiate a change in the addict's life. Only in this fashion, according to Morell, can the addict achieve the "individual and social well-being" that leads to successful, and complete recovery.

Robert Granfield and William Cloud, writing in the *Journal of Drug Issues*, provide a study of 46 alcoholics and drug addicts who escaped their addiction without the assistance of formalized treatment. According to Granfield and Cloud, the key to overcoming addiction lay in the addict's ability to create a drug or alcohol free identity. Once they were able to envision themselves as people who did not use drugs or drink, they created lives that did not involve such addiction, which notably included severing ties with all those people with whom they once drank or did drugs.

The next two articles in this section discuss the processes by which addiction is terminated. D'Arcy Jenish, writing for *Maclean's*, discuss a Toronto based self-help organization known as the Muckers which is really an off-shoot of the Alcoholics Anonymous' program. Employing Alchoholics Anonymous' twelve step program, the Muckers believe that Alchoholics Anonymous has strayed from its original simplicity. In response the Muckers "stick [strictly] to the original" Alcoholics Anonymous text, upholding its teachings as the necessary means to rid oneself of the cravings that lead to addiction.

As the Muckers accuse Alcoholics Anonymous of straying from their original course, Msgr. William O'Brien, co-founder and president of Daytop Village, Inc., asserts that the United States has replaced treatment with tough laws and incarceration. Rather than fund the treatment center, O'Brien remarks that politicians are building prisons. The result is a deep cut in the Substance Abuse and Mental Health Administration and an increase in prison building budgets.

Kicking Crack[1]

The headlines have died down, but more than ten years after crack first hit our neighborhoods, we're still reeling from its impact. No one could have predicted the power it continues to hold over our communities. Crack kills common sense, destroys families and infests our neighborhoods with crime. No one who tries crack is immune to its allure. Sisters—from senior citizens to executives to mothers and even beauty-contest winners—looking for a party in the pipe soon find themselves paralyzed by crack's grip.

Kicking crack is more than a notion. It's not unusual for an addict to relapse over and over again. Although crack stays in the body for less than a week, an addict can get treatment in a residential rehab center and leave thinking she's cured, only to find herself in the throes of painful psychological withdrawal from the drug. Cuts in federal funding mean few treatment centers are prepared to help recovering addicts deal with the realities they face once they're back on the streets. So it's no surprise that many crack victims find themselves smoking rock again—even after they've sworn that their last time as the last time.

"Getting clean can be as terrifying as getting addicted."

Still, despite the grim statistics, despite the horror stories, there are those who manage to crawl from under crack's heavy influence. Getting clean can be as terrifying as getting addicted. It takes courage, determination, a lot of nerve, a strong support system, faith and the willingness to keep trying, even if you fall off the wagon time after time. For many African-American women, help comes by adhering to the 12 steps espoused by Alcoholics Anonymous and Narcotics Anonymous, which encourage members to acknowledge they are powerless to fight their addiction without turning their lives over to a Higher Power. Often after losing themselves to drugs, women in recovery find their souls once more—and emerge from the experience happier and healthier than they were before they started using.

"With recovering addicts, we try to introduce a new reality that comes from hope," says Bobbi Owens, executive director of the Mini Twelve Step House in Los Angeles. "But at the same time, it's important for them to make a link between what it's like now and what it can be and will be like because they've made a choice to change."

These three sisters tell the stories of how they found recovery after living for years on the pipe:

---

[1] Article by Teresa Y. Wiltz, a writer for the Chicago *Tribune,* from *Essence* 26:82-4+ Ap '96. Copyright © 1996 Teresa Y. Wiltz. Reprinted with permission.

Diana Donnell, 44, Jennings, Louisiana, singer, clean for two years:

I'm from a little shipyard town in Louisiana. I was raised by my grandparents, hardworking, churchgoing people who gave us a good life. I was the second person in my family to go to college. When I went to college, I was like this Christian girl set free.

At the University of Southwestern Louisiana in the early seventies, I was the first Black to do a lot of things. I was the first Black cheerleader. The first Black sweetheart. The first Black on the homecoming court. Then in 1972 I was chosen Miss Black Louisiana. I sang. I did a lot of community work and demonstrated against the war. I was very proud of that.

But my years after that weren't as good as my beginnings. I had a son and got married. After that marriage broke up, I left my son with my mother, and I moved to Los Angeles, seeking fame and fortune as a singer. When that didn't pan out, I moved back home to Louisiana and straight into an abusive marriage. I had three daughters with a man who used drugs and abused me emotionally, mentally and physically for years. This wasn't the life I thought I'd have. I wasn't the person I thought I'd be.

The first time I used crack, I was driving through the back roads with my girlfriend. At first I would just lace some weed with crack. Then weed disappeared from the street. You couldn't find marijuana anywhere, only crack. I knew I was hooked when I would do everything and anything for it. I took great pride in paying for my own drugs. I'd haul scrap iron. I'd sew. I felt like as long as I worked hard and paid for my own drugs, it was nobody's business what I did. But my judgment was off, way off.

I stole my grandfather's checks, and I got into some legal trouble because of it. I'm still paying restitution. The last year I used, I was almost killed three times. One man was strangling me until, gasping for air, I agreed to let him rape me. After that I started selling my body. Being in a small town, you know who the tricks are. And they know to come looking for you when they get paid. Then in 1988, my only girlfriend, my best friend all my life, was brutally murdered in Baton Rouge over some cocaine. The first thing people said when they heard about it was, "They got Juanita, Diana's next." That made me angry. I felt like I had to use even more to show people not everyone would die from using crack.

I was totally frustrated and alone. I didn't care what I looked like. I was worshiping the drug that had become my god, my man, my friend. From the time I woke up until the time I went to bed, I put all my efforts into smoking. I was a connoisseur. I could always tell what it was cut with. When I would buy my rocks I would taste them, touch them with my tongue. Dealers didn't like that, but I didn't care. I wanted to know what I was getting.

But at some point you have to stop. Your body gives out on you. You can only get so high. When you try to get past the high, you become despicable, oblivious to the people around you.

I went into rehab the first time because I didn't like being a user. I couldn't face the person I had become. So I went into a residential program and stayed 33 days. I played the rehab game. You go to group therapy, you get into the groove of things. The problem is, in there you're in a protected environment. You're talking the talk but not walking the walk. When it comes time to get out, it gets difficult. You can't go into rehab as a user, come out as a nonuser and expect to be accepted as a nonuser by those who still use.

My husband was determined that I would fall. And I did fall. I ended up in the streets running from him. I had nowhere to go. I tried to ease my pain by escaping once more into a world of drugs. But I only managed to ease my way into a lifestyle that brought me greater pain.

When I was living in the streets, I ran into an old friend from high school. He would talk to me, reminding me of who I once was. He helped me to see *me* again.

But he was drinking heavily. So we started helping each other get clean. First I went into detox. Then we got help through a church. This preacher took a liking to the two of us and let us move into the church. I even became the church secretary. We had our own AA meetings. And I prayed. Sometimes I would dream I was high on crack. I knew I was ready for change when I woke up from the dream and said, 'Thank you, Jesus, it was only a dream."

I started singing again. I started liking me again. I started seeing that my children weren't lost to me. There was hope. I started practicing what they teach in rehab: Go to those people you have hurt and make amends.

Through it all, my mother never lost faith in me. I owe everything to her. I'm self-employed as a seamstress now. I sing in church. I'm going to court to get my four children back from my relatives. My children need me, and I need them. However long I have to wait, I'll have my children back. I have hope. A lot of hope.

God is very deep in my life. Whenever I become weak, feeling like there is no hope, instead of turning to the pipe, I just say, *Help me, God*. He sends me wonderful thoughts, and I maintain my sobriety. I'm proud of my life. Even the part with the drugs, because it's only by going through all those things that I know where I'm supposed to be now. I haven't given up, and I won't give up.

Dawn, 29, Los Angeles, assistant at a major movie studio, clean for four years:
The first time I tried crack. I was hanging out with my girlfriend at this rich guy's house in Beverly Hills. I remember this really sweet, sweet smell. I couldn't move. It was like I was flying away somewhere. The guy said to me, "Whatever you do, don't die."

But then it was over. After that, I found myself wanting to chase that feeling.

I come from an interracial family. My father's White; my mother's Black. I'm a movie brat. My dad's a film executive. I never knew what it was to need anything.

I started getting drunk when I was 9. By myself. I would sneak my dad's Jack Daniel's and drink it. I was such a loner. I would stuff my feelings inside and do things just for the thrill of it. I was the kid who would run across the street when the traffic light was red.

I was kicked out of my first private school while in the seventh grade. Soon I was hopping from private school to private school, learning enough about smoking pot and drinking and hanging out with rich white kids before I would get kicked out again.

"I got clean. I found a great job working in a hotel and I got into a spiritual practice..."

When I was 16, I got pregnant. I hid it for seven months, but my parents found out and made me give the baby up for adoption. That was so hard. After that, my rebellion kicked in. I dropped out of school and got my GED. One day I was hanging out at a friend's house, getting high on crack, when he blew his brains out. At first the police thought I had shot him. It was awful. You would think that would've slowed me down, but it didn't.

Because of my background, I never had financial responsibilities. I always had great jobs, made great money. Then, through my girlfriend, I met the man who would father two of my children. His name was Andre, and he had just gotten out of jail for selling drugs. He was drop-dead gorgeous. We moved into a drug dealer's house for a time and did drugs for 30 days straight. The day I found out I was pregnant, Andre got arrested again for selling drugs. I waited for him. I was in love, and my pregnancy inspired me: I got my own apartment. I got clean. I found a great job working in a hotel and I got into a spiritual practice, living a vegetarian life. I felt that this child would allow me to tell my parents, "You can't take this away from me." I was 23.

But six months later, Andre got out of jail. Within three days, he started getting loaded. I held out for a while, but soon after my son was born, I began dibbling and dabbling in crack again. And I got pregnant again. I was blessed when my second son was born drug-free. By this time, I had moved back in with my parents. Andre got arrested on drug charges again, and I crossed over the line. I was using every day. I would tell myself it was because I was in a relationship from hell. I didn't see the part I was playing in my own addiction.

At lunchtime, I would take the bus to the park, buy some crack and smoke it as I walked back to work. In the office I would be so high I couldn't sit still behind my desk. I'd be tweaking and twitching and biting my lips. Eventually I got fired because I stole money from them: $800. But they never pressed charges. These people still had such confidence in me. You see, I was a nice middle-class girl.

This disease had me believing that I was getting away with something. I started to believe I had some kind of power. It was like crack was saying "See, Dawn, see what you can get away with? See what I can do for you?"

Because I had a nanny, it was easy for me to push off my responsibilities. I wouldn't get out of bed to change a diaper, but I would get out of bed to cop a hit. And yet I adored my children. That's what was killing me. I would try to sit with them, but I would get this hunger, this urge to get high. Sometimes I would just sit and stare at them and cry, writing letters to them in case I died.

You could see my bones. You could see green in my color. I was crazy. Paranoid. And cocky. I thought I could go outside and beat up drug dealers and take their drugs.

The last four months of my using, I stayed loaded every day. Brushing my teeth and combing my hair were a chore. I pawned everything in the house. Stole from my mother. Turned the nanny on to crack to keep her mouth shut. Finally my mother told me I could either get help or go to jail.

"...I had to find a solution that went deep down inside of me to heal the feelings."

Then one day I drove by a rehab center, The Natural High, a men's recovery house. It was like I was divinely guided. I walked in with nothing but my roller skates and the clothes on my back, and they helped me find a residential facility.

I found recovery in South Central Los Angeles. After about six months of clean living, I got pregnant again. I didn't realize there was more to being sober than just not drinking and using. By the time I had been dry for 13 months, I hit a spiritual and emotional bottom. So I moved back home and got into a 12-step program. It saved my ass. It took me a year to go through all the 12 steps. During that time, I was introduced to the Agape Church of Religious Science. I did an inventory of my life and—what a surprise!—I found I could no longer blame anyone but me. The healing it brought into my household is just tremendous.

I found me. I found my self-respect. I found my inner voice. I'm proud to say I'm now a fully functioning mother and employee. I also joined the United Nation of Islam, and I'm taking courses at my church in prayer and meditation, which really helps. I still get agitated, and I get impatient. I want to get negative about things, but I realize drugs and alcohol lived deep down inside me. So I had to find a solution that went deep down inside of me to heal the feelings. I've learned that the past doesn't equal the future. I have a choice in how I live today.

Mia Mann, 30, Yonkers, New York, emergency medical technician, clean for four years:
I was raised in the church. No matter how bad my addiction got, I still made it to church on Sunday. I still made it to choir practice. I was always there, singing. I believed in God. Strongly.

A couple of times, though, I would be smoking and lose track of time. Then I'd end up high in church. I felt that there was no hope;

I was just going to be like this for the rest of my life. God can do anything—but I felt like He just couldn't help me. It seemed like every time I tried to kick crack, I would end up there again.

I used crack to medicate whatever I was feeling. It wasn't about partying. I was feeling lonely from my breakup with the father of my two children. I was living with my parents. I would buy the kids' Pampers and stuff, but my mother was doing everything else.

I knew I was hooked the first time I smoked crack. My best girlfriend gave me some. It was such a rush to my head, an unbelievable feeling. But in five minutes it was gone, and I wanted to do more. After that, whenever I had money, that's where I went: to get me some crack. And the more I did it, the more I wanted to stay high. Your body just craves it. I would buy crack before I would buy something to eat. I'd plan to spend $30 and end up spending $150. When you're using, you intend to do what you say, but it never seems to work out that way.

Six months into my addiction, I quit my job because I couldn't really get up in the morning. I felt like, *Oh please, so what.* I'd borrow money from my family to get high. I'd lie and say I needed it for the kids. I would wake up every morning, take a shower and go buy some rocks from the neighborhood crack house. Then I'd go to my friend's place, and we would smoke all day, until there wasn't anything left to smoke. I couldn't stop. There were times when I just smoked and smoked and smoked. I only associated with people who did what I did. My friends looked like they could handle it, and I thought I could handle it. But I couldn't.

Once I smoked 21 vials of crack. My heart was beating so fast it scared me. I was so deluded, I thought I could just go to the emergency room and say "I'm having chest pains." The doctor said, "Get real. You have a problem." When my high wore off, I finally broke down. I agreed to get treatment. My parents were shocked, hurt. "Not my little girl," they said. They knew I had a problem, but they hadn't known what the problem was. People don't like to face facts.

As long as I was in rehab, my recovery was working. I even got a job at the clinic. I met my husband there. We had a baby together. But I wasn't ready. Neither was he. We'd be all right for a little while, and then we'd start using again.

When you hear people saying every time you pick up the pipe, it gets worse, believe them. I ended up in a Harlem crack house, smoking for three days straight. I didn't eat. I didn't wash. I said, "I don't need these earrings. This bracelet. This chain." I never thought I would sell my things for drugs. And when the money was gone, I just felt, *Now what?* That day I told myself if I could find one quarter to make a phone call, would go back into rehab. I found my last quarter in a corner of my bag, and I made that call.

I had to find a new way to recover. The people at my old clinic didn't really help. If you relapsed, it was like, "You again?" I entered a 12-step outpatient recovery program, going from 2 P.M. to 6 P.M. each day, plus Narcotic⸱ ⸱ ⸱ ⸱⸱⸱ ⸱⸱⸱ ⸱lcoholics Anonymous meetings at least five ⸱⸱⸱⸱ ⸱⸱ople at the recovery program showered ⸱ ⸱⸱nselors weren't so much into the drugs I ⸱⸱⸱ ⸱e inter- ested in my everyday problems. Th ⸱⸱⸱ ⸱ to find out why you do what you do, anc ⸱⸱⸱ ⸱nd how you've dealt with your problems, ⸱⸱⸱ ⸱n."

I stayed clean for a year, but ther ⸱⸱⸱ ⸱ I called my counselors. They said, "Brush ⸱⸱⸱ ⸱plained that you mentally relapse before ⸱ ⸱⸱⸱ ⸱e drug. They put me in detox for seven d ⸱⸱⸱ ⸱day resi- dential program. They said, "You' ⸱⸱⸱ ⸱u." I'm really glad I went. They told me ⸱⸱⸱ ⸱bout the things I had done and to talk and ⸱⸱⸱ ⸱s to see the part I had played in them inst ⸱⸱⸱ ⸱.

I still had my problems. My hus ⸱⸱⸱ ⸱ted, and I was feeling *feelings*. But my p ⸱⸱⸱ ⸱s. I kept going to my meetings, getting stro ⸱⸱⸱ ⸱g strong in the community.

When I went into the program, ⸱⸱⸱ ⸱y kids to my mother's care. But it felt so g ⸱⸱⸱ ⸱he judge and have him say, "Here, you ca ⸱⸱⸱kids b ⸱k." I had asked God, *Lord, when You know* ⸱ ⸱y, give me a good place where my kids and I can ha⸱ ⸱⸱, and we can learn about one another. And that's what He gave me. Now I have a nice place of my own. I went back to school. I pay my bills. I can cry with my kids about my problems now. It's no secret. They know what I've been through, but now I know my Higher Power is God. The way I used to chase the drug, that's the same way I chase my recovery.

Portrait of a Killer

Crack has proven to be a drug like no other. "This is not a drug ⸱ play around with," says Salimah Majeed, executive director, African-American Family Services/Institute on Black Chemical Abuse in Minneapolis. "People say, 'I just use crack socially.' Well, they won't be using crack socially for long."

With crack, it takes much less time for the addiction to progress to the fatal disease stage than with other drugs. Alcoholics can take 25 years to hit rock bottom; crack addicts spiral out of control within three weeks to six months. Recent estimates indicate there are some 2.1 million cocaine addicts in this country, with an additional 4 million "occasional users." It's no secret brothers and sisters are overpresented in those num- bers.

While it's an equal-opportunity killer, crack has been particu- larly devastating for African-American women. Many sisters find smoking more palatable than injecting or snorting drugs.

Because crack destroys maternal instincts, a sister's addiction quickly affects others. Children are neglected or abandoned, and many end up in foster care. Others seek solace in gangs. And then there are the "crack babies" whose piercing shrieks echo through hospital words. It's not known what problems they'll face as they grow up.

If you or someone you know has a crack problem, these resources can help: **Cocaine Anonymous**, (800) 347-8998; **Narcotics Anonymous**, (818) 773-9999; **African-American Family Services/Institute on Black Chemical Abuse**, (612) 871-7878.

How to Quit the Holistic Way[2]

They've been minimized and they've been marginalized, but the fact is holistic therapies—including acupuncture, homeopathy, massage therapy, aromatherapy, yoga, nutrition therapy, and dozens more—have been gaining greater mainstream acceptance. According to a 1993 survey published in the *New England Journal of Medicine*, in 1991, about 21 million Americans made 425 million visits to practitioners of these types of alternative medicine; that's more than the estimated 388 million visits we made to all primary care physicians that year. Now a holistic approach—where an individual's situation and particular way of coping is addressed, and going cold turkey may not be necessary—is slowly beginning to influence the way people with addictions are treated. Holistic therapies are helping to bridge the gap between conventional, exclusively abstinence-oriented approaches and the newer, more controversial harm-reduction philosophy.

"Holistic therapies work to restore balance by connecting mind and body."

When addressing an addiction, all holistic techniques begin with the same basic philosophy people develop addictions to correct an "imbalance" within them. Addicts become stuck, unaware, and unable to deal with their thoughts, feelings, and actions. They may drink, take drugs, or eat to excess to disassociate from their deficiency. Holistic therapies work to restore balance by connecting mind and body. They take away some of the underlying causes of abuse by helping people become aware of and take responsibility for the way they think, feel, and act.

The goal of many holistic therapies is to restore the body to its naturally healthy state. The best treatments are not offered in isolation; they're carried out with psychotherapy or group therapy—especially when it's open to the holistic view of treating the entire person, not just the addiction—and other holistic therapies.

Holistic philosophy overlaps with the harm-reduction approach to addiction, which evolved out of a desire, about 10 years ago, to slow the spread of HIV/AIDS and hepatitis among injection drug users by dispensing clean needles. People running syringe exchanges realized they had an opportunity to provide additional services to drug users. Now a number of harm-reduction centers—offering programs including acupuncture, massage therapy, and substance use counseling; referrals to detoxification and treatment facilities; and caseworkers to help with housing, food stamps, and medical care—have sprung up in cities like New York, Chicago, Portland, Seattle, Los Angeles, Santa Cruz, San Francisco, and Oakland. Run by current and former drug users,

---

[2] Article by Marianne Apostolides, from *Psychology Today* magazine 29:35-42 + S/O '96. Copyright © 1996 (Sussex Publishers, Inc.). Reprinted with permission.

for current and former drug users, these centers don't demand that clients remain abstinent. From experience they know that no one can be forced into dealing with a problem, and that people who are treated with respect and who are educated about their choices can and often do elect to help themselves.

Holistic therapies do have their skeptics, of course. There's concern that these therapies haven't been properly studied or regulated. "As a general rule, holistic therapies are most helpful when they're used *in conjunction with*—not in place of—other treatments, says Barrie R. Cassileth, Ph.D., an adjunct professor of medicine at the University of North Carolina at Chapel Hill and Duke University, who has written extensively on alternative therapies and cancer treatment. Cassileth sees the need for methodologically sound, rigorous clinical tests before any claims about the capabilities of holistic treatments can be made. Frank Gawin, M.D., scientific director of a laboratory examining addictions at the University of California at Los Angeles, agrees. He's currently involved in a six-city study—the largest involving an alternative therapy—to determine the effectiveness of acupuncture on cocaine addiction. Dr. Gawin believes that holistic therapies should continue to be practiced while studies are underway, so long as people receive psychotherapy and are fully informed that these treatments have not been proven effective. "There are no magic bullets," Cassileth concludes. "People ought to be wary of those who say they have one."

Male alcoholics who've been married a long time drink less over the years. Women with a history of heavy drinking who've been married awhile don't seem to improve.

American college students spent $4.2 billion on booze in 1991—more than they spent on books.

Seven percent of adults—most of them alcoholics or problem drinkers—consume half of all the liquor sold in the United States.

Massage

It's too simplistic to say an addiction can be massaged away, but the power of this hands-on therapy is being tested on people dealing with anorexia, bulimia, smoking, and other addictions, with impressive results. The mind-body connection is all-important in massage, says Elliot Greene, M.A., past president of the American Massage Therapy Association. Greene says people with addictions can become trapped in a cycle of avoiding their problems and disassociating from their bodies. The experience of massage—where someone touches, respects, and cares for a person's body—can break that cycle, helping addicts reconnect physically and center themselves emotionally. The effect is a newly empowered person more able to talk about and come to terms with an addiction.

Massage may also have a powerful chemical impact on the body. By massaging the soft tissue, therapists release tension and get energy moving. The loosening of tight muscles sends the body a signal to cut down production of stress hormones, such as cortisol. This neurological response has a calming effect on body and mind. In addition, massage moves lymph through the body, assisting the body's natural cleansing process.

Various research is now testing the effectiveness of massage therapy. At the Touch Research Institute at the University of Miami Medical School, 48 different studies are currently underway to determine the effectiveness of massage on problems, such as anorexia and bulimia, drug addiction, asthma, and diabetes. In one ongoing study looking at massage's effects on tobacco addiction, smokers were taught to massage their ears and hands when they craved a cigarette. After one month, they had reduced the number of cigarettes smoked—and their cravings for them— by 40 percent. There will be a follow-up at three and six months to see if the results hold. "Massage provides a distraction that takes away from the nervous-habit aspect of smoking," says Tiffany Field, Ph.D., the institute's director.

A third of all smokers make serious attempts to quit each year. Eighty percent of them resume their habit within 12 months.

Childless smokers are more likely to quit successfully than smokers with kids.

A new vaccine halts cocaine use—at least in rats—by stimulating production of antibodies that keep the drug from entering the brain. Addicted rodents stop cocaine use within a week of vaccination.

Hatha Yoga

Hatha yoga, the yoga of postures—where people hold positions for varying lengths of time, stretching and contracting their muscles and breathing deeply—is one component of the ancient practice of yoga. It simulates the relaxing effects of the parasympathetic nervous system and removes tension from all the major muscle groups. According to Joseph LePage, founder and director of Integrative Yoga Therapy in Aptos, California, certain postures actually massage internal organs, helping dispel toxins that may have built up in the liver and kidneys from substance abuse.

"Hatha yoga allows people to get back in touch with themselves, and get into a frame of mind where they can experience what it is to be well, and not drug dependent or anxious," explains Peter Stein, M.A., addictions specialist at the North

Charles Institute for the Addictions, a private treatment facility in Boston, Massachusetts. According to a recently completed clinical trial by Howard Shaffer, Ph.D., director of the Division on Addictions at Harvard Medical School, hatha yoga is as effective as traditional group therapy in treating heroin addicts enrolled at a Boston methadone maintenance clinic. Those who practiced yoga for 75 minutes once a week and received individual therapy once a week reduced their drug use, criminal activity and cravings as much as those who went to group therapy once a week and had individual counseling.

Joyce, 37, a manager at a gourmet food store in the Boston area, has combined hatha yoga with talk therapy for four years as a part of her methadone maintnance progam. Although methadone has been essential to her getting off heroin, she now wants to give it up. "Yoga helps become more aware physically, and then become aware mentally of what's going on with me, and of how the things I do affect other people," she says "Five years ago, I'd have told you I'd be on methadone for the rest of my life. But now I'm in a different frame of mind."

Joyce has begun slowly detoxing off methadone, which is itself a physically addicting drug whose withdrawal symptoms are cold sweats, inability to sleep, impatience, and discomfort. "In yoga, you have to hold postures for so long, and while your holding them, you are saying to yourself 'I know this hurts, but I know I have to do in myself.'" That experience of feeling and withstanding the physical pain in hatha yoga helps Joyce know she can withstand the physical pain of methadone withdrawal.

In a recent study of 222 pathological gamblers, 65 percent said refraining from betting gave them "withdrawal symptoms" like insomnia, headaches, upset stomach, even sweating, and chills.

The typical compulsive shopper is a woman in her thirties who became a shopaholic as a teenager.

One-third of Gamblers Anonymous members have lost a job, 44 percent have stolen from work, and one-sixth have divorced.

Nutrition Therapy

"When people think of nutrition, I want them to think of the biochemical substances that are essential for maintaining optimal brain chemistry," says nutritionist Joan Mathews-Larsen, Ph.D., founder of the Health Recovery Center (HRC), a private abstinence-based addiction clinic in Minneapolis, Minnesota. After people change their diets and supplement their food intake with the right amount of amino acids, essential fatty acids, vitamins, and minerals, they can begin to deal with their alcoholism, drug abuse, anorexia, or bulimia, says Julia Ross, M.A., executive director of Recovery Systems, a private eating-disorder and drug-abuse facility in San Francisco, California.

With the proper nutrition and supplements, the brain manufactures chemical—like norepinephrine, a neurotransmitter that seems to increase energy and boost mood; serotonin, another important neurotransmitter; and endorphins, the brain's natural opiates—that are needed to regulate mood and behavior.

Optimal nutrition may also correct the possible deficiencies that contribute to alcoholism or substance abuse. "The question," says Alan Gaby M.D., editor of the *Nutrition and Healing* newsletter, "is what are the proper supplements? I treated an alcoholic who couldn't control his drinking, but with glutamine, an amino acid, he was able to go back to social drinking and handle it." For cocaine addiction, Dr. Gaby says the amino acid tyrosine is often recommended. Tyrosine is a building block for norepinephrine.

Richard Firshein, D.O., a New York City osteopath whose holistic practice emphasizes nutritional healing, says one theory is that addiction may be triggered by low levels of serotonin. By restoring healthy levels, one of the underlying causes of addiction can be taken away. Firshein prescribes a combination of amino acids and a high-carbohydrate diet to boost tryptophan, the building block for serotonin.

Vitamin C is sometimes used by nutrition therapists to moderate both the physical and emotional withdrawal symptoms of detoxification. "It was being used for some time with narcotics addicts," says Dr. Gaby. "The most dramatic case I've seen was a patient who sniffed morphine every day. He came to me on his second day of withdrawal. His shakes were so bad that he couldn't sit still. I gave him an intravenous injection of about 4 grams of vitamin C, along with magnesium, calcium, and B vitamins. About halfway through the injection he calmed down, and ultimately his withdrawal symptoms subsided. That lasted about 36 hours. He had to come back for three more injections over five days, but he essentially went through withdrawal without symptoms."

After detoxification, nutrients such as niacin, chromium, and magnesium are given to alleviate hypoglycemic reactions, which a high percentage of alcoholics, as well as a lesser number of amphetamine and heroin users, experience. Hypoglycemia, a metabolic condition that results in low levels of glucose in the brain, can cause depression, anxiety, panic attacks, and mood swings, perhaps bringing about more substance abuse.

For three years, Rita, now 34, tried unsuccessfully to stop drinking. First, she tried a traditional 28-day treatment center, where, she says, "they kept saying, 'You're helpless, you're helpless.' And to me that meant I might as well drink." After losing her job and having her husband give up on her, Rita eventually wound up at HRC. During the six-week program, she learned she had high levels of histamine—a neurotransmitter that regulates mood and energy—in her brain. This abnormally high level made Rita's mind race, and contributed to her obsessive-compulsive behavior. "I used alcohol to calm and soothe myself," she says.

By taking one methionine pill each day—an amino acid that reduces the effects of histamine on the brain—Rita says she no longer needs alcohol to stop her mind from racing. She also participated in cognitive-behavioral counseling to develop new ways of thinking and acting. "I don't feel I could've taken the nutrients without having some counseling," she says. "But I also know talk therapy alone wouldn't have been enough, because I've tried that." Three years later, Rita continues to take methionine and has remained sober. She and her husband reconciled, and their first child was born this past summer.

Rita's is not an exceptional case, according to Mathews-Larson, who claims that 75 percent of the people who complete her program are "abstinent and stable" three years after completing treatment.

Between a third and a half of teenagers who try cigarettes soon become regular smokers.

Cancer patients who remain disease-free for five years are considered "cured"—and the same may be true for alcoholics. Those who stay sober for five years have a relapse rate of only 10 percent.

In Russia, the average man drinks a liter of Vodka every four days—and lives only 57 years.

Acupuncture

Acupuncture's use as a treatment for addiction was discovered in 1972 by Wen, a Hong Kong neurosurgeon. Testing its use as an anesthetic, he accidentally determined—because many of his volunteers were opium addicts—that it reduced withdrawal symptoms such as nausea and the shakes. Since Wen's discovery, acupuncture has become the most widespread holistic therapy for treating addictions to cocaine, alcohol, nicotine, and heroin.

Like much of traditional Chinese medicine, acupuncture works on the theory that networks of energy called *chi*, flow through the body along natural pathways, and disease grows when that energy is out of balance or blocked. By inserting needles at precise positions along these pathways, acupuncturists aim to stimulate the body's flow of energy, restoring balance.

For an addiction, most people receive auricular (ear) acupuncture because *yin* energy—the nurturing energy that's damaged by an addiction—can be manipulated at points on the ear. Typically, an auricular acupuncturist will place five needles in the ear. The points used are: shen-men (the 'spirit gate'), an often-used acupuncture point that slows the heart rate and calms anxiety; the sympathetic nervous system point, which relaxes nerves, reduces 'fight or flight' panic, improves digestion, and aids the respiratory system; the kidney point, which helps release toxins through urine and is associated with restoration, rejuvenation, and a deep level of healing and purification of blood; the liver point, which cleanses the body of toxins and is related to emotional balance and stability; and the lung point, a nourishing organ that improves the immune system and eases breathing.

Acupuncturists learn how to touch and relate to their patients, respect their space, and express sympathy. In addition to the biological effects of acupuncture, this kind of care gives patients a sense of confidence, calmness, and motivation to start or continue treatment, says Michael O. Smith, M.D., a psychiatrist and director of Substance Abuse at the Acupuncture Clinic at Lincoln Hospital in New York City, where between 3,000 and 4,000 auricular acupuncturists have been trained.

"...acupuncture may help people stay off drugs after they've gone through withdrawal."

Acupuncture is used at all stages of an addiction, from the time people seek help to the time they are abstinent. It can ease the discomfort of withdrawal symptoms, including insomnia, muscle ache, profuse sweating, and nausea for heroin; depression, cravings, and fatigue for cocaine; and seizures, diarrhea, and hypertension for alcohol. Additionally, acupuncture may help people stay off drugs after they've gone through withdrawal. By enabling people to clear their minds and decrease stress, anxiety, depression, and cravings, acupuncture can help people deal with the issues that caused their addiction. "It helps people settle down and center themselves so they can participate in their own internal growth," says Dr. Smith. "They're less defensive, more thoughtful, and more open-minded."

In the last five years, acupuncture's use in addiction has spread to more than 300 clinics. Even the government has given its tacit approval of the therapy: almost half of the drug treatment facilities linked to U.S. drug courts include acupuncture in their programs. Yale University Medical School's Arthur Margolin, Ph.D., who, along with Dr. Gawin, is part of the six-city project looking into the effectiveness of acupuncture on cocaine abuse, says funding for this research came about because there's no pharmacological treatment for cocaine addiction—a vaccine has proven effective in rats—while heroin addicts are often treated with methadone. The problem, says Margolin, is that accurate clinical trials are difficult to design and assess. For example, the placebo in an acupuncture trial requires inserting needles into inactive points, but scientists are not certain which points are truly inactive.

Hypnosis

Hypnosis seems helpful in treating addictions, and the depression and anxiety associated with them, according to Michael Yapko, Ph.D., a psychologist with a specialty in hypnosis, and author of *Trance Work*. Hypnosis aids people with addictions because of its ability to facilitate a heightened state of consciousness. "During hypnosis," Yapko says, "people are intensely focused and their awareness deepened. But even in a trance they can have a conversation."

Not only does hypnosis help people develop specific techniques for changing their addictive behavior, but these techniques seem to take hold more strongly. "Situations, like being in a bar, feel more real than when you're just talking them through in therapy," says Helmut Relinger, Ph.D., a Berkeley, California, psychologist and hypnotherapist. "So people get to rehearse coping with their urges to use," which usually last only one to two minutes. The chance to imagine and truly feel yourself dealing with cravings while hypnotized can help you cope with them at other times.

"Other research indicates the ability of hypnosis to control the pain of drug withdrawal symptoms..."

Brian Alman, Ph.D., a psychologist and creator of Six Steps to Freedom, a program that incorporates self-hypnosis, meditation, and visualization to treat various addictions, says self-hypnosis "allows people to take a unique observer perspective on their own life. They can step back and watch what's going on without judging or criticizing themselves. Alman has begun a two-year study to compare the efficacy of his program with traditional inpatient treatment, AA, and no intervention.

When it comes to nicotine addiction, hypnosis results have been mixed, in part because not everyone can be hypnotized. It's been known for 20 years that people who are easily hypnotized are twice as likely to cut their smoking in half as those who aren't able to go under. Other research indicates the ability of hypnosis to control the pain of drug withdrawal symptoms: Studies on migraines, childbirth and dentistry show that hypnosis allows people to gain control over their fear and anxiety, thereby reducing pain.

Homeopathy

Homeopathy, a 200-year-old system of natural medicine, uses minuscule or extremely diluted amounts of substances that in their original concentration might actually produce symptoms of the disease being treated. This philosophy of "like cures like" doesn't mean a little heroin cures a heroin addiction. In fact, Ed Gogek, M.D., a licensed homeopath, cautions that homeopathy doesn't cure chemical dependencies. But it does work on other problems, like pain, anxiety, depression, and restlessness. In other words, homeopaths don't treat chemical dependencies, they treat the causes and *consequences* of addiction, whether to nicotine, cocaine, or food.

A homeopath takes into account a person's mental, emotional, and physical symptoms and uses remedies derived from plant, mineral, and animal sources that best fit a client's particular condition. For drug addiction, these substances may include tuberculinum, argentum, nitricum, arsenicum, or other materials equally unknown to most people. "Substances used in home-opathy help to express and dispel symptoms and regain balance," explains Martha Oelman, media liaison for the National Center for Homeopathy.

The effectiveness of homeopathy is still not clear. So far, the approximately 15 separate studies that have been rigorously reexamined show positive results for conditions like chronic pain, respiratory infections, and trauma.

A 1993 study by Susan Garcia-Swain, M.D., addiction specialist at St. Peter's Chemical Dependency Center in Olympia, Washington, examined 700 people overcoming drug addictions over a three-year period at the Starting Point addiction clinic in San Diego, California. One-third of her patients received counseling and one of 19 homeopathic remedies for addiction withdrawal symptoms; one-third received counseling and a placebo; and the last group received counseling only. The patients who received homeopathic remedies, says Dr. Garcia-Swain, were twice as likely as the others to remain sober after 18 months. Dr. Garcia-Swain says those people treated with homeopathic remedies were better able to benefit from other talk therapies because they were less guarded, more confident, and more inclined to continue in the program.

With a holistic approach to addiction, people with dependencies are given an opportunity to find their own rhythm to recovery. And when you're trying to kick a habit of any sort, that kind of flexibility can be the difference between success and failure.

Holistic Help and Where to Find It

To find out more about holistic therapies and practitioners in your area, try calling or writing the following organizatons:

Acupuncture
The American Academy of Medical Acupuncture
5820 Wilshire Boulevard, Suite 500
Los Angeles, CA 90036
(213) 937-5514

National Acupuncture Detoxification Association
3220 N Street, NW, #275
Washington, DC 20007
(503) 222-1362

Massage
American Massage Therapy Association
820 Davis Street, Suite 100
Evanston, IL 60201-4444
(847) 864-0123

Homeopathy
National Center for Homeopathy
801 N. Fairfax Street, Suite 306
Alexandria, VA 22314
(703) 548-7790

Hypnosis
The American Academy of Medical Hypnoanalysts
P.O. Box K
Ludlow, MA 01056
(800) 344-9766

Nutrition
Center for Addiction and Alternative Medicine Research
914 South Eighth Street, Suite D-917
Minneapolis, MN 55404
(612) 347-7670

Radicalizing Recovery: Addiction, Spirituality, and Politics[3]

Treatment centers and self-help recovery programs promote individual solutions to substance abuse through changing dysfunctional behavior and relying on spiritual beliefs and practices. The root problems are understood to be diseases within the person. However, the social conditions implicated in causing the addiction remain unaddressed. Although class, race, and gender do not predict substance abuse, many people entering clinics are from disempowered groups. Can social workers bring recovery and social justice methods together? What can radical social workers in the addiction-recovery industry do?

The interdependency of all individuals and organizations makes the elimination of addiction contingent upon basic social change.
—Stanton Peele, *Love and Addiction*

In their insightful critiques of therapeutic and spiritual solutions to addiction, feminists and other progressive political groups view such solutions as reformulating social issues ideologically to avoid political analysis and action. "Recovery thought," a worldview perpetuated in substance abuse treatment centers and self-help programs, assumes that current social and economic arrangements work for the general good; therefore, the addicted person must change. Social institutions that may cause and sustain substance abuse are not challenged: "The dominant culture is not threatened by sick people meeting together to get well."

Yet people are entering treatment centers and self-help programs in unprecedented numbers. In the 1980s the concepts of addiction ("the compulsive use of a chemical and its continued use despite adverse consequences") and recovery ("the behavioral and emotional change toward health and growth,") gained popularity. In the 1990s addiction treatment is a rapidly expanding industry, and recovery is the fastest growing social movement in the United States. In fact, many individuals live better lives because of their involvement in these activities. However, if social workers in the addictions field do not want their role limited to what social work pioneer Florence Kelley called "the wrecking crew"—those called in to clean up the damages the economic system perpetrates and perpetuates—politicizing treat-

[3] Article by Carolyn Morell, Ph.D., assistant professor, Social Work Program, Niagara University, from *Social Work* 41/3:306-12 My '96. Copyright © 1996 National Association of Social Workers, Inc. Reprinted with permission.

ment is necessary.

Although class, race, and gender do not predict addiction, many people entering clinics and joining recovery groups are from disempowered groups: women, people of color, unemployed and underemployed people, and poor people. Tena Okun (1992), training director of Grassroots Leadership, articulated the frustration felt by social justice activists: "These should be our people. So what is going on? Why aren't these same people flocking to our movement, to our organizations, to our causes?"

I live with this polarization of personal solutions and political explanations as a radical social worker in a hospital-sponsored outpatient chemical dependency clinic. With a foot in each world, I constantly wonder how these apparently opposite approaches might be integrated theoretically and practically. This article seeks answers to the question, What can radical social workers in the addiction-recovery industry do?

Definitions

The word "radical" may conjure up widely different images and meanings. Because radical people are portrayed negatively in the popular culture, the term may scare or repel some social work practitioners and clients. Because of the stigma associated with the word, a more neutral term, "progressive," has recently gained currency among reformers and social change activists. I am comfortable with both terms and use them interchangeably and in a broad, inclusive way in this article.

Radical social workers are not a homogeneous group; they disagree about such matters as how individual and social transformations occur, whether social workers should work inside or outside of society's welfare institutions, and the character of fundamental sources of oppression. Progressive social workers are united by their critical view of central social organizations such as capitalism, patriarchy, and institutionalized racism and the unnecessary human suffering they foster. These social workers share a vision of collective responsibility for both individual and social well-being and a "commitment to human equality." Although both radical and conventional social work attend to the alleviation of individual symptoms, radical social work pays more attention to oppression, that is, to the economic and political causes of personal problems.

A Sociospiritual Approach

Spiritual and political worldviews offer two vast and profound modes of understanding experience, and each knowledge system contains both empowering and disempowering tendencies. Social workers can blend the liberating aspects of both worldviews to promote individual and social well-being among each other and their clients. Whereas a political view directs attention to the material social organization of human life, a spiritual conviction directs attention to an experience that is before and beyond human social organization. Without a holistic perception that encompasses both the social and existential dimensions of experience, "we are without a sense of ourselves entire."

The concept of interconnectedness brings together the reformative trends found in these seemingly contradictory approaches. At the center of most great spiritual traditions (not specific religious ideologies) is a belief that human beings are united as expressions or emanations of a central energy or principle— Spirit, Creator, God, Goddess, Divinity, Force, Living Principle, Source, Life, Love. The recognition of humankind's fundamental relatedness motivates progressive political activity. "An injury to one is an injury to all" is a common phase heard among progressive social workers. Conviction about human interconnectedness provides will and courage to go against the grain in a culture that is committed to separating people by class, race and ethnicity, gender, age, and sexual orientation.

Divided, people suffer individually and collectively as they experience personal separation and oppression, both of which relate to addictive behavior. Yet substance abuse treatment and 12-step programs acknowledge and deal only with personal separation. Recovery programs such as Alcoholics Anonymous and professionally facilitated skills training and therapy groups break the emotional isolation between people. People in these groups cross diverse cultural and social boundaries and find their common humanity. These groups do not struggle to end exploitation and the social realities that relate to addiction, including unemployment and underemployment, homelessness, and inhumane urban conditions. Workers and clients alike see these problems as so intractable that action in this realm is perceived as a waste of time and energy. Some see the Serenity Prayer ("God, grant me the serenity to accept the things I cannot change...") as an injunction against social action. Thus, thorough recovery is derailed because attention is narrowly focused on personal solutions.

However, progressive social workers in addiction settings can help redress this imbalance by incorporating political education and opportunities for political action into all their activities. Social workers can change curriculum and counseling strategies to include consciousness-raising tactics that highlight humankind's interconnectedness and the necessity for collective action to change social circumstances hostile to recovery. Social workers can adopt Brazilian educator Paulo Freire's not-so-humble suggestion made at the 1988 World Conference of Social Workers: "The role of the educator, the dream of the educator, is the permanent transformation of the world."

"Conviction about human interconnectedness provides will and courage to go against the grain in a culture that is committed to separating people..."

Working with Groups

Without political education, addictive behavior is decontextualized. Historically, consciousness raising groups provided participants with contextualized experiences. Social workers engaged with oppressed populations in a variety of settings continue to promote this time-honored approach to helping people make connections between personal troubles and social issues.

Popular in the 1960s and 1970s, feminist consciousness-raising groups embodied many of the characteristics of today's self-help groups. While sharing their personal experiences, women obtained psychological help, positively redefined stigma, and increased self-esteem and self-acceptance in an environment that offered support and a nonjudgmental atmosphere.

In the conservative climate of the 1980s and 1990s, women's groups took an apolitical turn, introducing skills training as an approach to change. Skills training for both women and men continues today in substance abuse clinics in groups that address issues such as assertiveness, feelings identification, and self-esteem. Groups also offer opportunities to discuss the dynamics of power.

"Skills training for both women and men continues today in substance abuse clinics..."

However, unless such training explicitly deals with power, political realities are reduced to personal deficits and social relations are diminished to communication styles. Once personal issues are seen in light of power differences, skills training is expanded to include building competencies as social change agents. For example, when learning assertion skills, collective role playing is as important as individual role playing. Participants can practice ways to assert their needs as a group at their workplace, perhaps for a drug-free environment, safer working conditions, or more flexible hours.

In skills-training groups, social workers also can educate politically through sharing their progressive perspectives. For instance, one substance abuse prevention program I worked with targeted to women working in the home offered feminist-oriented minilectures. One lecture, called "Doing Good and Feeling Bad," summarized the work of feminist psychologist Jean Baker Miller (1976), who pointed out that women are assigned the role of giving, which is not recognized as a real activity and is often punished, devalued, and denied, leaving women feeling bad. Helping others develop is seen as not doing anything; working is the only activity that is directly self-enhancing. The progressive value orientation was made clear—everyone, men and women, must be givers and receivers, and ultimately, power must be shared equally. The women in the group not only learned new skills, but also apprehended a possible new self-definition that moved beyond a "woman's proper place." The essence of feminist consciousness is this "apprehension of possibilities."

Through bibliotherapy social workers can introduce clients to progressive writers of all colors, ages, genders, classes, and sexual orientations; for example, bell hooks's (1993) *Sisters of the Yam: Black Women and Self-Recovery* provides excellent material for presentation to African American women in treatment. Through these writings, clients may see themselves as "an ensemble of social relations" and may think about how their identities are constructed from social experiences, including the dynamic of class, race and ethnicity, and gender.

Another way to stimulate thinking about social variables related to addiction is to use "guided inquiry" in group work. Questions about how gender socialization (or social class location or ethnic and racial background) affects present feelings and experiences can be explored by guiding discussion around topical queries. For example, in the blanks in the following questions could be substituted such words as male, female, gay, lesbian, African American, Latino or Latina, poor, working class: "What did it mean to be_____in your family?" "What direct and indirect lessons did you learn about being_____?" "What happened when you deviated from gender role norms?" "How does your drinking or drugging behavior connect to your identity as_____?" "How is your personal pain connected to being_____?" "How is your personal happiness connected to being_____?" Such questions increase awareness of how social inequality and socialization interact with substance abuse problems.

"Clients and workers can join together in dialogic relationships..."

Working with Individuals

Although social workers live in a world of diagnostic manuals, third-party payments, and medicalized language and practices, radical workers can engage in political practice when assessing and counseling clients. Because common assessment procedures tend to locate the source of addiction within the client rather than within the interaction between the person and his or her surrounding context, progressive social workers can use the dialectical method of therapist Marsha T. Linehan (1993) to restore missing parts to the historical formation of addiction:

> Dialectical assessment requires that the therapist, along with the patient, constantly look for what is missing from individual or personal explanations of current behaviors and events. The question always being asked is "What is being left out here?" The assessment does not stop at the immediate environment or at the historical family or other past learning experiences (although these are not ignored); it also examines social, political, and economic influences on the patient's current behavior.

How social workers interact with clients in individual sessions makes a difference. Clients and workers can join together in dialogic relationships in which clients are given choices and share in assessments. Motivational interviewing, a nonauthoritarian approach to helping individuals discover their own motivations and resources to overcome addiction seeks to be democratic in spirit. Rather than labeling clients "resistant" and confronting their denial, Miller and Rollnick used five general principles in their work: express empathy, develop discrepancy, avoid argumentation, roll with resistance, and support self-efficacy. In motivational interviewing worker and client become "coinvestigators linking client thoughts, feelings, and behavior to the problem situation." As with Linehan's (1993) dialectical method, motivational interviewing provides opportunities to link the subjective experience of substance-abusing clients with the primary structures of oppression.

In their roles as brokers and advocates, social workers can refer clients to community resources for political education. For example, at the University of Buffalo, the Introduction to Women's Studies course is offered through the continuing education department. The class is educational and therapeutic, and others like it could be wonderful resources for some clients.

Promoting an Engaged Spirituality

"Many recovery programs do not attempt to impose a narrow belief system on people."

Among radicals, the lack of appreciation for the spiritual emphasis in recovery programs is based on connection of the term "spirituality" to organized religion and theology, the understanding that specific religious beliefs exclude many who need help, a sense that "otherworldliness" precludes necessary politicization of this life, and fear of the power of right-wing religious ideology. These are real concerns, but they are not factors inherent in recognizing a spiritual dimension in life. Many recovery programs do not attempt to impose a narrow belief system on people.

Whether thought of as God or as the vitality that results from communing with others, spirituality can inspire and sustain people to move beyond external and internalized oppression. Many people in substance abuse treatment are dispirited. Beliefs and experiences that connect them to others and challenge discouragement can be thought of as spiritual; they invigorate and empower people. Although organizations and leaders may exploit religion and use the term "spiritual" for their own enrichment, there is also evidence that people seek a deeper dimension to life. People draw on this dimension for satisfaction, understanding, and comfort. Rather than simply resisting spiritual discourse, progressive social workers can overcome the false separation between politics and spirituality by focusing on interconnectedness.

The goodness-of-fit between spiritual and political activities is displayed by the many people who enter the social justice movement because of their religious affiliations and spiritual beliefs. The congeniality of worldviews is also demonstrated in the writings of many people of color for whom spiritual beliefs and activities play a central role in the struggle against racist oppression. With the current emphasis on respecting diversity, social workers must honor the important role that spirituality plays in the lives of people of all cultures.

African Americans addressing addiction may provide a model for radicalizing recovery. Spirituality, along with African American history and communal values, is an indispensable tool for resisting and overcoming slavery to drugs and genocide. For example, Reverend Cecil Williams (1992), minister of Liberation at Glide Memorial Church in San Francisco, founded an innovative recovery program that combined individual healing and social change. In the late 1980s more than 600 people marched on Valencia Gardens, a troubled housing project in San Francisco, to call out the good news of recovery to the people addicted to crack cocaine who lived there. Each marcher was committed to absolute, unconditional acceptance of the people they met there. Marchers brought "paintbrushes and gallons of paint. Others bore heaping plates of fried chicken and potato salad." They arrived carrying banners declaring their nonviolent battle cry, "The User Needs Recovery," and "Welcome Home to Recovery," and they sang songs of freedom. Marchers surrounded the project and, using bullhorns, shouted to those inside, "C'mon down. Join us. It's recovery time. We know who you are. You are our sons and daughters. It's time for you to take control of your lives." One by one, as people slowly came out of the projects, they were put on the stage and given a microphone. They talked. They ate home-cooked food. They agreed to come to the church.

Williams (1992) articulated a new way to think about recovery that involves four steps: (1) recognition (not powerlessness), (2) self-definition (not society's definition), (3) rebirth (facing the pain and telling the truth), and (4) community (moving further into relationship with people of all colors). Political empowerment is the only route to recovery, and this empowerment is braided with spirituality. Social workers in conventional substance abuse programs need to know stories such as this one. At a minimum, social workers can discuss them with colleagues and clients. Those who dare may be inspired to organize similar outreach efforts.

Collaborating at the Policy Level

The sociospiritual approach depends on the availability of substance abuse treatment for those who need it. The number of facilities has never been adequate, and with the growth of managed care, insurers are reducing benefits, causing clients to be prematurely terminated from treatment. Yet this crisis provides an excellent opportunity for progressive social workers to engage in political struggle on the health care issue. Colleagues or clients who might not ordinarily engage in political action are more likely to become involved by writing letters and signing petitions to government representatives. Workers could attend public hearings and give testimony of their need for a comprehensive continuum of health care services. Workers could talk about this issue in the groups they facilitate and in this way empower the addictions community to effect history.

Another policy issue is the question of what constitutes treatment. Part of the hesitancy to fund lengthy treatment is based on the medical model of addiction. Most substance abuse programs provide psychosocial services along with medical care. Health care insurers do not view skills training and psychoeducational groups as medical care and are unlikely to do so unless evidence of their effectiveness is shown. However, some of the most creative programs, like the one at Glide Memorial Church, lack evidence of effectiveness because of the lack of evaluation of treatment processes and outcomes. Radical social workers can advocate for more alternative programming together with funds for research. With empirical data in hand, the collective clout of addiction staff can alter the definition of treatment.

Conclusion

People's lives are made through both subjective and objective transactions between inner and outer realities that are constantly developing processes rather than static structures. A person is not an isolated individual but an ever-changing "self-social unity," both an object of the prevailing social order and a subject able to move beyond it.

"The personal self is injured by the social world."

People construct themselves out of social experiences, including the dynamics of class, race, and gender. Such factors may be associated with negative self-understanding related to prejudice and limited opportunity. The personal self is injured by the social world. Self-love requires transcending this injury. Spiritual traditions and practices provide ways to experience self beyond self-hatred, but such practices do not eliminate the external causes of self-loathing.

In the sociospiritual approach advocated in this article, addiction is seen as a deficiency in spirit and in power. The medical aspect of addiction is not denied or ignored but is instead understood not to be all encompassing. Substance abuse is a condition that needs liberation (release from domination by a foreign power such as a substance, a psychological condition, or a social order), a process that requires both a change in consciousness and a change in circumstance.

Despite the millions of dollars spent on drug interdiction, prisons, treatment centers, and self-help books, addiction continues to expand as a personal and social tragedy. Society must do more and do it better. The self-help movement teaches the power of bringing individuals together and emphasizing spiritual values. The feminist, African American, and other progressive movements teach the power of politics and social structure. Social workers need to bring recovery and social justice methods together. A sociospiritual approach to addiction—with its emphasis on interconnectedness—offers this opportunity.

The Elephant That No One Sees: Natural Recovery Among Middle-Class Addicts[4]

This paper examines the characteristics of middle-class alcoholics and drug addicts who terminate their addictions without the benefit of treatment. Using what is commonly referred to as "natural recovery" processes, respondents terminated their addictions without formal treatment or self-help group assistance. Data for this study are based on in-depth interviews with 46 alcoholics and drug addicts who were identified through snowball sampling techniques. First, we examine the postaddict identities of our respondents to see how they view themselves in relation to their addictive past. Next, we explore the reasons respondents gave for avoiding treatment and self-help groups. We then examine the factors in our respondents' lives that promoted natural recovery. Finally, this paper concludes with a discussion of the relevance of our findings to clinical treatment and social policy.

Introduction

Social deviance literature typically portrays drug and alcohol addicted individuals as possessing distinct subcultural characteristics that marginalize them from the nonaddicted world. Whether this marginalization occurs because of a personality profile which predisposes an individual to addiction or whether it follows from being labeled and stigmatized as "an addict," the outcome is thought to be the same. Such individuals are considered to be distinctly different from the majority of the population. Indeed, the social deviance literature has played a role in classifying addicts as "other" thereby contributing to the production of an outsider status. However, as Waterston (1993) has recently argued, such portrayals have contributed to the "ghettoization" of drug users and to the construction of a false separation between 'them and us.'"

While the social deviance paradigm of addiction has produced insightful material documenting the lifestyle, experiences, and world views of drug and alcohol addicted persons, this literature has excluded groups not conforming to the image of social disparagement. For instance, the social deviance perspective has been instructive in expanding our knowledge of "bottle gangs" and other alcoholic subcultures, "crack whores" or crack-distributing gangs, and the slum-dwelling heroin addict who injects in order to either enhance his/her social status or simply to escape

---

[4] Article by Robert Granfield, assistant professor of sociology at the University of Denver, and William Cloud, associate professor in the Graduate School of Social Work at the University of Denver, from *Journal of Drug Issues* 26/1:45-61 Winter '96. Reprinted with permission.

the hopelessness of his/her own economic poverty. Although such groups can be classified as "hidden populations" due to their powerlessness and poverty as well as the fact that these groups are largely omitted from national surveys, their actions are frequently visible. Inner-city heroin addicts, coke whores, and skid row alcoholics often come in direct contact with social control agents such as the police, the courts, treatment programs, hospitals, and researchers. Precisely because these groups are classified as deviant and are "othered," they are subject to social inspection and identification.

Often absent from the research on hidden populations are those drug addicts and alcoholics who fail to fit into the previously constructed categories that are consistent with current models of deviance. One such group that falls into such a category is the population of middle-class addicts. For instance, some heroin-addicted women from middle-class backgrounds are often able to avoid immersion into a heroin-using subculture, and also have better chances of recovery. According to these authors, "it is possible for them to readjust more readily, because they often possess the resources necessary to start a new life." Such limited subcultural involvement may also result in an increased ability to circumvent detection. Similarly, many high-level drug dealers may remain hidden due to the secretive nature of their activity. Thus, many drug users and drug dealers avoid detection because they occupy otherwise legitimate social roles and lead basically straight, middle-class lives. In fact, recent scholarship has removed drug use from the world of deviance and has advanced alternative perspectives including the arguments that addiction is an act of cultural resistance, or one that locates addiction in the larger social, political, and economic contexts. Such views remove the unique characteristics associated with addiction and places it within the context of conventional social life.

"...many drug users and drug dealers avoid detection because they occupy otherwise legitimate social roles..."

One population that remains hidden due to the fact that they deviate from socially constructed categories regarding addiction are middle-class drug addicts and alcoholics who terminate their addictive use of substances without treatment. Research exploring the phenomena of natural recovery has found that significant numbers of people discontinue their excessive intake of addictive substances without formal or lay treatment. While it is difficult to estimate the actual size of this hidden population because they are largely invisible, researchers agree that their numbers are large and some even contend that they are substantially larger than those choosing to enter treatment facilities or self-help groups. Some have estimated that as many as 90% of problem drinkers never enter treatment and many suspend problematic use without it. Research in Canada has shown that 82% of alcoholics who terminated their addiction reported using natural recovery.

Research on natural recovery has focused on a variety of substances including heroin and other opiates, cocaine, and alcohol.

Much of this literature challenges the dominant view that addiction relates primarily to the substance being consumed. The dominate addiction paradigm maintains that individuals possess an illness that requires intensive therapeutic intervention. Failure to acquire treatment is considered a sign of denial that will eventually lead to more advanced stages of addiction and possibly death. Given the firm convictions of addictionists as well as their vested interests in marketing this concept, their rejection of the natural recovery research is of little surprise.

Research on natural recovery has offered great insight into how people successfully transform their lives without turning to professionals or self-help groups. The fact that people accomplish such transformations naturally is by no means a revelation. Most ex-smokers discontinue their tobacco use without treatment while many "mature-out" of a variety of behaviors including heavy drinking and narcotics use. Some researchers examining such transformations frequently point to factors within the individual's social context that promote change. Not only are patterns of alcohol and drug use influenced by social contexts as Zinberg (1986) illustrated, but the experience of quitting as well can be understood from this perspective. Others have attributed natural recovery to a cognitive appraisal process in which the costs and benefits of continued drinking are assessed by alcoholics.

"Failure to acquire treatment is considered a sign of denial that will eventually lead to more advanced stages of addiction and possibly death."

Perhaps one of the most detailed investigations of natural recovery is Biernacki's (1986) detailed description of former heroin addicts. Emphasizing the importance of social contests, Biernacki demonstrates how heroin addicts terminated their addictions and successfully transformed their lives. Most of the addicts in that study as well as others initiated self-recovery after experiencing an assortment of problems that led to a resolve to change. Additionally, Biernacki found that addicts who arrest addictions naturally utilize a variety of strategies. Such strategies involve breaking off relationships with drug users, removing oneself from a drug-using environment, building new structures in one's life, and using social networks of friends and family that help provide support for this newly emerging status. Although it is unclear whether the social context of those who terminate naturally is uniquely different from those who undergo treatment, it is certain that environmental factors significantly influence the strategies employed in the decision to stop.

While this literature has been highly instructive, much of this research has focused on respondents' circumvention of formal treatment such as therapeutic communities, methadone maintenance, psychotherapy, or regular counseling in outpatient clinics. Many of those not seeking professional intervention may nevertheless participate in self-help groups. Self-help groups have been one of the most popular avenues for people experiencing alcohol and drug problems. This may be due in large part to the fact that groups such as Alcoholics Anonymous (AA), Narcotics Anonymous (NA), or Cocaine Anonymous (CA), medicalize substance abuse in such a way as to alleviate personal responsibility and related guilt (Trice and Roman 1970). Moreover, these groups contribute to the cultivation of a support community which helps facilitate behavioral change.

Despite these attractions and the popularity of these groups, many in the field remain skeptical about their effectiveness. Research has demonstrated that addicts who affiliate with self-help groups relapse at a significantly greater rate than do those who undergo hospitalization only. Some have raised concerns about the appropriateness of self-help groups in all instances of addiction. In one of the most turgid critiques of self-help groups, Peele (1989) estimates that nearly half of all those who affiliate with such groups relapse within the first year. Peele contends that these groups are not very effective in stopping addictive behaviors since such groups subscribe to the ideology of lifelong addiction. Adopting the addict-for-life ideology, as many members do, has numerous implications for a person's identity as well as ways of relating to the world around them.

Somewhere between the two positions of skepticism and optimism are the findings of Emrick et al. (1993). In one of the most comprehensive analyses of AA participation to date, their meta-analysis of 107 various studies on AA effectiveness report only a modest correlation between exposure to self-help groups and improved drinking behavior. They additionally point out the compelling need for further research on the personal characteristics of individuals for whom these programs are beneficial and those for whom they are not.

Given the emerging challenges to the dominant views of recovery, research on recovery will be advanced through an examination of those who terminated their addictive use of alcohol and drugs without the benefit of either formal or informal treatment modalities. While research has provided insight into those who reject formal treatment modalities, we know little about the population who additionally reject self-help groups, particularly those from middle-class backgrounds. This paper examines the process of natural recovery among middle-class drug addicts and alcoholics and first explores the identity of previously addicted middle-class respondents in relation to their past addictions. Next, respondents' reasons for rejecting self-help group involvement or formal treatment are examined. Strategies used by our respondents to terminate their addictions and transform their lives are then examined and the implications of our findings in relation to current addiction treatment are presented.

"...addicts who affiliate with self-help groups relapse at a significantly greater rate than do those who undergo hospitalization only..."

Method

Data for the present study were collected from a two-stage research design involving 46 former drug addicts and alcoholics. The initial stage of this study involving 25 interviews explored 3 primary areas. These areas included elements of respondents' successful cessation strategies, perceptions of self relative to former use, and attitudes toward treatment. The second stage of the study sharpened the focus of the exploration within these three areas. This was accomplished by constructing a new interview schedule designed to capture the most salient themes that emerged from the first stage of the study. In each phase of this study, lengthy, semistructured interviews with respondents were conducted to elicit thickly descriptive responses. All interviews were tape-recorded and later transcribed.

Strict criteria were established for respondent selection. First, respondents had to have been drug or alcohol dependent for a period of at least 1 year. On average, our respondents were dependent for a period of 9.14 years.

Determination of dependency was made only after careful consideration; each respondent had to have experienced frequent cravings, extended periods of daily use, and associated personal problems due to their use. Second, to be eligible, individuals had to have terminated their addictive consumption for a period of at least 1 year prior to the interview. The mean length of time of termination from addiction for the entire sample was 5.5 years. Finally, the sample includes only individuals who had no, or only minimal, exposure to formal treatment. Individuals with short-term detoxification (up to 2 weeks) were included provided they had had no additional follow-up outpatient treatment. Also, individuals who had less than 1 month exposure to self-help groups such as AA, NA, or CA were included. Some of our respondents reported attending one or two of these self-help group meetings. However, the majority of our respondents had virtually no contact with formal treatment programs or self-help groups.

Respondents in this study were selected through "snowball sampling" techniques. This sampling strategy uses referral chains of personal contacts in which people with appropriate characteristics are referred as volunteers. Snowball sampling has been used in a variety of studies involving hidden populations. In particular, snowball samples have been employed in previous studies of heroin users and cocaine users. In the present study, snowball sampling methods were necessary for two reasons. Since we were searching for a middle-class population that circumvented treatment, these individuals were widely distributed. Unlike those in treatment or in self-help groups, this population tends to be more dispersed. Also, these individuals did not wish to expose their pasts as former addicts. Very few people were aware of a respondent's drug- and alcohol-using history, making the respondent reluctant to participate. Consequently, personal contact with potential respondents prior to the interview was necessary to explain the interview process as well as the procedures to ensure confidentiality. While there are limitations to this sampling strategy, probability sampling techniques would be impossible since the characteristics of the population are unknown.

All of our respondents in the present study report having stable middle-class backgrounds. Each of the respondents had completed high school, the majority possessed college degrees, and several respondents held graduate degrees. Most were employed in professional occupations, including law, engineering, and health-related fields, held managerial positions, or operated their own businesses during their addiction. Of the respondents participating in this study, 30 were males and 16 were females. The age range in the sample was 25 to 60 with a mean age of 38.4 years.

Forming a Postaddict Identity

Research within the tradition of symbolic interaction has frequently explored the social basis of personal identity. Central to the symbolic interactionist perspective is the notion that personal identity is constituted through interaction with others who define social reality. From this perspective, the self emerges through a process of interaction with others and through the roles individuals occupy. Symbolic interactionists maintain that the self is never immutable, but rather change is an ongoing process in which new definitions of the self emerge as group affiliation and roles change. Consequently, identities arise from one's participating within social groups and organizations.

"Symbolic interactionists maintain that the self is never immutable, but rather change is an ongoing process..."

The perspective of symbolic interaction has frequently been used when analyzing the adoption of deviant identities. For instance, the societal reaction model of deviance views the formation of a spoiled identity as a consequence of labeling. Reactions against untoward behavior in the form of degradation ceremonies often give rise to deviant identities. In addition, organizations that seek to reform deviant behavior, encourage the adoption of a "sick role" for the purposes of reintegration. AA, for instance, teaches its members that they possess a disease and a lifelong addiction to alcohol. Such organizations provide a new symbolic framework through which members undergo dramatic personal transformation.

Consequently, members adopt an addict role and identity, an identity that for many becomes salient. One respondent in Brown's study, for instance, indicated the degree of engulfment in the addict identity:

> Sobriety is my life's priority. I can't have my life, my health, my family, my job, or anything else unless I'm sober. My program [participation in AA] has to come first...Now I've come to realize that this is the nature of the disease. I need to remind myself daily that I'm an alcoholic. As long as I work my program, I am granted a daily reprieve from returning to drinking.

Brown's (1991) analysis of self-help programs and the identity transformation process that is fostered in those settings demonstrates that members learn that they must constantly practice the principles of recovery in all their daily affairs." Thus, it is within such programs that the addict identity and role is acquired and reinforced.

If the addict identity is acquired within such organizational contexts, it is logical to hypothesize that former addicts with minimal contact with such organizations will possess different self-concepts. In the interviews conducted with our first set of respondents, a striking pattern emerged in relation to their present self-concept and their past drug and alcohol involvement. They were asked, "How do you see yourself now in relation to your past?" and, "Do you see yourself as a former addict, recovering addict, recovered addict, or in some other way?" A large majority, nearly two-thirds, refused to identify themselves as presently addicted or as recovering or even recovered. Most reported that they saw themselves in "some other way." While all identified themselves as being addicted earlier in their lives, most did not continue to define themselves as addicts. In several eases, these respondents reacted strongly against the addiction-as-disease ideology, believing that such a permanent identity would impede their continued social development. As one respondent explained:

> I'm a father, a husband and a worker. This is how I see myself today. Being a drug addict was someone I was in the past. I'm over that and I don't think about it anymore.

These respondents saw themselves neither as addicts nor ex-addicts; rather, most references to their past addictions were not central to their immediate self-concepts.

Unlike the alcoholics and drug addicts described by Brown (1991) and others, they did not adopt this identity as a "master status" nor did this identity become salient in the role identity hierarchy. Instead, the "addict" identity was marginalized by our respondents. Alcoholics and addicts who have participated extensively in self-help groups often engage in a long-term, self-labeling process which involves continuous reference to their addiction. While many have succeeded in terminating addiction through participation in such programs and by adopting the master status of an addict, researchers have raised concern over the deleterious nature of such self-labeling. Peele (1989), for instance, believes that continuous reference to addiction and reliance on the sick role may be at variance with successful and enduring termination of addictive behaviors. Respondents in the first stage of the present study, by contrast, did not reference their previous addictions as being presently central in their lives. Their comments suggest that they had transcended their addict identity and had adopted self-concepts congruent with contemporary roles.

During the second phase of the study, the question around identity was reconstructed. Since most respondents in the first sample often made extensive and unsolicited comments about how they currently view themselves in relation to their past experiences (former addict, recovering addict, recovered addict, or other), a decision was made to reshape this question for use with the second sample. The question then read, "How do you see yourself today in relation to your own put experiences with drugs and alcohol (e.g., addict, recovering addict, person who had a serious drug and/or alcohol problem or, do you see yourself in some other way)? Please discuss as it relates to your current identity." The solicited responses from this second sample did not differ dramatically from the unsolicited responses from the first sample. Essentially, their former identities as addicts were not currently central in their lives but rather had been marginalized, as had been the case with the first sample of respondents.

Also, during the second stage of the study, an additional question about "addict identity" was constructed and asked. The question read, "To what extent do you freely discuss your previous drug and alcohol experiences with others? Please elaborate." The majority of these respondents were quite selective about with whom they discussed these previous drug experiences. Some stated that they shared these experiences with very close friends. Others stated that they discussed these matters only with people who had known them as addicts. Still others reported that they discussed these experiences with no one. Again one could conclude, as was the case with the first sample, that this second group minimized these experiences in terms of how they presently view themselves.

The fact that our respondents did not adopt addict identities is of great importance since it contradicts the common assumptions of treatment programs. The belief that alcoholics and drug addicts can overcome their addictions and not see themselves in an indefinite state of recovery is incongruous with treatment predicated on the disease concept which pervades most treatment programs. Such programs subscribe to the view that addiction is incurable; programmatic principles may then commit addicts to a life of ongoing recovery, often with minimal success. Some have suggested that the decision to circumvent formal treatment and self-help involvement has empirical and theoretical importance since it offers insight about this population that may be useful in designing more effective treatment. While research has examined the characteristics of individuals who affiliate with such groups, few studies have included individuals outside programs. Therefore, there is a paucity of data that examines the avoidance of treatment. We now turn to an examination of respondents' attitudes toward addiction treatment programs.

"...the decision to circumvent formal treatment and self-help involvement has empirical and theoretical importance..."

Circumventing Treatment

Given the pervasiveness of treatment programs and self-help groups such as AA and NA, the decision to embark upon a method of natural recovery is curious.

Some of our respondents in the first stage of the study reported having had direct exposure to such groups by having attended one or two AA, NA, or CA meetings.

Others in this sample, although never having attended, reported being indirectly familiar with such groups. Only two of them claimed to have no knowledge of these groups or the principles they advocate. Consequently, the respondents, as group, expressed the decision not to enter treatment, which represented a conscious effort to circumvent treatment rather than a lack of familiarity with such programs.

In order to explore their decisions to bypass treatment, we asked what they thought about these programs and why they avoided direct involvement in them. When asked about their attitudes toward such programs, most of them commented that they believed such programs were beneficial for some people. They credited treatment programs and self-help groups with helping friends or family members overcome alcohol or drug addictions. Overall, however, our respondents in the first sample disagreed with the ideological basis of such programs and felt that they were inappropriate for them.

Responses included a wide range of criticisms of these programs. In most cases, rejection of treatment programs and self-help groups reflected a perceived contradiction between these respondents' world views and the core principles of such programs. Overcoming resistance to core principles which include the views that addiction is a disease (once an addict always an addict), or that individuals are powerless over their addiction, is imperative by those who affiliate with such programs. Indeed, individuals who subscribe to alternative views of addiction are identified as "in denial". Not unlike other institutions such as the military, law school, or mental health hospitals, self-help groups socialize recruits away from their previously held world views. It is the task of such programs to shape its members' views to make them compatible with organizational ideology. Socialization within treatment programs and self-help groups enables a person to reconstruct a biography that corresponds to a new reference point.

Respondents in this sample, however, typically rejected specific characteristics of the treatment ideology. First, many expressed strong opposition to the suggestion that they were powerless over their addictions. Such an ideology, they explained, not only was counterproductive but was also extremely demeaning. These respondents saw themselves as efficacious people who often prided themselves on their past accomplishments. They viewed themselves as being individualists and strong-willed. One respondent, for instance, explained that "such programs encourage powerlessness" and that she would rather "trust her own instincts than the instincts of others." Another respondent commented that:

> I read a lot of their literature and the very first thing they say is that you're powerless. I think that's bull.... I believe that people have power inside themselves to

make what they want happen. I think I have choices and can do anything I set my mind to.

Consequently, these respondents found the suggestion that they were powerless incompatible with their own self-image. While treatment programs and self-help groups would define such attitudes as a manifestation of denial that would only result in perpetuating addiction, they saw overcoming their addictions as a challenge they could effectively surmount. Interestingly, and in contrast to conventional wisdom in the treatment field, the overwhelming majority of our respondents in the first sample reported successful termination of their addictions after only one attempt.

"...discomfort with the cultural aspects of these programs was often keenly felt by the women..."

They also reported that they disliked the culture associated with such self-help programs. In addition to finding the ideological components of such programs offensive, most rejected the lifestyle encouraged by such programs. For instance, several of them felt that these programs bred dependency and subsequently rejected the notion that going to meetings with other addicts was essential for successful termination. In fact, some actually thought it to be dangerous to spend so much time with addicts who continue to focus on their addictions. Most of our respondents in this first sample sought to avoid all contact with drug addicts once they decided to terminate their own drug use. Consequently, they believed that contact with addicts, even those who are not actively using, would possibly undermine their termination efforts. Finally, some of these respondents reported that they found self-help groups "cliquish" and "unhealthy." One respondent explained that, "all they do is stand around smoking cigarettes and drinking coffee while they talk about their addiction. I never felt comfortable with these people." This sense of discomfort with the cultural aspects of these programs was often keenly felt by the women in our sample. Most women in this group believed that self-help groups were male-oriented and did not include the needs of women. One woman, for instance, who identified herself as a lesbian commented that self-help groups were nothing but a bunch of old men running around telling stories and doing things together." This woman found greater inspiration among feminist support groups and literature that emphasized taking control of one's own life.

During the second stage of the study we decided to separate and sharpen our focus on what appeared to be three prominent overlapping themes around attitudes toward treatment. We asked these respondents why they chose not to undergo formal treatment or participate in self-help groups. We also asked about their general impressions of formal treatment, separate from their impressions of self-help groups. We then asked them specifically about their impressions of AA, NA, and other 12-step programs.

The principal reason reported for not undergoing formal treatment was that nearly all of the 21 respondents in the second sample stated directly or in some variation that they felt that they could terminate their addiction without such interventions. Some stated that treatment was not a viable option since it was either too expensive or essentially unavailable. While some of these respondents registered positive attitudes regarding varying treatment modalities, these respondents, nonetheless, reported that such treatment was not necessary in their individual case. In the case of respondent evaluation of 12-step programs, the second sample of addicts was not as critical as the previous sample. However even among the second group, most believed that the principles espoused by these programs were at variance with their own beliefs about the recovery process.

The Elements of Cessation

The fact that our respondents were able to terminate their addictions without the benefit of treatment raises an important question about recovery. Research that has examined this process has found that individuals who have a "stake in conventional life" are better able to alter their drug-taking practices than those who experience a sense of hopelessness. In their longitudinal research of cocaine users, these authors found that many people with structural supports in their lives such as a job, family, and other involvements were simply able to "walk away" from their heavy use of cocaine. According to these authors, this fact suggests that the social context of a drug user's life may significantly influence the ability to overcome drug problems.

"...the social context of a drug user's life may significantly influence the ability to overcome drug problems."

The social contexts of our respondents served to protect many of them from total involvement with an addict subculture. Literature on the sociocultural correlates of heavy drinking has found that some groups possess cultural protection against developing alcoholism. In addition, Peele (1989) has argued that individuals with greater resources in their lives are well equipped to overcome drug problems. Such resources include education and other credentials, job skills, meaningful family attachments, and support mechanisms. In the case of our first 25 respondents, most provided evidence of such resources available to them even while they were actively using. Most reported coming from stable home environments that valued education, family, and economic security, and for the most part held conventional beliefs. All of our respondents in the first group had completed high school, nine were college graduates, and one held a master's degree in engineering. Most were employed in professional occupations or operated their own businesses. Additionally, most continued to be employed throughout their period of heavy drug and alcohol use and none of our respondents came from disadvantaged backgrounds.

It might be concluded that the social contexts of these respondent's lives protected them from further decline into alcohol and drug addiction. They frequently reported that there were people in their lives to whom they were able to turn when they decided to quit. Some explained that their families provided support; others described how their nondrug-using friends assisted them in their efforts to stop using. One respondent explained how an old college friend helped him get over his addiction to crack cocaine:

> My best friend from college made a surprise visit. I hadn't seen him in years. He walked in and I was all cracked out. It's like he walked into the twilight zone or something. He couldn't believe it. He smoked dope in college but he had never seen anything like this. When I saw him, I knew that my life was really screwed up and I needed to do something about it. He stayed with me for the next two weeks and helped me through it.

Typically, respondents in our first sample had not yet "burned their social bridges" and were able to rely upon communities of friends, family, and other associates in their lives. The existence of such communities made it less of a necessity for these individuals to search out alternative communities such as those found within self-help groups. Such groups may be of considerable importance when a person's natural communities break down. Indeed, the fragmentation of communities within postmodern society may account for the popularity of self-help groups. In the absence of resources and communities, such programs allow individuals to construct a sense of purpose and meaning in their lives. Respondents in our first sample all explained that the resources, communities, and individuals in their lives were instrumental in supporting their efforts to change.

In some cases, these respondents abandoned their using communities entirely to search for nonusing groups. This decision to do so was often triggered by the realization that their immediate social networks consisted mostly of heavy drug and alcohol users. Any attempt to discontinue use, they reasoned, would require complete separation. Several from this group moved to different parts of the country in order to distance themselves from their using networks. This finding is consistent with Biernacki's (1986) study of heroin addicts who relocated in order to remove any temptations to use in the future. For some women, the decision to abandon using communities, particularly cocaine, was often preceded by becoming pregnant. These women left boyfriends and husbands because they felt a greater sense of responsibility and greater meaning in their new maternal status. In all these cases, respondents fled using communities in search of more conventional networks.

In addition to relying on their natural communities and abandoning using communities, these respondents also built new support structures to assist them in their termination efforts. They frequently reported becoming involved in various social groups such as choirs, health clubs, religious organizations, reading clubs, and dance companies. Others from this group reported that they returned to school, became active in civic organizations, or simply developed new hobbies that brought them in touch with nonusers. Thus, respondents built new lives for themselves by cultivating social ties with meaningful and emotionally satisfying alternative communities. In each of these cases where respondents formed attachments to new communities, they typically hid their addictive past, fearing that exposure would jeopardize their newly acquired status.

During the second stage of the study we further examined two of the above themes. The first theme that was revisited dealt with "specific strategies used to remain abstinent." Overwhelmingly for this group, severing all ties with using friends emerged as the most important strategy one could undertake in successfully terminating addiction.

The next theme around elements of cessation that was further examined among this second sample included "resources that were perceived as valuable in the process of recovery." After giving examples of resources discovered in the first stage of the study (e.g., family), these respondents also reported that identical or similar resources had been very useful in their own struggles to overcome addictions. They reported being able to draw upon their families, job skills, formal education, economic security, and other conditions that had been identified as instrumental resources by the first sample. Interestingly, will power and determination emerged as important internal resources during the second stage of the study. However, these should be viewed cautiously since "determination" was given as an example of a possible internal resource during the interviews with the second sample.

Given the apparent roles that severing ties with using networks and having resources play in the natural recovery process, one might draw the compelling conclusion that those individuals from the most disadvantaged segments of our society are also least likely to be in a position to overcome severe addiction problems naturally. Unfortunately, these individuals are also at greatest risk for severe drug and alcohol problems, least likely to be able to afford private treatment, and least likely to voluntarily seek public treatment.

Discussion and Implications

While the sample within the present study is small, there is considerable evidence from additional research to suggest that the population of self-healers is quite substantial. Despite empirical evidence, many in the treatment field continue to deny the existence of such a population. The therapeutic "field" possesses considerable power to construct reality in ways that exclude alternative and perhaps challenging paradigms. As Bourdieu (1991) has recently pointed out, such fields reproduce themselves through their ability to normalize arbitrary world views. The power of the therapeutic field lies in its ability to not only medicalize behavior, but also in the ability to exclude the experiences and world views of those who do not fit into conventional models of addiction and treatment.

Finding empirical support for natural recovery does not imply that we devalue the importance of treatment programs or even self-help groups. Such programs have proven beneficial to addicts, particularly those in advanced stages. However, the experiences of our respondents have important implications for the way in which addiction and recovery are typically conceptualized. First, denying the existence of this population, as many do, discounts the version of reality held by those who terminate their addictions naturally. Natural recovery is simply not recognized as a viable option. This is increasingly the case as media has reified dominant notions of addiction and recovery. Similarly, there is an industry of self-help literature that unquestionably accepts and reproduces these views. Denying the experience of natural recovery allows treatment agencies and self-help groups to continue to impose their particular view of reality on society.

"...there is an industry of self-help literature that unquestionably accepts and reproduces these views."

Related to this is the possibility that many of those experiencing addictions may be extremely reluctant to enter treatment or attend self-help meetings. Their resistance may stem from a variety of factors such as the stigma associated with these programs, discomfort with the therapeutic process, or lack of support from significant others. Whatever the reason, such programs do not appeal to everyone. For such people, natural recovery may be a viable option. Since natural recovery demystifies the addiction and recovery experience, it may offer a way for people to take control of their own lives without needing to rely exclusively on experts. Such an alternative approach offers a low-cost supplement to an already costly system of formal addiction treatment.

A third implication concerns the consequences of adopting an addict identity. While the disease metaphor is thought to be a humanistic one in that it allows for the successful social reintegration of deviant drinkers or drug users, it nevertheless constitutes a deviant identity. Basing one's identity on past addiction experiences may actually limit social reintegration. The respondents in our sample placed a great deal of emphasis on their immediate social roles as opposed to constantly referring to their drug-addict pasts. Although there is no way of knowing, such present-centeredness may, in the long run, prove more beneficial than a continual focusing on the past.

Fourth, for drug and alcohol treatment professionals, as well as those who are likely to refer individuals to drug and alcohol treatment programs, this research raises several important considerations. It reaffirms the necessity for individual treatment matching. It also suggests that individuals whose profiles are similar to these middle-class respondents are likely to be receptive to and benefit from less intrusive, short-term types of interventions. Given the extent of the various concerns expressed by these respondents around some of the possible long-term negative consequences of undergoing traditional treatment and related participation in self-help programs, the decision to specifically recommend drug and alcohol treatment is a profoundly serious one. It should not be made capriciously or simply because it is expected and available. A careful assessment of the person's entire life is warranted, including whether or not the condition is so severe and the absence of supportive resources so great that the possible lifelong identity of addict or related internalized beliefs are reasonable risks to take in pursuing recovery. Overall, the findings of this study as well as previous research on natural recovery could be instructive in designing more effective treatment programs.

Finally, the experiences of our respondents may have important social policy implications. If our respondents are any guide, the following hypothesis might be considered: those with the greatest number of resources and who consequently have a great deal to lose by their addiction are the ones most likely to terminate their addictions naturally. While addiction is not reducible to social class alone, it is certainly related to it. The respondents in our sample had relatively stable lives: they had jobs, supportive families, high school and college credentials, and other social supports that gave them reasons to alter their drug-taking behavior. Having much to lose gave our respondents incentives to transform their lives. However, when there is little to lose from heavy alcohol or drug use, there may be little to gain by quitting. Social policies that attempt to increase a person's stake in conventional life could not only act to prevent future alcohol and drug addiction, they could also provide an anchor for those who become dependent on these substances.

Further research on the subject of natural recovery among hidden populations such as the middle class needs to be conducted in order to substantiate the findings we report and related conclusions. One important direction the researchers are presently pursuing is to differentiate the natural recovery experience of individuals who have been addicted to different substances. Such research could increase understanding of how different hidden populations overcome the addictions they experience.

Back to Basics for Addicts[5]

"Up there," says James, a slim, muscular Bay Street executive in his early 40s, as he points to a gleaming office tower in Toronto's financial district. "That's where I work. Up on the 50th floor." On a noon-hour stroll through a downtown park, James admits that he's lucky he still holds a job anywhere. For years, he confides quietly, he was addicted to cocaine, a problem he kept concealed from his blue chip employer. At the height of his addiction, he confesses, he routinely blew $1,000 a weekend on the potent white powder. By Monday morning, he was exhausted, often unable to work. But a year ago, after numerous attempts to quit, James turned to a small but growing self-help organization called The Muckers Anonymous Inc. "My cravings went away and never returned," he says. "It was like someone with terminal cancer waking up one day to discover the disease was gone. It was remarkable."

There is, however, nothing remarkable about the Muckers' technique. According to a 52-year-old recovered alcoholic named Jim, who helped start the Toronto-based group in early 1995, the Muckers rely on intense study of the 57-year-old book *Alcoholics Anonymous*, known to AA adherents as the Big Book, and the 12-step approach outlined in its first 103 pages. Nevertheless, the group has become embroiled in a dispute with AA and several other self-help groups that resembles a battle between fundamentalist and mainstream Christians. Among other things, those groups contend that the Muckers, so named because they frequently muck up the Big Book by underlining key passages and phrases, have a zealous approach to recovery from addiction that excludes anything but the 12-step method. "There's been a huge backlash from the established groups," says James.

Last fall, AA representatives in Toronto removed the Muckers from their list of approved groups after discovering that their meeting covered various kinds of addictions, rather than just alcoholism. In May, AA ousted two members from elected positions as co-ordinators of treatment centre meetings because they had been espousing the Muckers' philosophy. Representatives of AA are reluctant to comment on the Muckers or to discuss the relative merits of their approaches. "The Big Book hasn't changed," said Ron, a high-ranking official for eastern and central Ontario. "It's worked for almost 60 years."

Some treatment centres have also rejected the Muckers. Alpha House Inc., a rehabilitation facility treating various addictions, has instructed staff and residents to avoid the Muckers. "The bottom line is that Muckers seem to be obsessed with their way

[5] Article by D'Arcy Jenish, from *Maclean's* 109:63 O 21 '96. Reprinted with permission.

being the only way," states a memo to employees. On the other hand, the Donwood Institute, a well-established Toronto recovery facility, has allowed the Muckers to hold weekly meetings, which Donwood clients can attend. "Some of them found it quite helpful," says Dennis James, vice-president of the Donwood's health recovery program.

The Muckers contend that they are maintaining the original traditions of AA. They charge that AA has drifted away from the Big Book and the 12-step approach that its founders, Bill Wilson, a New York City stockbroker, and Bob Smith, a physician from Ohio, developed in the mid-1930s to cope with their own alcoholism. According to the Muckers, many AA groups pay lip service to the sanctity of the Big Book but no longer insist that a recovering alcoholic must use it. "AA's message has become broader and diluted," says John, a 35-year-old alcoholic, drug addict and staunch Mucker. "We stick to the original text."

The cornerstone of the Mucker approach is a process called "booking," in which a member of the group works one-on-one with a recovering alcoholic or addict. They spend up to three hours a day, usually over a two- to three-week period, studying the Big Book, line by line and phrase by phrase. Among other things, the recovering addict must admit personal failings and weaknesses and make amends to people he has harmed through his addiction. Some Muckers who belonged to AA say they became disenchanted by that organization's move away from its original policy of one-on-one therapy in favor of personal or group study. And some longtime AA members confirm the trend. "You just don't see a lot of people going through the Big Book one-on-one anymore," said Gord, who has belonged to AA for 35 years.

The Muckers have been booking about 100 people a month, according to Jim, and the fellowship now has about 2,000 members, almost all in the Toronto area. Some recently recovered addicts say they have experienced moments of profound spiritual contentment while being booked. "I had this sense of absolute peace," recalls Tory, a film-maker in his mid-30s who was battling alcoholism and heroin addiction. "I couldn't see anything or hear anything. It was almost like the first few seconds of a drug overdose." Since then, Tory says, he has not been tormented by his old cravings. And for that, he is both relieved and grateful.

"...many AA groups pay lip service to the sanctity of the Big Book but no longer insist that a recovering alcoholic must use it."

The Crisis in Drug Treatment:
An Interview with
William O'Brien[6]

Msgr. William B. O'Brien, a priest of the Archdiocese of New York, is co-founder and president of Daytop Village Inc., one of the oldest and largest non-profit drug treatment programs in the world. Founded in 1963, it operates 28 facilities in five states, as well as facilities abroad. Monsignor O'Brien is also president of the World Federation of Therapeutic Communities and the author, with Ellis Henican, of You Can't Do It Alone: The Daytop Way to Make Your Child Drug-Free *(1993). The interview took place at Daytop's headquarters in New York City. The interviewer was George M. Anderson, S.J., an associate editor of* America.

How are we now addressing drug addiction in the United States?
We're in a fortress mode, building more and more prisons to handle the drug problem. The American people are on a high. They think that law enforcement can solve a major social problem like drug abuse, and politicians are following suit, insulating the public from the truth—that American society is in trouble—to make them feel good with simplistic solutions. As one example, the Governor of New York, George Pataki, has taken $60 million out of drug treatment funds to build another prison.

What is the cause of this one-dimensional view?
It's a shortsightedness that stems from an unwillingness to sit back and appraise the situation, a shortsightedness made worse by the American way of opting for a push-button resolution to a complex problem instead of studying it first to see the best way of handling it. If you look at the drug abuse problem you see that there is a continuum from the minimally dysfunctional, to the median, to the maximal. When you have family breakdown to the extent we now have in America, the minimally dysfunctional will become maximally dysfunctional and in need of jail cells, given our present emphasis on incarceration as a supposed solution.

It's a battle of philosophies, really. The current way is to impose control from outside the person, by putting him or her in a cell. The Daytop way, on the other hand, is to intervene in the person's life by changing destructive life patterns, building in self-discipline and boundaries with the help of a therapeutic community.

---

6 Article by George M. Anderson, from *America* 174:10-13 Mr 16 '96. Reprinted with permission.

This is not happening?

No, and the net effect of the hard-hat war on drugs approach is that we go crashing into poor neighborhoods with undercover officers looking to make arrests. They'll set up some poor addict on the street with a fake drug deal and then lock him up. For 12 years we've been filling our prisons with vulnerable, low-level addicts. By doing so, we've treated them to a university course in crime, so that when they're finally released, they hit the streets as new members of the crime network. We've positioned them to be accomplished criminals.

There's a place for prisons for hardened, violent, recidivistic offenders, but 80 percent of those we're putting away don't need to be there. We package everyone together into one category and lock them up. It's going to yield huge negative dividends in terms of crime, especially in regard to children who are growing up now. When they reach adolescence, given the sociopathology that's out there and the breakdown of families, they'll represent a tidal wave of criminal activity like nothing heretofore recorded.

You've mentioned that New York State is cutting funds for treatment to build another prison. What has been the attitude of the Federal Government?

The drug crisis has been off the Federal radar screen for five years. Like the states, they want to do the criminal justice number, which is typical, because the Government never deals with people anyway, but with damage control. At present, the House of Representatives is talking about cutting 18 percent from the budget of the Substance Abuse and Mental Health Administration, which funds a number of drug treatment programs around the country. Our own programs will be decimated as a result of Federal and state cuts.

What will state and federal cuts mean for addicts on waiting lists for treatment?

We ourselves have a waiting list of about 460, which shows the extent of the need. Everyone has to be interviewed, and we try to interview as quickly as possible. But by the time the appointments come up, half the people on the list have disappeared. They've either returned to drugs on the street, are doing burglaries to pay for their habit or are dead or in jail.

Regarding addicts in jail facing drug charges, there has been much favorable publicity about the so-called drug courts. How do you feel about them?

Drug courts do represent a hopeful breakthrough, and they're in use in various jurisdictions in the country, including here. Five years ago the Brooklyn district attorney, Charles Hynes, began the Drug Treatment Alternatives to Prison program, and it's now in the other boroughs as well. Defendants who've been arrested for B felony drug sales to undercover officers are given a choice between prison and a residential drug treatment program like ours or Phoenix House or Samaritan Village.

Defendants who complete the 15 to 24 months of treatment have their charges dismissed—even if they had a prior felony, so long as it was nonviolent. Those who leave the program go back to jail, and some do so deliberately, because the treatment program can be tougher than prison. You'll hear them say that doing time in prison is easier, because all they have to do is lay up. The Brooklyn D.A.'s office did a study of its program last year and found that offenders who completed the program had a much lower recidivism rate than the ones who didn't take part in it. But budget cuts are now threatening drug courts too.

"...the poor do have a high incidence of vulnerability.

Some prisons in the country have in-house drug rehabilitation programs. Are they effective?
Only if the authorities turn over the whole prison to you as a treatment center. We pioneered a program at Wallkill, N.Y., a medium security facility. It ran for eight years, with a special cell-block for the Daytop residents. They took the program so seriously that they gave up their chance to move to better cells in other parts of the building, just to stay on the program's cellblock. But in the long run we weren't making the progress we wanted because they were being badgered by negative inmates they'd meet in the dining hall and elsewhere. To make matters worse, some of the guards were bringing in drugs. So we pulled out.

Who in the general population are most vulnerable to becoming addicted to drugs? The poor?
Given the level of drug dealing that goes on in poor neighborhoods, it's true that the poor do have a high incidence of vulnerability. But again, the main source of vulnerability lies in the brokenness of families. American families are in such a sorry state, so broken and non-nurturing, that they're letting these emotionally throw-away kids float away, until peer pressure takes over and they slip down into the drug population. The power of peer pressure was the subject of a U.N. study a few years back. It concluded that parents have a primary influence over children only up to age seven. After that, peers take over.

William F. Buckley Jr., the editor at large of the conservative *National Review*, has been calling for some form of legalization of drugs. Do you agree with him?
No. I'm against legalization. Can government get into the business of licensing death? Frank O'Connor, who was president of the New York City Council some years back and later a judge, had a nephew who was treated at our Daytop facility on Staten Island. The nephew was present at a congressional hearing while still in treatment, and one of the congressmen asked him his opinion about legalization. He answered: "Are you telling me that the government is considering licensing my death?"

England tried legalization and failed. It has to do with the way drug tolerance prompts escalating dosage levels to produce the high that addicts seek. Addicts in Great Britain would go to clinics and finally reach the maximum level of prescribed heroin, short of lethal dosages; then they'd go back to the streets for additional heroin, because their tolerance had increased and they wanted more to handle the new stress they were consequently feeling. When you're dealing with tolerance, the English system is fraught with fallacies. Here in the United States in the 19th century, opiates were freely available in candy and grocery stores for just a few pennies. Many women were taking them, mostly for premenstrual syndrome problems, and would end up falling out of windows or burning themselves, because they were taking more and more as their tolerance increased, and were becoming dysfunctional.

As the oldest and one of the largest drug treatment programs in the nation, has Daytop undergone many changes in the three decades of its existence?
When we started in 1963, we focused on hardcore addicts, the maximally dysfunctional. But by 1971, we began differentiating and working also with the median group—drug abusers who still had some semblance of family and job or school. Our full program lasts 18 months. The longer residents stay with us, the deeper we penetrate in regard to values, goals and overcoming limitations to self-discipline. A Johns Hopkins University study of Daytop found that 85 percent of those who completed the full 18 months stayed off drugs. Even those who dropped out after six months showed a lot of improvement.

We found that there were some, the minimally dysfunctional, who responded well to shorter-term treatment, 30 to 90 days. It's a matter of different strokes for different folks. But with us it's always tough love. John Chancellor, the senior commentator for NBC Nightly News whose son graduated from Daytop, spoke at the dedication of our facility in Dallas. In his talk he emphasized that the law enforcement solution hasn't worked; what has worked is treatment through the tough love approach that teaches self-discipline, total honesty and acceptance of responsibility.

Over the years there have been changes regarding treatment for women. We've always been coed, but in the beginning, the women who came to us had often been brutalized by men who used them as a meal ticket on the streets. That attitude carried over into the treatment. In group discussions, the men would call the women everything in the book. If a woman wore a pretty dress to group—maybe the last remnant of her pride—they'd say she was flaunting her sexuality. So she'd give up the dress and appear in a baggy T-shirt and rumpled jeans, denying her femininity.

After five or six years, that changed. Now we have a women's division and women residents have their own retreats and staffing and programs. We teach parenting too, and offer family

"Here in the United States in the 19th century, opiates were freely available in candy and grocery stores for just a few pennies."

therapy. Drug use represents a cry of anguish, and we have to respond, telling the parents, "Your child is slowly dying."

Drug abuse is closely linked with the transmission of the AIDS virus. Has AIDS had an impact on the program?
A huge impact. Our decison to accept people who were H.I.V.-positive came about through a young Puerto Rican named Sammy. I was visiting our entry center in Far Rockaway, Queens, N.Y. About 60 kids were in the dining room socializing, but I noticed one boy in the corner all by himself. I went over right away, because in Daytop, the worst thing you can do is withdraw. I asked him what was the matter, and he said, "I just came back from Beth Israel Hospital and the doctor says I have AIDS." So I arranged to call everybody together, the Daytop family, to ask their opinion about what we should do. When they heard about Sammy, the kids broke down in tears and said, "We want to love our AIDS brothers and sisters two times as much."

Now we have a whole division of AIDS counsellors. Two administrators in different parts of the country are H.I.V.-positive and so far nonsymptomatic. The dark side of the story is that we bought 32 plots in a cemetery in Liberty, N.Y. We buried six people there this past fall. The inscription on the headstones includes the words: "Daytop. We have loved much." Sammy died about eight years ago and is buried there. During his final days in the hospital, there was a Daytop person with him 24 hours a day, and 600 people came to his funeral. Now we've established the Sammy Award for the most outstanding resident of the year.

The Catholic Church puts great emphasis on family. Has the church spoken out much on the subject of drug addiction and its harmful effect on families?
Until four years ago, the Catholic bishops never mentioned drugs; and when they subsequently did, they said very little, even though drugs are eating away like a cancer at the heart of family life in America. The Pope and the Italian bishops have been much more vocal. The Pope, in fact, addressed the Italian Federation of Therapeutic Communities last year when it commemorated the World Day against Drugs sponsored by the United Nations. Many treatment centers in Italy have been provided by the church.

The Pope spoke of drugs as a symptom of what he called "a culture starved of genuine values" and praised the therapeutic community concept. There are now 119 treatment centers in Italy. The church here could have tremendous leverage in addressing drug addiction, which is on the rise. Heroin use has increased and is now on a par with cocaine. Hospital emergency room episodes are up—this is the only reliable indicator we have. But the good guys, the bishops, aren't speaking out enough.

Bibliography

An asterisk (*) preceding a reference indicates that an excerpt from the work has been reprinted in this compilation.

Books and Pamphlets

Allen, Karen M. Nursing care of the addicted client. Lippincott-Raven '96.

Anderson, Neil T., Quarles, Mike & Quarles, Julia. Freedom from addiction; breaking the bondage of addiction and finding freedom in Christ. Regal '96.

Bellenir, Karen, ed. Substance abuse sourcebook; basic health-related information about the abuse of legal and illegal substances such as alcohol, tobacco. Omnigraphics '96.

Bonner, Adrian & Waterhouse, J. M. Addictive behaviour; molecules to mankind: perspectives on the nature of addiction. St. Martin's '96.

Caldwell, Christine. Getting our bodies back; recovery, healing, and transformation through body-centered psychotherapy. Shambhala '96.

Chandler, Lynette S. & Lane, Shelly J. eds. Children with prenatal drug exposure. Haworth '96.

Doweiko, Harold E. Concepts of chemical dependency. Brooks/Cole '96.

DuPont, Robert L. The selfish brain; learning from addiction. American Psychiatric '97.

Edwards, Griffith & Dare, Christopher, eds. Psychotherapy, psychological treatments, and the addictions. Cambridge Univ. Press '96.

Fisher, Gary L. & Harrison, Thomas C. Substance abuse; information for school counselors, social workers, therapists, and counselors. Allyn & Bacon '97.

Flores, Philip J. Group psychotherapy with addicted populations; an integration of twelve-step and psychodynamic theory. Haworth '97.

Free-Gardiner, Linda. Trust the process; how to enhance recovery and prevent relapse. Newjoy '96.

Gossop, Michael. Living with drugs. Arena '96.

Gruenewald, Paul J. Measuring community indicators; a systems approach to drug and alcohol problems. Sage '97.

Gutman, Bill. Harmful to your health. 21st Cent. '96.

Hogue, Michael D., ed. Points of light; a guide for assisting chemically dependent health professional students. American Pharmaceutical Assn. '96.

Institute of Medicine (U.S.)/Committee on Opportunities in Drug Abuse Research. Pathways of addiction; opportunities in drug abuse research. National Acad. '96.

Kinney, Jean. Clinical manual of substance abuse. Mosby '96.

Konkol, Richard J. & Olsen, George D. eds. Prenatal cocaine exposure. CRC '96.

Langton, Phyllis Ann. The social world of drugs. West '96.

Miller, David K. & Blum, Kenneth. Overload; attention deficit disorder and the addictive brain. Andrews & McMeel '96.

Miller, Norman S., ed. The Principles and practice of addictions in psychiatry. Saunders '97.

Myers, Arthur. Drugs and emotions. Rosen '96.

Pagliaro, Ann M. & Pagliaro, Louis A. Substance use among children and adolescents; its nature, extent, and effects from conception to adulthood. Wiley '96.

Peters, Ray DeV. & McMahon, Robert J. eds. Preventing childhood disorders, substance abuse, and delinquency. Sage '96.

Pike, R. William. Facing substance abuse; discussion-starting skits for teenagers. Resource '96.

Read, Edward M. Partners in change; the twelve step referral handbook for probation, parole, and community corrections. American Correctional Assn. Hazelden Foundation '96.

Rotgers, Frederick, Keller, Daniel S. & Morgenstern, Jon, eds. Treating substance abuse; theory and technique. Guilford '96.

Siegal, Harvey A. & Rapp, Richard C., eds. Case management and substance abuse treatment practice and experience. Springer '96.

Stares, Paul B. Global habit; the drug problem in a borderless world. Brookings Institution '96.

Strazzabosco-Hayn, Gina. Drugs and sleeping disorders. Rosen '96.

Underhill, Brenda L. & Finnegan, Dana G. eds. Chemical dependency; women at risk. Haworth '96.

Walters, Glenn D. Substance abuse and the new road to recovery; a practitioner's guide. Taylor & Francis '96.

Watkins, Kathleen Pullan & Durant, Lucius. Working with children and families affected by substance abuse; a guide for early childhood education and human service staff. Center for Applied Res. in Educ. '96.

White, William L. Pathways; from the culture of addiction to the culture of recovery: a travel guide for addiction professions. Hazelden-Pittman Archives '96.

Additional Periodical Articles with Abstracts

For those who wish to read more widely on the subject of Substance Abuse, this section contains abstracts of the additional articles that bear on the topic. Readers who require a comprehensive list of materials are advised to consult the *Reader's Guide to Periodical Literature* and other H.W. Wilson indexes.

Prozac: the verdict is in. Nancy Wartik. *American Health* 15:58-61 + N '96

It has been ten years since Prozac, the highly celebrated antidepressant, first hit the market. Since it was first introduced, Prozac has been glorified as a miracle cure and vilified in a backlash centering on claims that it makes some users violent. It has also been attacked as a so-called happy pill—a quick fix that enables users to ignore the psychological issues that are causing their depression. Even with its image tarnished, however, the drug prospers. With 1995 sales exceeding $2 billion, up 24 percent from 1994, it is the second-largest moneymaking drug in America. The drug has especially touched the lives of women, mostly because they are twice as likely as men to suffer from major depression and tend to have higher rates of other disorders for which the drug is now prescribed, such as dysthymia, some forms of anxiety, severe PMS, and bulimia. The writer examines some of the claims that have been made about the drug.

No to drug legalization. R. Emmett Tyrrell. *The American Spectator* 29:16-17 Ap '96

In a symposium in the *National Review*, William F. Buckley came out in favor of legalizing drugs because he feels that a war against drugs has been lost. Discussions about legalization is 1960s nonsense, however. To legalize is to sign the death warrants of those compulsive people in society who have a low tolerance for drugs. If the laws regarding possession are draconian, they can be liberalized but should not be eliminated. Drug traffickers are killers and should be punished for preying on the weak and spreading a vice, which encourages the flight from personal responsibility that is today endangering free society. One can witness the appalling consequences of drug use in the condition of the inner cities, and these wretched scenarios should not be encouraged in the rest of America.

Unsafe at any speed. James Bovard. *The American Spectator* 29:48-9 Ap '96

Current U.S. drug policy is a case study in contradiction. Parents face the worst of both worlds: poor, self-defeating government drug education programs and the massive doping of children with government-approved drugs. The forced medication of hyperactive and allegedly hyperactive school children, in the form of Ritalin, is soaring. Ritalin is an amphetamine-related stimulant that is being prescribed mainly in response to an alleged epidemic of Attention Deficit Disorder. Meanwhile, federal, state, and local governments and private donors are spending around $700 million on the Drug Abuse Resistance Education program each year, but a study conducted by the Research Triangle Institute found that the program has been much less effective at discouraging drug abuse than other "interactive" teaching methods.

A magic bullet for heroin addiction? Neal Sandler. *Business Week* 48 D 9 '96

A new treatment for heroin addiction is producing results. The ultrarapid opiate detoxification therapy was developed in 1988 by Juan Jose Legarda, a Spanish expert in drug rehabilitation who established the Center for Research & Treatment of Addiction

(CITA). Under the CITA treatment, addicts are put under a general anesthetic for six hours so they do not suffer withdrawal symptoms. During that time, they are given naltrexone, a drug that blocks the desire for heroin. Patients are then given naltrexone daily for six months, in addition to drug counseling. The treatment has been administered to some 5,000 heroin addicts at clinics mainly in Israel and Italy but also in Britain, Germany, Spain, the Netherlands, and America. Studies in Italy and Israel have found that around 65 percent of addicts stay clean after 18 months, says Moshe Zerzion, medical director of CITA. That figure compares with a success rate of about 20 percent for ordinary methods.

A drug by any other name: generics. Melanie Scheller. *Current Health* 23:30-1 D '96

Generic drugs are essentially chemical clones of drugs sold under a brand name, but they cost less. On average, generic drugs are 30 percent cheaper than their brand name counterparts. The reason for this lies in the lengthy research drug manufacturers must carry out before their products can be sold legally in America. Before being marketed, a drug must be approved by the Food and Drug Administration (FDA). It takes an average of 12 years to complete the studies required by the FDA, at an estimated cost of $231 million per drug, a cost that is factored into the drug's final price. The company that develops a new drug obtains a patent that gives it exclusive rights to sell the drug for 17 years, at which time other companies can sell clones. The safety of generic drugs, their effectiveness, and the cases in which they are unsuitable are discussed.

Recognizing signs of drug abuse. Judy Monroe. *Current Health* 16-19 Sept '96

According to the Substance Abuse and Mental Health Services Administration, 23 million Americans aged 12 years or older have taken illegal drugs during the past year. Abusers take drugs for nonmedical purposes, which can result in the impairment of their physical, emotional, mental, or social well-being. Teens who suspect that a friend is using drugs should talk to the user about their concerns. They should try to stay calm, factual, and honest when discussing their friend's behavior and its day-to-day repercussions. They should also try to guide their friend to sources of help such as treatment referral or support groups. Information is provided on the major illegal drugs of abuse: cannabis, depressants, hallucinogens, narcotics, and stimulants.

Recreational drugs: an alluring threat to your body chemistry. Linda H. Hamilton. *Dance Magazine* 88-91 Jan '96

Seductive new names and increased potency are giving many drugs a dangerous new appeal. A whole new group of upper- and middle-class Americans are now developing a taste for heroin. As its average purity has risen to 60 percent, heroin can now be inhaled, lessening the risk of AIDS from contaminated needles. Alcohol and marijuana remain as popular as ever, and hallucinogens, such as Ecstasy, appeal to a small, but avid and growing audience. In recent years, "smart drugs," described by their sellers as nutrient based energy boosters, have also been popular in clubs in San Francisco and elsewhere. The long-term benefits or possible dangers of these drugs have never been studied. Advice and information relating to dancers and drugs is provided.

Blunted. Kierna Mayo Dawsey. *Essence* 73-74+ Aug '96

After years of steady decline, the National Institute of Drug Abuse (NIDA) reports that marijuana use has increased since 1993 among young people, with the rate of use among black youngsters also high. According to NIDA, chronic use of the drug may produce depressions, anxiety, delayed puberty, reduced sperm production, disruption of the menstrual cycle, and personality disturbances. In addition, besides possibly landing in jail, buyers of marijuana have no insurance that the drug they purchase is not mixed with an unknown substance with unpredictable results. Moreover, according to research by the Center of Psychosocial Studies in New York, people who smoke marijuana daily use the drug to avoid dealing with their difficulties, and the avoidance makes their problems worse.

Evening out the ups and downs of manic-depressive illness. Ricki Lewis. *FDA Consumer* 30:26-9 Je '96

Manic-depressive illness, also known as bipolar disorder, affects 1 percent of the U.S. population at some time. Researchers estimate that of the 2 million people in America suffering from the condition, one-third of them receive no treatment. For many years the standard treatment has been lithium, which is the best-studied drug to treat manic-depressive illness and which is effective in the acute treatment of mania and in long-term prevention of relapses. Lithium does, however, cause significant side effects in some people. In May 1995, the FDA approved the antiseizure drug Depakote for the short-term treatment of manic-depressive illness, and it may be helpful for some of the 30-40 percent of sufferers who do not respond to lithium. The writer discusses the diagnosis of manic-depressive illness, the history of drug treatment for the condition, and the side effects of drug treatment.

Preventing childhood poisoning. Audrey T. Hingley. *FDA Consumer* 30:6-11 Mr '96

Accidental poisonings, especially of children, are a household hazard. Supplements containing iron are the main cause of pediatric poisoning deaths for children under age six in America. The FDA is attempting to protect children from iron poisoning by proposing regulations that will make it more difficult for small children to gain access to high-potency iron products, but there is also concern about other drugs. According to George C. Rodgers, medical director of the Kentucky Regional Poisoning Center, antidepressant drugs can cause problems for children and adolescents, and the marketing of pediatric vitamins so that they look like candy is worrying. He adds that the tendency of children to mimic their parents can also be a problem if the parents take pills. Advice on combating and treating childhood poisoning is provided, as is information on progress against poisonings.

U.S. drug policy: addicted to failure. Mathea Falco. *Foreign Policy* 102:120-33 Spr '96

The perceived connection between drugs and foreigners still encourages the U.S. government to try to prevent drugs from entering the country through the use of diplomacy, coercion, money, and military force. This supply-side approach to the control of drugs has been thoroughly tested by Democratic and Republican administrations, but it is fatally flawed for several reasons. In the first place, the economics of drug cultivation militate against sustained reductions in the supply of drugs.

What is more, America consumes a relatively small share of global drug production, and the annual U.S. drug demand can be supplied from a comparatively small growing area and transported in a few airplanes. In any case, the price structure of the drug market severely curtails the potential impact of interdiction and source-country programs. International narcotics control can be useful, but it is important to remember that enduring answers to the U.S. drug problem are at home in the form of drug-prevention and treatment programs.

Keeping a child's spirit alive. Anita Bartholomew. *Good Housekeeping* 222:28 My '96

When Grace Jones's 15-year-old daughter Jennifer, nicknamed J. J., died from inhaling Freon, a gas that works as a coolant in air conditioners, she began a crusade to keep her daughter's spirit alive. Among other activities, she lobbies local newspapers to run articles alerting parents to the practice, called huffing, and telling them where to get help, and she puts reporters in touch with experts and other mothers whose children have died from inhalants. She is currently taking her crusade nationwide by asking President Clinton to help raise national awareness of the problem, a request she bolstered with hundreds of petitions from around America.

Miracle or menace? Marisa Fox. *Harper's Bazaar* 78 + My '96

Melatonin, a hormone that occurs naturally in the body, is a growing obsession in America, despite the lack of complete knowledge of its effects. It is known with some certainty that melatonin can control the body's natural clock but not how it affects many conditions connected to these biological cycles. The substance promises to fight jet lag, improve sleep, act as an aphrodisiac, boost the immune system, prevent cancer, fight AIDS, act as birth control, and sustain youth. Richard Wurtman, M.D., has discovered that melatonin can have many side effects, including hangover-like symptoms, reduced body temperature, and a reduced sex drive. Canada, Great Britain, and France have limited or banned sales of the hormone, but in the United States melatonin is considered a dietary supplement, exempting it from the strict FDA scrutiny to which drugs are subject.

Contras, crack, the C.I.A. Robert Parry. *The Nation* 263:4-5 O 21 '96

Regardless of assurances of a thorough federal investigation into recent allegations of a CIA-contra-drug connection, government documents show that Ronald Reagan's Justice Department ignored many eyewitness accounts of the link. The issue rose to national prominence when the San Jose *Mercury News* revealed that Nicaraguan contra leaders financed their war by smuggling into America, with near impunity, the cocaine that fueled the crack epidemic in Southern California. Typical of evidence that the government has long turned a blind eye to such events is the case of FBI informant Wanda Palacio. A verifiable account she gave to Massachusetts senator John Kerry in 1986, which implicated the CIA in numerous drugs and weapons deals with the rebels, was handed to William Weld, then assistant attorney general for criminal affairs. Wearied by his department's challenges to her credibility, Palacio returned home to Puerto Rico. Weld, now Republican governor of Massachusetts, is to challenge Kerry for his Senate seat. News of the CIA cocaine link may soon be resonating through the state elections.

Crack reporting. David Corn. *The Nation* 263:4-5 N 18 '96

A story in the San Jose *Mercury News* has forced Congress to consider a matter it would rather not, led a public too often deceived to think the worst, and motivated the press to come to the partial defense of the national security elite. The story by Gary Webb alleged that a California drug ring operated by Nicaraguan exiles helped bring about the crack epidemic in urban America and gave millions in drug profits to the CIA-backed contras. As a result of the story, a session of the Senate Intelligence Committee was held, the atmosphere of which reflected the intense reaction to the story in black communities nationwide. Many citizens have voiced outrage, some mischaracterizing the series as proving that the CIA engineered the epidemic, and the establishment media has rushed to debunk the stories or declare them nothing new.

People of the opiate: Burma's dictatorship of drugs. Dennis Bernstein and Leslie Kean. *The Nation* 263:11-12 + D 16 '96

The State Law and Order Restoration Council (SLORC), the ruling dictatorship of Burma—or Myanmar—has integrated the rapidly expanding heroin trade into the permanent economy of the country. The country has more than doubled its illegal drug exports since the SLORC takeover in 1988, and the U.S. Embassy in Rangoon reports that the area under poppy cultivation in Burma rose by two-thirds between 1987 and 1990. Moreover, a study by the International Monetary Fund refers to major expenditures unaccounted for by Burma's government. The integration of drug money into the national economy is further highlighted by a recent economic report from the U.S. Embassy in Rangoon: The Country Commercial Guide, published in July, states that at least 50 percent of the Burmese economy is unaccounted for and extralegal. Meanwhile, the heroin pipeline from Burma to America is fully open, and mainlining heroin has become fashionable among young Americans.

Misfire on drug policy. William F. Buckley. *National Review* 48:70 F 26 '96

The bipartisan Council on Crime in America has exploded in opposition to the call for an approach to drug legalization made by seven writers in a previous issue of this journal. The council contends that the war on drugs has certainly not been lost, but an examination of the formal aspect of this war is needed. If something is illegal, then the law that makes it so is effective to the extent that it jails those who break it, thereby hypothetically reducing the number of offenders. The members of the Council on Crime in America fail to grasp this reality. In 1985, 811,000 drug-related arrests were made. By 1994, that figure had risen to 1.35 million. This does not mean that the war on drugs is being successful; an effective law reduces, rather than increases, the number of offenders who have to be arrested.

The pot war in England. William F. Buckley. *National Review* 55 Dec 31 '95

The November 11 editorial of *The Lancet*, Britain's preeminent medical publication, stated that while cannabis per se is not hazard to society, driving it underground may be. The editorial was picking up on the proposal by the Labour MP Clare Short that cannabis be legalized. Short cited the Dutch stance on the issue and *The Lancet* pointed out that the decriminalization of soft drugs in the Netherlands has not led to a rise in the use of hard drugs. The calm acceptance by the medical community of the relative harmlessness of cannabis is striking.

The war on drugs is lost. Steven B. Duke. *National Review* 48:47-8 F 12 '96

Part of a cover story on the war on drugs. The only benefit to the United States in maintaining drug prohibition is the psychic comfort people derive from having a permanent scapegoat. The prohibitionist claim that legalization of narcotics would lead to huge numbers of addicts has no basis in the history of America or that of other cultures. There are a number of inconsistencies in the position conservatives commonly take on drugs and related issues, including preaching "individual responsibility" while ardently punishing people for the chemicals they consume, revering the right to one's property while supporting drug forfeiture, and supporting schemes to "devolve" matters from federal to state and local government but failing to apply this principle to drug prohibition.

Crime and drugs. *Nation's Business* 85:24+ F '97

Part of a special section on challenges facing the United States. Business must increase its involvement at the local level and keep up pressure on federal lawmakers to keep crime and drug problems high on their list of concerns. Although the incidence of violent crime and drug abuse in America started falling significantly in the early 1990s, polls show that the majority of Americans do not believe that these problems have lessened. In a large number of communities, businesses are proving to be a key part of local anticrime coalitions, and entrepreneurial firms are providing numerous high-technology products and services that are permitting the dynamics of free enterprise to help reduce crime.

Hidden addictions alert! Robert Kanigel. *New Choices* 60-62 May '96

Although statistics say addiction to drugs and alcohol is less prevalent among older adults than any other group, physicians, substance-abuse counselors, and public health officials now worry that these statistics do not fully reflect reality. Abuse or misuse of mood-altering prescription drugs such as tranquilizers is widespread among retirement age adults. Too often, older drug and alcohol abusers encounter doctors who prescribe tranquilizers they do not need, overlook indicators of heavy drinking, or dismiss it as harmless. The usual alarms alcoholics and addicts set off—absenteeism from work, erratic behavior, brawling, drunk driving—are not the same for retirees. Consequently, family members should be on the lookout for behavior that might anticipate a flight into substance abuse.

Gone country. Bruce S. Feiler. *The New Republic* 214:19-20+ F 5 '96

The suburban, middle-aged themes of family and renewal in country music today might be the clearest reflection of many of the anxieties and aspirations that have just begun to rise to the surface in American politics. To begin with, legions of new fans, both Southern and Northern, conservative and liberal, have flocked to the music in recent years. Country music is now the dominant radio format in America, with 42 percent of all radio listeners tuning into country radio every week.

There are several theories to explain this growth in country music's popularity. One is the idea that as baby boomers aged and moved to the suburbs, they became increasingly interested in the themes of country music, as opposed to what most pop music focused on: drugs, sex, and other forms of license.

Maturity diminishes drug use, a study finds. Christopher Sale Wren. *New York Times* 28 Feb 2 '97

A study of five researchers at the University of Michigan's Institute for Social Research found that substance abuse increases when adolescents break free of parental restraints but diminishes once they mature and take on new responsibilities of love and marriage. The study confirmed that those who give up drugs and alcohol after using them as teens are more likely than other young adults to return to substance abuse after personal setbacks, such as a divorce. The findings appear in Jerald G. Bachman's "Smoking, Drinking and Drug Use in Young Adulthood: The Impacts of New Freedoms and New Responsibilities."

Pill-popping deals by prescription. Allen R. Myerson. *New York Times* 3 Mr 2 '97

The less-publicized Mexican-American drug trade is one in which American retirees and drug-dealing youths purchase large amounts of easily available prescription drugs for use or sale at higher prices in America. This market has similar dynamics to the violent trade in illicit drugs: cheap and ample supply in Mexico, high demand in America, and little regard for legalities. A recent study estimated that visitors legally brought back from Nuevo Laredo some 4 million Valium tablets through Laredo in a one-year period.

+ **Welfare's drug connection.** Joseph A. Califano. *New York Times* 23 Ag 24 '96

The welfare reform legislation passed by the Republican Congress and signed by President Clinton ignores the fact that substance abuse and addiction have changed the nature of poverty in America. As a result, the new law will most likely thrust thousands of women and children into homelessness and will crush state and local foster care systems, which are already striving to care for their charges.

Drugs & the CIA. Murray Kempton. *The New York Review of Books* 43:65 N 28 '96

Tim Golden of the *New York Times* says that he can discover no evidence that the CIA acted as a crack wholesaler in America's inner cities. This follows an increasing number of reports stating that the CIA stimulated the crack epidemic in the inner cities by flooding these areas with cocaine and funding arms for the Nicaraguan contras with the profits. Although both the CIA and the government that funds it have no more concern for the well-being of America's poor than for the poor of Latin America, the idea that the government damaged the poor by deliberately stimulating drug sales is fantastical. In fact, the government damages the poor by removing children's welfare entitlement and guaranteeing Medicare to all 70 year olds, regardless of their ability to pay for health care themselves.

+ **Communities against crime.** Marc Kaufman. *Parents* 71:50-2 Je '96

With good reason, fear of crime is rampant among parents raising children in cities. The Council on Crime in America reports that over 43 million crimes were committed in 1993 and that 10.8 million of them were violent. Increasingly, children are involved, and young teens are far more likely to be the perpetrators and the victims of such crime. Convinced that the police and the criminal-justice system cannot stem the tide, millions of parents are banding together to fight back. Often the battles concern quality-of-life issues, and sometimes the issue is garage break-ins, drug selling, or the constant troubles coming from an out-of-control home. For a surprisingly large number of families, the answer has been to buy homes in a gated community, others have joined neighborhood and town watches, and still others have embraced a more aggressive neighborhood activism. These three solutions to violent crime are discussed.

Clinton pushes military aid: human-rights abusers lap it up. Eyal Press. *The Progressive* 61:20-2 F '97

Under the guise of the drug war, the Clinton White House is supporting repressive security forces responsible for human-rights abuses throughout much of Latin America. The renewed war on drugs fuels repression, comes at an enormous cost to U.S. taxpayers, and does little to stop the flow of drugs. Nonetheless, President Clinton has found it much easier to win elections by being a tough guy than by explaining the intricacies of the issue. It is unlikely that Clinton will shift to a more enlightened policy now that he is reelected, however. To reorient drug policy, he would have to push hard against a Republican Congress that is delighted about the scandals surrounding him, and he would have to risk challenging the Right's terms of debate on drug policy.

Guatemalan hit squads come to the U.S.A. Martha Honey and Ricardo Miranda. *The Progressive* 60:22-6 Je '96

According to former Guatemalan intelligence and military officers, human rights activists, and a former Drug Enforcement Agency agent, the Guatemalan military has been sending intelligence branch hit-squads into America to intimidate or eliminate its opponents. On January 5, 1996, a bomb was planted in a car outside Jose Pertierra's home in a suburb of Washington, D.C. Pertierra represents Jennifer Harbury, a Harvard-educated lawyer whose Guatemalan guerrilla husband, Efrain Bamaca, was killed by the Guatemalan army, allegedly under orders from a paid CIA informant. Harbury has been waging a relentless, high-profile campaign since 1992 to uncover the truth about her husband's capture, torture, and murder. One line of investigation by the FBI into the bombing reveals evidence of a campaign of low-intensity warfare being waged by Guatemala's military in Washington, which is aimed at silencing critics of the military and winning favor with U.S. government officials and Guatemalans residing in the Washington area.

The return of reefer madness. Mike A. Males and Faye Docuyanan. *The Progressive* 60:26-9 My '96

The "teenage drug crisis" is a fabrication that has been manufactured for political ends. Health and Human Services Secretary Donna Shalala, the police, sheriff's deputies, drug counselors, and school officials have joined together to proclaim a war on drugs in the schools. The reality is, however, that three decades of drug-fatality statistics reveal that youths have not played a serious part in the country's drug-abuse problem for 20 years. The annual media circus that now surrounds the release of the University of Michigan's "Monitoring the Future" survey of 50,000 junior and senior high school students is actually the government's overreaction to increases in the occasional use of marijuana. There is a large and growing drug-abuse crisis in America, but its essential elements are hard drugs, middle-aged men, and Vietnam. The government does not wish to confront the drug legacy of the Vietnam War, however.

Doing methadone right. Ethan A. Nadelmann and Jennifer McNeely. *The Public Interest* 123:83-93 Spr '96

Methadone-maintenance programs are poorly utilized in America despite their proven effectiveness in rehabilitating heroin addicts. Enrollment in methadone programs is linked to significant reductions in death, crime, and disease, yet several studies have shown that methadone programs have been hindered by state and federal regulations, prejudice toward methadone users, ignorance of scientific research, and ideological assumptions that belie good medical practice and common sense. Methadone should be deregulated and put back under the control of the medical community.

Ritalin alert. Denise Dowling. *Seventeen* 62 Feb '96

Ritalin—the brand name for methylphenidate, or MPH—is employed to treat Attention Deficit Disorder (ADD) but can be dangerous and even addictive when used by those who do not have ADD. Ritalin abusers are using it as a party drug, crushing the tablets into a powder to be snorted. For them, Ritalin acts as a stimulant like cocaine, but overuse can result in seizures, hypertension, and even strokes. The Substance Abuse and Mental Health Services Administration says that Ritalin-related visits to hospital emergency rooms in 1994 increased 214 percent over 1993. Meanwhile, a national advocacy group called Children and Adults with Attention Deficit Disorder is calling on the federal government to make Ritalin more available to ADD patients.

Rehab centers run dry. Elizabeth Gleick. *Time* 147:44-5 F 5 '96

Managed care has led to a sharp drop in the number of inpatient treatment programs in substance abuse clinics in America. According to Monica Oss, editor of *Open Minds*, a behavioral-health-industry newsletter, the average number of patient bed days dropped from 35 to 17 between 1988 and 1993. This has caused many facilities around the country to reinvent themselves. Nearly all insurers and doctors acknowledge that some of the changes being imposed by managed care are long overdue, and addiction specialists concede that some scamming went on in the for-profit recovery business, but they maintain that for some patients it was necessary to spend a month in a placid, nurturing environment away from all their former temptations.

+ **Just saying "no" to the sick and suffering.** *The Washington Monthly* 38 Oct '95

The refusal to permit medical use of marijuana is an example of the drug war's stupidity. Thousands of Americans insist that marijuana effectively treats pain, muscle spasms, skin rashes, inflammations, seizures, and the intense nausea that often accompanies chemotherapy. Moreover, it is far safer and causes fewer side effects than many legal painkillers. Nevertheless, the Drug Enforcement Administration classifies marijuana as a Schedule I substance, which means that it is considered a drug with the highest potential for abuse and no medical uses. Doctors are not allowed to prescribe it, patients are not legally permitted to smoke it, and researchers are not allowed to study it.

Index